The Paradox of Meaning

Cultural Poetics and Critical Fictions

by

JOHN MOSS

TURNSTONE PRESS

Turnstone Press
607 – 100 Arthur Street
Artspace Building
Winnipeg, Manitoba
R3B 1H3 Canada
www.TurnstonePress.com

Turnstone Press gratefully acknowledges the assistance of the Canada Council for the Arts, the Manitoba Arts Council and the Government of Canada through the Book Publishing Industry Development Program for our publishing activities.

Le Conseil des Arts du Canada depuis 1957 | The Canada Council for the Arts since 1957

Cover photograph:
Stephen C. Moss, "Portrait of the Author as Landscape"

Design: Manuela Dias

This book was printed and bound in Canada
by Hignell Printing for Turnstone Press.

Canadian Cataloguing in Publication Data

Moss, John, 1940–

The paradox of meaning

Includes bibliographical references and index.
ISBN 0-88801-230-6

I. Title

PS8576.07863A16 1999 C814'.54 C99-920038-0
PR9199.3.M665A16 1999

to Beverley
for being in my life and for all that we share

. . . between meaning and being falls the shadow of time . . .

—Jorges de Cuchilleros,
The Inventions of Time
trans. Luis E. Melendez
Madrid: Prado Editores, 1948

Meaning?

—Robert Kroetsch,
in conversation, Montreal, 1976

CONTENTS

FOREWORD

THE INTERRELATED CONCERNS of this book are first and foremost cultural. They have to do with literature, especially Canadian literature. They have to do with language, especially Canadian, and with narrative form. They have to do with the illimitable capacity of the imagination to apprehend written words as reality; and with gender and nationality as conditions of being, inseparable from the shape and content of the stories we tell to make ourselves real. They have to do with moral responsibilities of the critic, the writer, and the written; and they have to do with a profound commitment to the primacy of *being* over *meaning*, presence over imminence, engagement over memory or dream.

This collection of writings is an argument for 'book' as genre. The essays and rhetorical imaginings that I call 'critical fiction' assembled here relate in ways that challenge generic convention, perhaps even subvert the notions of genre we use to distinguish between prose and poetry, fiction and exposition, creative writing and critical commentary. They reflect upon one another, and occasionally borrow from one another, placing passages from one context in the entirely different light of another to tease out nuances of significance, elicit alternative responses not anticipated in the original. Although written over a period of nearly two decades, everything here is of a piece; and this, for want of a better word, is a book.

The coherence of the book and its significance in the world both depend on the reader's pleasure. I hope each part will stand on its own as a play of language and idea, appealing, as intended, on emotional, intellectual, and imaginative planes to a greater or lesser degree, simultaneously. Some, such as the early essay "Bushed in the Sacred Wood," are essentially exposition; others, like "Waves Break Stone," fall into a category usually called 'creative writing.' Yet "This Is a Poem," the piece on Robert Kroetsch that I offer as a prelude to the book as a whole, evades categorization. It is certainly rhetoric, pursues a plausible if improbable argument, interrogates, speculates, expostulates as an essay. At the same time, it develops a whimsical narrative that is sometimes more serious than it seems, sometimes less. And it is a heartfelt personal meditation in the belletristic tradition, meant perhaps to beguile the reader as much as to persuade or perplex. Different as they are, these selected writings share in voice and values to an extent that pleasantly surprised me when I gathered them together.

Development over the period separating the earliest piece from the most recent is evident in the progressively more relaxed articulation of ideas and in the gradual conflation of imaginative and intellectual responses to the same perceived conditions of language and culture, moral responsibility and personal being. I am struck more by the consistency of my concerns and my desire to give them robust expression than by shifts in aesthetic, ideology, or imagination. I find the recent writing more complex and inherently more interesting. At the same time, I find the personality informing the earliest writing one that my present self can accommodate. This book represents an evolution of sensibility and perhaps the acquisition of maturity, but it also embodies the fullness of an intellectual and imaginative life, not as progression or improvement but as a process of growing awareness.

There seems no point in rehearsing the arguments pursued since if you have made it this far you will likely prefer to discover on your own what the book is about, beyond what is already apparent by brief perusal of the Table of Contents and a review of the descriptive paragraph at the beginning of this Foreword. In keeping with a desire to encourage these writings to speak among themselves, I have arranged them not by chronology or strictly by theme but for resonance that will make the diverse conversations among them more than the sum of their separate noise. If the genre is book, then the form is orchestral, however modest the music.

There is evident here a Canadian nationalism that will make some readers uneasy. It is not, however, a political nationalism but rather a desire to examine and share the genius of Canadian experience from a particular perspective, Canada as a country rather than a state, as landscape rather than geography, as a culture of infinite particularities, a community of endless diversity, a lovely and necessary and breathtakingly beautiful land. Some readers will find the feminism awkward, and I make no apology for the muted anger that occasionally informs my writing, nor for the relentless concern; I am a male of a particular age, and with the best intentions may sometimes stumble in reaching for a wholeness to human experience so long denied us.

Readers may find it a little odd that someone obviously the product of southern Ontario, with roots in Waterloo County extending through eleven generations, should show a disproportionate interest in Prairie writers and Arctic places. My response is embedded in what follows, but in brief, it is because I find that the most exciting Canadian writing, as opposed to writing-in-Canada, comes out of the West, and in particular out of the wonderfully shape-shifting mind of Robert Kroetsch; and because in over a dozen forays into the Arctic in all seasons, and in scores of books, I have discovered there among landscape and words a version of myself I am comfortable to live with and access to elusive characteristics of Canada as a northern nation not readily apprehensible elsewhere.

And finally, some readers may find the syntactical play excessive, and I confess, yes, and invite your indulgence. Writing that satisfies is seldom easy; nor is it transparent, pretending not to be there. Share in the enthusiasms for subjects of inquiry, in expressions of attitude, and in the exhilarating convolutions of language itself. Forgive the crankiness and eccentricities—if I can barely contain my fury over Margaret Atwood's banal critical reflections on Canadian nordicity, I applaud her genius elsewhere as a writer of fine true fictions and superb poetry. If the book seems occasionally driven by personal obsessions, I hope more often it is eclectic and generous. Enjoy the diversity, the refusal to be neat. This is a selection, not the whole canon. Some of the pieces have been extensively rewritten and all have been altered at least a bit from original publication. I owe much to many, but I am especially indebted to my daughters, Julia Moss and Laura Moss, both now professionals in the field, for their critical advice and affectionate forbearance over the years, and to my wife, Beverley, to whom this book is dedicated with deepest affection.

PRELUDE

This Is a Poem

(This piece might be called critical fiction, writing that collapses the conventions separating literary criticism, the belletrist essay, and imaginative narrative. The result is a pale reflection, perhaps, of a Borgesian short story or possibly, in the end, it may fulfill its desired fate to be a poem. Reading it now, you generously complete a paradox of indeterminacy, for it was written to be delivered orally, as the closing address following a lovely medley of formal papers and creative readings at the symposium "A Likely Story," held at the University of Waterloo as a tribute to Robert Kroetsch, June 12-15, 1997. The proceedings were subsequently published in The New Quarterly, *Spring 1998.)*

TIME IS LATE, so listen quickly. You know how some essays consist of a really good title—usually it's enigmatic and profoundly allusive—followed by ten or fifteen pages of explication? I've done a few of those and they are immensely satisfying. The more I thought about offering an essay in honour of Robert Kroetsch's seventieth birthday, however, the more inviting it seemed to do something radical, perhaps a whole paper of titles, page after page of phrases stolen from Kroetsch or inspired by Kroetsch, each title followed by a trenchant expository caption. Between these corollaries, a third notion occurred to me as more appropriate yet: there must be a title that could stand alone, a singularity consisting of all possible enigmas relating to the subject of Kroetsch. The title itself would be the text in its entirety, beyond which, in a subversion of syntax, there could be nothing more to say. Think of it. Words freed from the impetuous narratives implicit in grammar, in an infinite helix of ambiguity; a proto-title containing Kroetsch as a subject of discourse, yet allowing him to exist as a probable entity outside the text.

I once read poetry to an audience in Winnipeg. Kroetsch was in the second row, hair clenched; the intensity of his attention, as it always is, a compliment. Kroetsch laughed at a cryptic allusion to Wittgenstein. It wasn't meant to be a joke but at least he was listening.

Having posited my project as a focus of thought, I began to assemble the ingredient elements of diction with which to construct the panacetic Kroetschean title. At first this seemed an easy task. Words surged forward onto the computer screen from among the more familiar recesses of my mind in a critical mode. After accumulating a number of these, words like 'labyrinth,' 'paradigm,' 'doppelgänger,' and 'palimpsest,' I realized I would have to rise above the analogical deceptions of grammar by cataloguing my vocabulary according to the lexographical status and the metaphoric implications of each word in an endless variety of discontinuous contexts. I also realized the fruitlessness of thinking my private fund of words might coincide with Kroetsch's.

Since I would be working in English, the one language Kroetsch and I have in common despite our coincident ancestry amid the various strains of German endemic to Waterloo County, it seemed easiest to take up the thirteen-volume *Oxford English Dictionary* as a guaranteed repository of the words we might share. Since the *Oxford*, however, is based on principles determined by a parochial geo-historical elite convened under the sly British rubric 'The Philological Society,' once I had copied all its words onto my hard drive and arranged them in all possible categories of signification, using Web space for storage, I was compelled to supplement my compilation with Canadian variants, especially those resonating of childhood in Heisler, Alberta or Blair, Ontario, in the thirties or forties, respectively. My insistence on the Canadian component undermined many of the Oxford words, which then had to be culled from the original lists and inserted in new categories under such headings as 'imperialist anachronisms,' 'Anglo-Irish subversions,' 'alien sophistries,' and 'post-colonial lacunae.'

Needing a conceptual centre from which to measure the efficacy of words arranged by inference alone, in defiance of syntax, I momentarily fixed on Kroetsch the man as a rhetorical device. I wrote Kroetsch and asked if I could inhabit his life. I offered to be unobtrusive; to live it as if it were my own. He demurred through strategic silence. I may have had the wrong address, for he is the most generous man I have encountered among letters or words and among the most adventurous. I cannot believe he would have been able to resist my suggestion, as I was offering an exchange such that he could live a discrete portion of my own secret life for a while, perhaps when I was nineteen and thought myself tragically invulnerable or when I was fifty-six and refigured utterly by the inventions of love.

This was the situation. The categories into which I had parcelled out my word list were more numerous than the words they quantified. Think about it: there are only so many words to draw on for a monographic title, even allowing for future vocabularies, but their usage is apparently infinite. All words could be put in a big enough book, but no library could hold all the books they might breed. How, then, to disperse words into subsets in such a way as to direct their usage into an enigmatic cluster that would displace or subsume all previous and all possible projects on Kroetsch? My initial impulse to dispense with syntax seemed in retrospect anarchy. Yet I reasoned that only in the absence of rules do meaning and non-meaning confer, and only in such ambiguity could my ambitious project possibly succeed. By side-stepping grammar, I reasoned, words could merely be words.

In the presence of Kroetsch things are not that simple. Infinite galaxies of language refused to yield order. I suspected verbs were the problem. Before I could catalogue the discontinuous categories of all possible words that might apply to Kroetsch as a subject, I would have to subdue the motion of certain among them, to force them into uncharacteristic stillness. Nouns are still by definition; spacial, potential. The verb brings stillness alive, contributes the chaos of context. It is temporal, and tricky to deal with, even in titles of modest intent. Success, I suspected, for a project as daunting as mine, lay in bringing time to a standstill. But you will see my problem: what is only spacial or exclusively temporal cannot exist in itself, has no existence at all. Still is still only in relation to motion. Movement moves relative only to stasis. The delights of anarchy were beginning to wane. I would have to acknowledge grammar even if I refused its existential determinations. Words are never only words, I discovered.

Perhaps print would induce an illusion of stillness that syntactical evasions abjured; language inscribed on paper, not merely the patterning absence of light on a screen. Paper, as the Inuit say, stays put. Time, say the Irish, can be folded away on a bookshelf. Such was my strategy, then, as I shifted technologies and took up a pen. If I could reduce from three to two the dimensions of motion, then verbs might as gerunds seem still while nouns might appear unquiescent. (Think of it: on descent into a two-dimensional world of print, time, normally opaque, is faded to the utter limits of transparency; words become passages, paragraphs are places, ink an ontology, and from the position of text the contours of earth are impossible. On the page, lateral progress on the surface of the planet is a lovely illusion, connections are made in the mind, and the protuberant world is reduced to abstraction.) I used to think you could become what you write, find your way home on the page.

This was not the case. As I began writing, real things receded; my project seemed more elusive than ever. Nothing was gained from the shift in venue. Paper, it seems, offers only a brief premonition of how in the future we might see ourselves think—I returned to my Macintosh Powerbook, where in ways semioticians could never have dreamed, words come and go with lives of their own. I compiled a few titles at random: Reading Robert Writing; Enkroetsching the Cosmos; The Danger of Merely Living; The Shivaree Is Pronounced a Success; The Vernacular Imagination; Escape from Transcendence; The Fear of Paradise; The Despair of the Poet on Meeting Reality; A Typewriter Full of Words. Fragments, at best. I realized if I kept this up long enough to conjure all conceivable titles, I would not have everything. The illimitable possibilities of absolute singularity remained inaccessible. The only thing for it was to devise syntactical rhythms that would encourage words to be anything they wanted, yet more precise in the process, and unending in their particularity. Rather than turn away from grammar, I would orchestrate the parodic subversions implicit in all authoritarian systems. And thus, I reasoned, with leaps in both logic and faith, I would have to deal with irony, head on, if I were to devise a title that would apprehend our experience, in being Canadians, with Robert Kroetsch as our defining moment.

Whoa, I thought. Is that like saying he's Mr. Postmodern?

Caught in the snare and delusion of my own rhetoric, suddenly I realized, Kroetsch is not Kroetsch. I wasn't sure whether I meant the man or his canon or his cultural presence, or possibly all three. But of the essential paradox I was certain. Robert Kroetsch is a verb: in the incendiary fusion of writing and living that relates to his name, we witness a syntactical paradigm for what it means to be wholly engaged in the nexus of world and earth; Kroetsch, an empowering euphemism for being-in-time; not Heidegger, here, but Canadian maverick, and the hell with transcendence. What could be better, I thought, than such metamorphosis?

During the epiphany of discovering that Kroetsch is not Kroetsch, I was forced to reflect on something that had happened in the present tense, that I wrote as a poem. Sometimes poetry is the best way of saying things, especially for Canadians.

I decided it could wait. My project demanded the urgency that only the past can sustain.

It is not hard to place Kroetsch in a specific past but it is difficult to keep him there. I remembered him speaking in Grant Hall at Queen's University, October 27, 1995. In my memory I knew what he was going to say before he said it. That's when I realized it was Jacques Derrida I had heard in Grant Hall on October 27th. It is important to locate time and place in a text, to establish distance between an event being described and the event of its description. Narrative in the present tense lacks credibility—pretending, as it does, that writing, the written, and reading could be simultaneous. There is little substance to the statement 'Derrida speaks in Kingston,' whereas the statement that Kroetsch spoke in Kingston, Ontario, October 27, 1995, is irrefutable, even if he was never there. In using the past tense, narrative pushes the text ahead of the event while maintaining that the event precedes the reading that brings it into presence: we do not read the past as a past that has not yet happened; we read the past as a future that has already occurred.

Imagine Robert Kroetsch in Grant Hall, hunched under the mantle of diffidence he wears like Clark Kent's cape forgotten in a hasty change, chortling in anticipation of his own jokes so that we laugh with him and obscure the punchlines; Kroetsch, the shy extrovert, flashing his wicked grin into dark caverns of possibility beyond the balcony, enunciating with covert glee a dirty word, then muttering a mitigating theoretical context so that we share the grimace of his embarrassment; Kroetsch, in Kingston, Ontario, seeming for some reason the displaced Prairie love-child of Evelyn Waugh and F. Scott Fitzgerald; Kroetsch, the verb, in public apprehension. I can imagine not having seen all this, but eliminating myself from the scene does not make the Kroetsch we imagine less real. One way of locating someone is to identify his absence.

I recall being with Kroetsch in another context. This one I'm not making up; David Arnason and Dennis Cooley were there.

We were drinking beer and yarning about a previous gathering they had had. Kroetsch and Arnason had got into a discussion of grammatical proprieties in a common project, and Cooley had been arbiter. Arnason, where Kroetsch had had 'had,' had had 'had had.' 'Had had' had had the sanction of Cooley until, as he said, he had noticed Kroetsch, where Arnason had had 'had had,' had had 'had.' 'Had had' had had more credibility as Prairie vernacular, Cooley had thought, but such was no longer the case. Listening to them—I don't remember where it was, actually; I may be making this up—I remember my confusion about whether their earlier gathering had been in Winnipeg or somewhere else. Even our own place, out of time, can be empty.

I have heard Margaret Atwood speak in Grant Hall. She was amusing and clever, her talk reminiscent of the way you sometimes rehearse a conversation after it has happened, giving yourself all the best lines. I remember Atwood's hair, rampant, but not whether it was in style; aggressive hair, like Spenglerian gyres of history, comes into its own from time to time, without reference to moral context. Listening to Derrida, I did not think Atwood out of place at the edge of my mind, a persona for my fugitive and inattentive selves. Thinking of either, I do not find it inappropriate to remember Kroetsch speaking in Grant Hall.

This, however, gets away from my narrative. Kroetsch's personality was becoming syncretic poesis, so to speak, a structural paradox lending shape to my enterprise, without margins. It seemed hardly delusion that I could lie among words for aesthetic effect and words would become Kroetsch, or he become words. Reconsidering the Derrida episode, I was beginning to suspect that if I were to locate Kroetsch, at all, it would be as a future event, perhaps a work of art. Derrida spoke of lies and the future, of truth and the true. There, then, I thought, Kroetsch as a title awaits at the intersection of what is true and the truth. And that, I thought with brief satisfaction, will be a critical moment, where literature and life ingenuously open to each other, fully justifying my persistence in an enterprise of this magnitude.

Though we may lie among words, words do not lie. I was prepared to move ahead on this. But I can hear you saying to yourself, words lie on the page. That is yet to be determined, I will answer. Derrida spoke of the lie on October 27th at Queen's University in Kingston: since intentionality is a defining characteristic of the lie, he said, the future will decide its histories. The great man punctuated the air with crook'd index fingers, contextualizing quoted statements by Hannah Arendt, by others. What has been said in the past is pushed ahead of him, into the abyss of his own impending argument. Literature, while intentional, does not lie, he declared, but is not true, or else it would be something else. Truth, paradoxically, is ambiguous and absolute, but the true is relative, mutable, and transient. Literature is not true, but in literature one may experience the truth. What has been said in the past anticipates what Derrida will say. What he says will anticipate the past. As he spoke a conversation fell into place.

Derrida is proving as much a distraction in the present account of my enterprise as he was to the project itself, which was threatening to collapse under the exponential accretions of its own relentless success. Avaunt, Derrida! Avanti, Kroetsch! Like Conrad Black, not yet a peer of the realm, I wanted a title that would declare the future subsidiary, and everything preceding redundant. I wanted a title that would articulate and resolve all the anomalies surrounding Kroetsch as Kroetsch, if such could be said, surrounding Kroetsch as a verb, Kroetsch as art, Kroetsch as Canadian. Imagine the cosmology of word-combinations I constructed to address these anomalies. Abjuring the big bang theory of finite reality, I opted for endless parallel worlds of meaning, anti-meaning, and non-meaning from which revelation might appear. Unfortunately, no title came that seemed adequate. You can imagine the frustration that brought me back, eventually, from the abyss of intellectual opacity to consider the possibility that resolution of my problem lay, not in an open time-space continuum, but in language, itself, as a territorial imperative.

Proceeding inductively, I had arrived at the proposition that Kroetsch's major impact has been on language as the location of our collectivity, the region of our elusive confraternity as Canadians. He has given other Canadian writers, through critical rhetoric and by creative example, sanction to write in our own cadence and idiom. From outside Canada, where less emphasis is on the mimetic characteristics of our writing and more attention is devoted to its aesthetic achievement, Kroetsch is celebrated as an outstanding artist. Within Canada, he is appreciated on a more esoteric plane, for his revolutionary liberation of the vernacular imagination. It did not seem surprising to me, then, that his popular success at home would be in inverse proportion to the astonishing extent of his achievement. The proof of our freedom is in not knowing we are free. I felt goosebumps of satisfaction, but apprehensive. How could this be conveyed? This is Canada, I reasoned. Kroetsch's influence has not been absolute—how much could I expect language to convey about language? Short of including the entire Kroetsch canon in my title, along with everything that has been said or thought about him, and including his entire life insofar as words could contain it, with enough elasticity to allow for all that refused to be named, I could feel the grail slipping from my grasp, Canada subsuming us both.

Briefly in need of assistance, I turned to Dennis Cooley, a Kroetsch cohort and the foremost thinker on the subject of writing Canadian. With relief such as one invariably feels at finding an ally in an unlikely event, I read Cooley's argument that in this country we tend to receive literature only with our eyes and, in our writing, seldom show that we are listening to ourselves, our neighbours, speak. This gave me something I could run with. Much of our writing is done in what we call, with disheartening acquiescence, Canadian English. And of course there are some, such as John Metcalf, who write what might best be described as English-in-Canada. Not many write the language we use among ourselves. There are few who gather us in a text the way Joyce and Yeats do for Ireland, Faulkner for the American South. There are few who have made English a Canadian word.

At first you might think of Margaret Atwood. There is immediate recognition in Atwood's language of the times we live in, but there is no place, except the place described. Atwood's language reassures the decentred Canadian reader by insisting there is no centre. Michael Ondaatje does the same by making all things familiar, because the words are. Ondaatje's language may evoke specificity, but the reality is textual. Place is the place that is named; time, the times specified. The indiscriminate intimacy of Atwood and Ondaatje is part of their charm, part of their genius, perhaps, and may in some measure account for their immense popularity everywhere they are read. However, they speak to us, not for us. We listen; we listen in. That's the way we have learned to imagine people in the real world talk among themselves.

And then there is Kroetsch. Kroetsch listens; Kroetsch is a listening. Spoken and written language in Kroetsch's writing imply each other. When I read Hemingway's Africa, I hear Northern Michigan, early this century. When I read Achebe's Africa, I hear post-war Oxford. And when I read Kroetsch, I hear Heisler, Alberta, and if Robert Kroetsch were to write of Africa, or Alice Springs, I would still read among his words the sounds of Alberta. Language does this—not imagery but diction; not description but inflection. Idiom does this—spontaneity, at the expense of artifice; familiarity at the expense of formality; the feel of words, not fey intimations of meaning; pleasure in the noises of the living, at the expense of beauty, right reason, and ultimate ends. Such is the writing of Kroetsch and the life it conveys, the lives it becomes.

Now you might argue that we are not all from Heisler. But we are; and Heisler, of course, is us, born of the same ragged and distended history, cradled by the same sprawling discontinuities of landscape, nurtured by the same crazy-quilt culture, stupidly accommodating iconography and wondrous polyphony as we drown out national anthems in the dissonant squalor of regional bickering. Of course this is us. Do you think for one minute the Strauss boy, pissing clean over the principal's new car in Heisler, is not an intrinsic part of my own heritage, growing up in Blair, Ontario? Or yours in Leaside or in Chicoutimi, or on the banks of the Mirimachi?

Writers become the creations of what they write. Margaret Laurence created Morag Gunn, but now that Margaret's gone, she is Morag's progeny. Robert Kroetsch has re-created written language as a living space so well, for his Canadian compatriots, the writer tends to disappear among words, albeit some of them shaped as a familiar persona. Perhaps, I thought, being language while you are demonstrably not only of the world but in it is not all it should be. You can explicate Kroetsch as a text, but for all the generosity with which he shares his life, you will have missed the man. When you hear someone speak honestly, you attend to the words that lie between you, conversation inseparable from experience, between recollection and anticipation, history and dream. This is how you read Kroetsch reading you. This makes some people nervous, particularly in Ontario. He puts himself on the line. Take, these are my words. Kroetsch is a listening.

All my life I waited for the revolution. I tried to sing the revolutionary anthem but I didn't know the words. We are post-revolutionary, now. Those of us who survive gather to celebrate or grieve. An undertaking such as I had devised could never be more than an incomplete memoir, and I feared that perhaps what I was left with, if failure to say everything seemed likely, was silence. Given Kroetsch as model and motive, however, as subject and object combined, given Kroetsch as a verb and a listening, that seemed unlikely. My project was doomed, perhaps, to failure from the start for its colossal immodesty, yet I took comfort in the knowledge of my pivotal role in the turning of time. One writes to remind the dead they are not alone; but one also writes to remind the unborn they might never have been. Posterity will owe us more than we could possibly say. I was moved at last to poetry.

CRITICAL WORDS

Bushed in the Sacred Wood

(My perspective in this essay, originally written for publication in The Human Elements II, *edited by David Helwig and published by Oberon Press in 1981, reflects values and concerns of a time when critical responses to Canadian literature were undergoing close and necessary scrutiny. Others pursuing similar interrogations into the 'thematic' approach include Frank Davey, Russell Brown, and, more recently, Robert Lecker in* Making It Real. *While the significance of what follows may have shifted a little, from polemical to historical, I think the project itself is still disconcertingly immediate and relevant.)*

The resources of English-Canadian literary criticism are no longer adequate to the achievement of the literature. The boom years of Canadian self-consciousness have passed and sales of Canadian books are down; critical commentary is in a state of exhaustion. Responses that were apparently valid only a short time ago now seem inappropriate and often at odds with the function of good criticism. Access to the literature is threatened; appreciation is on increasingly tenuous grounds. In order to discover why, and then perhaps what may be done, the characteristics common to so-called thematic criticism of the early 1970s in English Canada invite consideration. In the tenets of its phenomenal success lie the sources of our present condition.

Critical evaluation at the time was based primarily on social or rhetorical utility rather than on aesthetic achievement. Is a work quintessentially Canadian, or marginal? Is it pedagogically attractive; that is, would it teach well, illuminate society, illustrate real life from a Canadian perspective? Does it reinforce the generalizations, the thematic schemes and cultural constructs that provide its critical context? The evaluation of art as art, even the appreciation of craftsmanship, of style and technique, were seldom allowed to intrude on the critic's role as mediator between the literature and society, explicator of its usefulness. Excellence was largely a matter of sympathy, and achievement the measure of a work's participation in the tradition, as critically defined. Based on ingenious schemes that were devised to contain an impossibly diverse literature and to define an improbably diverse society, an orthodoxy evolved. It is this CanLit orthodoxy that today threatens Canadian literature by limiting access to it, obscuring genuine works of merit while distorting the significance of secondary works, and constricting its future development.

Critics as different as D.G. Jones and Robin Mathews developed criteria for the appreciation of Canadian letters that in effect created a hierarchy of literary values based on concepts of nationality. Both men skillfully explicated the national character. Margaret Atwood, in *Survival*, casually drew our collective caricature. Frank Davey incisively defined us through our lack of definition. Criticism as caricature, or as a mirror, or as chiaroscuro portraiture, criticism that seeks to define rather than illuminate, particularly when its object is a nation, can become comfortably insular.

Critics of the early seventies more than ever before asserted Canadian nationality as both the object of critical inquiry and its beneficiary. Criticism became the expression of an ebullient chauvinism that had about it more than a touch of paranoia. Behind each declaration of our sovereign differences, swarming hints of our inferiority struggled for articulation and were necessarily quelled. These were not the times for humility or doubt. Yet any conception of culture as a phenomenon continuous beyond our borders, of continuity from our own literature to another, made us feel unspeakably colonial. We therefore in a cultural revolution of extreme but subtle importance severed our own tradition from those that threatened to overwhelm it.

If we must have connections with the outside world, let them be with Commonwealth literature, Australian, Nigerian, West Indian, where we can, more likely, hold our own. By consensus among Commonwealth specialists not only American literature but British literature, as well, is excluded. The effect is a curious lateral context without depth: we move from Margaret Laurence to Patrick White to Chinua Achebe to V.S. Naipaul, without reference to Melville or Twain or to Dickens or Trollope or Fielding. We have divorced Canadian literature of the past, present and, by implication, the future, from some of the greatest creations of human-time; seeking authority instead in archetypes, in Biblical or in allegorical allusions, and in our own generalized experiences of Canadian social, geophysical and historical realities. Shakespeare, Milton, Whitman threatened our integrity as Canadians, whereas the word of God or C.G. Jung, the Indian or Inuit personification of nature, the collective experience of Canadian 'folk' all served to reinforce our existence. Bear in mind that we had, culturally at least, been a spectral presence in the world until this time, the lumbering shadow of several empires, and our writers as well as our critics struggled artfully to make us whole: the writers would provide substance and dimension but it was up to the critics to outline the form, to define our shape.

The effect of this insularity, born out of pride and fear in strident combination, was the critical perception of Canadian letters in a literary vacuum. There was no standard of comparison, no established source of criteria for critical judgement, no perspective from which to approach a work, nor context within which to examine it, that was not arbitrarily devised. Critics seemed to be judging the size and shape of a constellation in the firmament, without regard either to their own arbitrary perspective or to the containing universe. It is a ludicrous task if you think about it; constellations do not exist except as imposed patterns of coherence. Yet we, that is, the critics, devised ingenious constellations to cast upon our literature, then assessed each separate work as it conformed to the design. Critics of the early seventies served profound social needs of their time but left such a distorted perception of our literature that it will take a determined effort to offset it in the future.

Those not caught up in the enthusiasms and anxieties of Canada of less than a decade ago have trouble understanding critical response to our literature at the time. They tend to assume Northrop Frye was somehow responsible—more because Frye's reputation would legitimize what they regarded as questionable practices, rather than for any evidence of his influence. If Frye generalizes about the literature and society, and so do these others, then Frye must be their source. But of course Frye responded to the same socio-cultural conditions as the others; he did not create them. Frye on Blake, Milton, and Shakespeare is a very different phenomenon from Frye on Canadian literature, about which he generalizes with as much careless aplomb as the least of his apparent followers.

The outsider is often puzzled by the very concept of a Canadian literature. Random works may command attention: *Fifth Business*, for instance, bears up under disinterested scrutiny; *Wacousta* appeals as a literary curiosity; Pratt's poetry stands apart from referents and antecedents in the way a Tom Thomson painting does, satisfying, from a present perspective, without jarring a pre-fixed sensibility. But what of all those other Canadian works, clearly secondary, derivative, provincial? Canadian criticism to date has no response to the unconverted, many of whom readily accept the value of inferior works in the major traditions—who often, in fact, make their living explicating these works in Canadian universities. Critics of Canadian literature, in cleaving from the mainstream, in devising arbitrary criteria of evaluation, in subverting worth to rhetorical utility, have generated an orthodoxy that bewilders outsiders. Instead of proselytizing for the literature among the literate, as it intends to do, such criticism limits access to it, particularly to the often delightful secondary works which are celebrated for the wrong reasons, ones to which the uncommitted reader is quite probably indifferent.

For those caught up in the CanLit syndrome, the distinction between literature and its social and historical contexts became blurred. Connections established by the so-called thematic critics as rhetorical devices seemed the truth, at the time. The most exciting writing of the sixties and early seventies apparently affirmed the importance of certain themes and motifs in what came to be called "the Canadian experience." Furthermore, the same predilections could readily be discovered in our literary past—the land was monstrous and Indians personified the land, and if the land was also beneficent and Indians the embodiment of natural good, contradictions could be subsumed merely by expanding the margins of the rhetorical scheme. The Canadian imagination, it turned out, was populated by wolves in snow, fool-saints and gothic bastards, slumbering giants and victims in a curious display of quasi-sexual positions, all preoccupied with survival, isolation, the body odour of race, wanderlust, even sex and violence.

For a brief period it was not only appropriate but essential to confuse content with context, to place arbitrary perimeters around the literary tradition, then use that tradition to define our social history. It seemed necessary to confuse content with critical criteria, assessing by the extent of its conformity a work's artistic significance. The conditions of our cultural history engendering such criticism passed, however. Its purpose, to redeem the literature from the darkness of colonial imperialism and assert its social worth as the voice and vision of national sovereignty, was served. Less than a decade later, such a response seems inadequate, both to the literature and the society.

Once an orthodoxy has set in, it is difficult to dispel. Adversaries of the so-called thematic critics proved ineffectual. This is because they offered only the vaguest of alternatives, the most tentative of new directions. And this is so because critics of thematic criticism, for all their ingenuous self-righteousness, have never really accounted for the origins of the response they perhaps justifiably despise, nor accounted for its apparent success, nor for its residual attractions. Without knowing where the 'thematic' response originates, nor why it was appropriate to the social, cultural, and even literary needs of its time, their call for change amounts to little more than an expression of contempt for our mutual blindness. What we need is someone to turn on the lights.

Mitigating against the darkness, thematic criticism has offered readers, teachers, critics, even writers a coherent guide through Canadian literature that for all its being arbitrary is no less a convenience. Teachers in particular enjoy the benefits of a critical rhetoric that emphasizes content over form, and subverts aesthetic judgement to the criteria of schematic generalization. Literature is reduced to a pedagogical tool: *The Stone Angel* illustrates themes, motifs, literary devices all of which confirm that it is indisputably Canadian. "Keine Lazarovitch 1870-1959" illuminates similar themes and motifs, uses similar devices, and is likewise empirically a Canadian work. Both Laurence's novel and Irving Layton's poem fit into a scheme of things, to several schemes, in fact. They are eminently teachable: critical systems that make them so, and offer them as prototypes in retrospect of an entire tradition, will not easily be abandoned. That these two works are excellent art is fortunate.

Other works that also reinforce one system or another and are not of the same quality, however, are taught as if they were. The best works are often taught for the wrong reasons, and works that do not fit are not taught. While *The Man from Glengarry*, for instance, might be a suitable novel for either a grade ten class or a graduate seminar, for very different reasons, it is taught in that broad area between, as if it were a worthwhile work of art in its own right, which is questionable. And contrarily, *Lives of Girls and Women*, which is superb art, is sometimes used as a source for discussion of social hygiene in grade ten, and as an example of aesthetic sophistication in graduate school, and for both it is inappropriate. And the novels of Mavis Gallant and Hugh Hood are consigned to limbo, beyond schematic rhetoric, outside the proscriptive tradition—and so, too, with the poetry of Joe Rosenblatt and even of Gwendolyn MacEwen.

In the classroom or wherever else the Canadian sensibility has been conditioned by so-called thematic criticism, there is little room for creative eccentricity, or for a critical revision of the past to handle our shifting perspective upon it, or for renewed congress with other traditions and the outside world. The current environment is not a healthy one for Canadian writers, the best of whom have left behind the thematic preoccupations writers shared with critics in the recent past. John Metcalf's 1980 comic novel, *General Ludd*, is brilliant—and has been casually denigrated or simply ignored: it belongs in company with the more sardonic works of Evelyn Waugh, but alongside *Sarah Binks* and *Cocksure* it seems merely out of place. Insights from the larger world are allowed to intrude as little as possible on the Canadian sensibility, it seems.

Only an enlightened anarchist like George Woodcock appears able to appreciate fully Matt Cohen's *The Colours of War*, or to question honestly the achievement of Rudy Wiebe's *The Scorched-Wood People*. Experimentation has been discouraged, although orthodoxy does admit exceptions: Robert Kroetsch and Michael Ondaatje are the best examples of formally innovative writers who have captured critical attention. In both cases, however, and with *The Double Hook* as well, invention is inseparable from a strong thematic thrust, which itself is highly conventional and very 'Canadian.' Other experimental writers of the sixties and the early seventies either faded, like Graeme Gibson and Douglas LePan, rose phoenix-like from their own burned-out embers as darlings of other genres, like Leonard Cohen who became a pop star and Scott Symons who became an avatar of antique furniture, or they adapted, like Matt Cohen, or became, like bp Nichol and George Bowering, members of the permanent avant-garde.

The problems of the critic of Canadian literature today are in good part a legacy of the so-called thematic criticism of our immediate past. While close attention to text or to a single author's canon avoids much of the confusion, as soon as comparative evaluation is attempted, the exhaustion of previous approaches becomes all too apparent. The further a work lies outside the thematic constructs of CanLit, the more pronounced the difficulty. For me as a critic, personally, this was brought home not long ago when I was set the task of writing a comprehensive critical piece on John Glassco.

Glassco is a writer about whom I once admiringly wrote that his genius lay in the consumption of his own life in order to have something to write about, a man who literally lived for his art, and whom I applauded for the dispassionate elegance of his style and for his elliptical insights into the creative sensibility. Yet more recently, in a commentary on Glassco's erotic fiction, I denounced the lifelong waste of his talent and judged his literary achievement trivial at best. Now, as I circled the man and his work, trying to resolve discrepancies of response, to separate personality from aesthetics, I became aware of being encircled myself. The many emanations of John Glassco refused to coalesce into a critical artifact. Instead, my assumptions, judgements, perceptions, were deflected back and were, it seemed, found wanting.

The inevitable response was intemperate. I wrote as follows:

> It is difficult to ignore John Glassco. A minor poet, bloodless pornographer, elegant hack riding on the reputations of such truly creative eccentrics as Beardsley and von Masoch, smug memoirist, amateur translator, gourmand, titillating darling of a Presbyterian *literati*, Glassco so squandered his talent, so indulged his appetite for public self-abuse, that he achieved the rare status in Canadian letters of 'failed celebrity.'

And so it went. Having previously acclaimed *Memoirs of Montparnasse*, I now assailed the personality informing it—being a memoir, this seemed a valid if confused critical approach. My notes teemed with comments about the book as a compendium of menus, about its author's staggering lack of imagination, about his role as a petty whore slithering through decadence that he had not the wit to enjoy nor the sensitivity to condemn.

Eventually sense prevailed and it became apparent just how far afield frustration had led me from legitimate critical function. Such recognition, however, raised more problems than it answered, and their resolution superseded the enigma of John Glassco in engaging my interest as a critic. Why is it so difficult to reconcile John Glassco's achievement with his failures? Why does his writing often seem to be both, at the same time? Why does Glassco seem so large and yet peripheral in Canadian letters, while in an international context he is small but comfortably ensconced? Why do the careless achievement and unrealized potential evident throughout his work both fascinate and repel? Why does the man so much intrude in the consideration of his literary canon? Somehow taste and judgement have fallen askew in the Canadian context, both of each other and of their informing principles.

In the context defined by Laurence and Layton, Glassco seems, at best, amiss. Among concepts of Canadian regionalism and/or the garrison mentality, among newly perceived mythologies of a communal personality, amidst schemes of themes, doctrines of aesthetic relativism and cultural utility, Glassco defies coherent appreciation. But as a decadent among decadents, an eroticist in the tradition of literary eroticism, an ironist, memoirist, belletrist, an apostle of esoteric hedonist subgenres, against the criteria of these contexts his achievement falls into perspective. The present critical climate in Canada, however, would hardly admit the practice of such urbane and cosmopolitan criticism as Glassco's work demands.

We have isolated our literature from world literature, cut our tradition away from the mainstream and run it through a mill-race, through the flume of historical necessity, to drive the wheels of national self-consciousness. But the mill grinds slower now, on other power, and the backwater in the race threatens to stagnate. It is time to open the floodgate.

The critical past cannot simply be repudiated, if radical change is to take place. Long before the vogue of thematic criticism, Canadian critics displayed a penchant for rhetorical generalizations and a distaste for aesthetic evaluation. From the beginning, taste, informed by a knowledge of The Great Tradition, and judgement, based on the social function of a critic within a perpetually fledgling society, bore little relation to each other. The critic, attracted by educated taste to particular works of art, then suspended critical judgement in deference to the demands of his or her society and discussed the literature in terms of cultural history. The critic as parochial historian, art as artifact—these premises dominated until well after World War

II, when our traditional sense of continuity with the British tradition attenuated, then severed. Finding us adrift on murky waters, critics like Carl Klinck and Desmond Pacey took soundings and with little reference to our former anchorage charted the topography of our own obscured past. Their purpose was literary in the broadest sense: theirs was not so much an aesthetic as a documentary function.

Preceding critics had likewise placed more emphasis on enthusiasm than aesthetic evaluation while struggling, often brilliantly, toward a coherent sense of a developing tradition. Sarah Duncan, writing in the 1880s, was perhaps the first modern Canadian critic, that is, the first to write self-consciously of literature from a Canadian perspective. Her work, never collected, was followed in this century by volumes with expansive titles like *Headwaters of Canadian Literature, An Outline of Canadian Literature,* and *Canadian Writers.* Such names as Archibald MacMechan, Lorne Pierce, Arthur Phelps, Pelham Edgar, A.J.M. Smith, and E.K. Brown ring through our cultural history, not ringing the changes but at least tolling our distinctive presence.

It was not until the late 1940s, however, when Canada culturally roused itself out of protracted adolescence, that criticism of Canadian letters took on the airs of a literary discipline. Through the inspired diligence of Klinck, the casual authority of Pacey, the professional zeal of people like Roy Daniels, Clara Thomas, Elizabeth Waterston, and Malcolm Ross, a lively awareness was generated of major works and key figures in the Canadian literary past. Yet the tradition itself remained amorphous; any claim it lay to achievement or coherence seemed pretentious and at the same time provincial. The critic was trapped by our cultural history in the role of apologist—until the sixties came and then the seventies and our writers and critics alike proclaimed Canadian reality as real, and proclaimed it good.

For a time, thematic criticism seemed to animate us and yet to absolve us from the burden of being ourselves, free us from the outside world, celebrate the best we had and were. Criticism, literature, and society seemed in perfect harmony. The querulous opponents of so-called thematic criticism would do well to consider how this came to be. Critics of thematic criticism like Frank Davey, the editor of *Open Letter*, W.J. Keith, the editor of *University of Toronto Quarterly*, and Barry Cameron, the editor of *Studies in Canadian Literature*, for all their articulate opposition, have failed to consider the implications of thematic criticism's apparent appropriateness and its undeniable success during the preceding decade. Yet it is there that the resolution to the muddle that such opponents offer as an alternative will most probably be discovered.

What is it that has nurtured thematic criticism in the bush garden of Canadian letters? The literature is diverse and so are the critical responses to it. Book-length studies like *Butterfly on Rock, Patterns of Isolation, Vertical Man; Horizontal World, The Haunted Wilderness, Harsh and Lovely Land, The Ancestral Present, Unnamed Country*, personal anthologies like *Odysseus Ever Returning, Articulating West, Another Time, The World of Canadian Writing*, extended essays like Frye's seminal conclusion to *The Literary History of Canada*, Dennis Lee's *Savage Fields* and "Cadence, Country, Silence," and Warren Tallman's "Wolf in the Snow," teacher handbooks like *Survival*, or the series on Canadian themes written by committees and published by the Writers' Development Trust, all these, it seems, fall under the versatile rubric 'thematic criticism.' Each gathers a variety of works into a rhetorical context. Each relates one work to another according to the configuration of its argument. Each treats literature in effect as a system, obscuring rather than enhancing the luminescence of individual works, particularly those that lie outside its rhetorical design.

At the extreme, this leads to the estimation of Hugh MacLennan as peripheral, while the critic's friends write works apparently the very embodiment of Canadian experience. More often, it merely lends to the literature itself an aura of insularity that is erroneous and demeaning. Literature becomes the vehicle of archetypal visions, patterns, regional idiosyncrasies, Heideggerian paradigms, and socio-cultural obsessions. Art becomes secondary. Some critics have conscientiously attempted to counter this, but so long as systems are promulgated, their needs demand to be served.

The prolific creation of rhetorical contexts was in part because there were none extant. Each critic approaching the literature had to decide for himself/herself the perimeters within which to work, the criteria, even the vocabulary to be used. Our cultural history yielded up no established literary tradition and certainly not a critical tradition. Canadian achievement was at the nether edge of a much larger and indifferent world. Separate works seemed, particularly to sensibilities conditioned from abroad, to relate far more to movements elsewhere than to each other. Thus early critics were forced to provide arbitrary connections among them, based not on literary but on socio-historical principles. The context and the criteria for literary appreciation necessarily came from abroad and inevitably our achievements here seemed rather paltry and peripheral. Nonetheless, attempts were made to see the literature as a whole. When, however, the time came to see it also as worthwhile, it was necessarily divorced from all others.

For cultural survival we rejected as tyranny anything that threatened to overwhelm us. The question in the early 1970s was not whether we were good enough but how our qualities could best be appreciated. If critical perception of Wordsworth defines a particular tradition, then, axiomatically, the criteria of that tradition will hold Wordsworth paramount. What chance has anyone else but to be considered below Wordsworth on a Wordsworthian scale; what chance has a Canadian in comparison with those from whose achievement the scale is made? The problem was not that Buckler might be inferior as an artist, but that he is not so Lawrencian as D.H. Lawrence, not as Wolfish as Thomas Wolfe. Similarly Sinclair Ross might empirically be a better artist than Sinclair Lewis, but against the awesome presence of the American tradition in our consciousness, Ross's Horizon seems provincial and Lewis's Main Street apparently runs through the cultural heartland. How could we fairly appreciate Canadians in alien contexts, using for judgement criteria derived from alien achievements? The answer of course lay in reducing the outside world to a level of inconsequence, simply by ignoring its existence. Our culture could stand alone—otherwise, it seemed, it would not be allowed to stand at all.

Taste might be informed by alien experience, but judgement would serve Canadian needs.

Encouraged by, or perhaps in response to, the maturity of a new wave of Canadian writers, typified by Margaret Laurence, Al Purdy, and the precocious Margaret Atwood, each of whom seemed to turn away from international response and write to us alone, critics shrugged off the Leavisites' Great Tradition and, with only a vacuum to take its place, devised systems of their own. Rhetorical generalizations no longer provided merely a framework to meet the needs of a gradually coalescing culture; they now defined that culture, asserted its sovereignty. Thematic schemes created critical contexts and provided criteria of evaluation without reference to the larger world. Critical systems served an obvious social function and the literature served to illuminate the systems. For a brief period a symbiosis seemed apparent among Canadian society, its literature, and the criticism that mediated between the other two.

There was an express need in the early seventies for a cultural identity in English Canada to appease our fears of separatism and to perpetuate Centennial self-love. Historically, perception of the collective identity in Canada has always been at odds with social reality. By the seventies this discrepancy had become acute and not only critics but writers of the time rushed to reconcile our strong sense of self with our apparent lack of definition. Critics discovered systems, themes, patterns, visions which held our literature together. And writers like Margaret Laurence in *The Diviners*, Rudy Wiebe in *The Temptations of Big Bear*, Al Purdy with *In Search of Owen Roblin*, David Helwig in *Atlantic Crossings*, Margaret Atwood in *The Journals of Susanna Moodie*, they too, sensitive to their social environment, discovered through their art patterns of identity in Canadian experience.

To some extent, thematic criticism is in direct response to the thematic predilections of Canadian writers. In the past, when our literature was necessarily derivative as a consequence of our colonial condition, form and style sustained our continuity with the Imperial source, while content expressed our differences. The legacy of this is that even now the most fiercely independent Canadian writers tend to express their sovereignty in content, and form remains reassuringly conventional. Good experimental work is rare in Canadian literature: among novels there are exceptions like *Tay John, By Grand Central Station I Sat Down and Wept, The Deserter, The Double Hook, Beautiful Losers, Five Legs* and *Coming through Slaughter*, all of which seem aberrations; in poetry, the *Martyrology* of bp Nichol, the works of bill bissett and Daphne Marlatt seem equally eccentric. Much more in conformity with the tradition as presently perceived are the pellucid prose of Alice Munro, the strong characterizations of both Laurence and Davies, the arresting strategies of Kroetsch, the strident attitudes of Richler. More central among poets are Nowlan, Layton, Livesay, Purdy, all of whose work demands close attention to what is said, far less to how; or Reaney, Macpherson, Avison, and Page, whose pyrotechnics reinforce the content of their poetry rather than embody it. In good part, critics have addressed content in Canadian writing because that is what predominates.

Criticism in response to content, to fulfill a social need, to fill a critical vacuum and construct a coherent literature of our own—such criticism is no longer adequate. As Wilfred Cude argues in his recent book, *A Due Sense of Differences: An Evaluative Approach to Canadian Literature*, excellence demands analysis, and the end of analysis should be explication of excellence. The refusal of Canadian critics to treat our literature seriously, as literature, earns Cude's wrath. It also provokes him to write excellent criticism; rhetoric, he reserves for the articulation of critical theory and the disparagement of current critical practice in Canada. The literature is never used to make his case: rather, his treatment of it provides the example of how it should be treated.

Perhaps the best forums for criticism as it is presently being written are the most arbitrary: learned journals or anthologies like *Contexts of Canadian Criticism* and *The Canadian Imagination*. Encyclopedic handbooks such as *Survey* and *From There to Here* nicely beg the question, while at the other extreme, specific social and cultural concepts are readily promulgated in works quite unambiguously designed as rhetorical vehicles—for example, Ronald Sutherland's *Second Image* and *The New Hero*, D.J. Dooley's *Moral Vision in the Canadian Novel*, and Robin Mathews' *Canadian Literature: Surrender or Revolution*.

It is time now that Canadian literary criticism serve the literature itself, time to stop considering literature a map of our collective consciousness; a mirror of our personality; a floodlight illuminating the national sensibility. It is time to consider Canadian literature as literature and not another thing. Schools may continue to use art as an exercise in civic awareness or moral development, the Canada Council may continue to endow talent on the basis of regional representation and the influence of referees, the Governor General's Award may continue to pass predictably among kith and kin, but Canadian criticism must learn to correlate, discriminate, evaluate. The responsible Canadian critic must force the reintegration of taste and judgement in his or her own work and demand it of his or her peers. The literature demands it. Works of Canadian literature must be celebrated for their excellence as works of literature. They must be appraised in relation to other works in the Canadian tradition but also to the best works anywhere in their genre, of their kind. Nationality must be recognized as having more to do with nationalism than with art. If we cannot be worldly and urbane as critics, then we should abjure the critical function, or at least more modestly address problems within our grasp.

Northrop Frye, who has become something of a false prophet, was true in his time. Offering by example modes of perception that effectively denied the necessity of explication or aesthetic evaluation, validating cultural generalization as a critical instrument, lending credibility to the serious consideration of Canadian literature, he served a vital purpose. Now, if we must discover a critic to emulate, one whose approach is cosmopolitan and urbane, one who does not shy away from evaluation and who is skeptical of critical schemes and cultural generalizations, we might do no better than to take another look at George Woodcock, who has been a critic practising among us for a generation.

Thoroughly informed about even the most obscure reaches of Canadian literature, at home with the best of British, American, and European literature and cultural history, insistent that these are not separate but interpenetrating realities, Woodcock has often seemed a curious anomaly. As the editor of *Canadian Literature* for nearly two decades and the prolific author of critical books and anthologies, he has been at the very centre of the CanLit boom, yet distinctly an outsider. When MacLennan was passé, he wrote on MacLennan. If Lowry seemed an imposition on Canadian hospitality, he welcomed him among us. He celebrated the polish of Purdy's poetry, the humanity of Klein. He elevated James De Mille, for *A Strange Manuscript Found in a Copper Cylinder*, to a peerage that includes Butler, Lytton, and Mallock. While more parochial critics have justly celebrated Matt Cohen's *The Disinherited* and *The Sweet Second Summer of Kitty Malone*, Woodcock went on (or back) to assess *Korsoniloff* in the context of the nouvelle vague fiction of Duras, Sarraute, Butor. Cohen's critically assaulted novel *The Colours of War*, Woodcock suggests, wryly echoes Voltaire's achievement in *Candide*, and discredits the novel's adversaries. Unfettered by rigid systems of literary response and social utility, George Woodcock is a superb model for the Canadian critic at the present time.

Our literature has come of age. It no longer needs a protective environment, favoured treatment. The same critical procedures that a short while ago were essential to its development and to our perception of it now inhibit its appreciation. It is time to assess Sheila Watson in relation to Jean Giono and not just the shaman and scripture, time to enjoy *Roughing It in the Bush* as a sentimental romance, time to recognize the radical genius of Elizabeth Smart. It is time to acknowledge that we are the heirs to a living past, citizens of the larger world.

'The Canadian tradition' is a term of convenience, not definition. 'Canadian literature' is a critical concept, not a limit of creation. 'Canadian' is a label of affiliation, not a quality of being. It is time for Canadian literary criticism to recognize these precepts and respond to them, for the sake of the literature, for the sake of excellence, for the appreciation of art as art and not another thing.

To Criticize the Critics: Cooley, Rooke, Atwood and Lecker

(To criticize the critic, for a critic, is a chance to acknowledge the art of the craft, to push at its edges, test its reach. For the critic as reviewer it means uncharacteristic humility to address, writ large, what he or she for the moment writes small; but it is also a licence to prescribe limits, proclaim values and goals. Of criticism I have reviewed over the years, three of the following works have most elicited the wonderful dread of admiration—the desire to share enthusiasm for someone doing better what I aspire to do well. In contrast, the fourth, number three in this arrangement, aroused the greatest anger for its facile and dangerous subversion of critical responsibilities. My review of Dennis Cooley's The Vernacular Muse *appeared in the* Journal of Canadian Poetry, *Volume III, 1987; the review of Constance Rooke's* Fear of the Open Heart *was published in the* Globe and Mail, *February 3, 1990; the review of Margaret Atwood's* Strange Things: The Malevolent North in Canadian Literature *was published in* Canadian Forum, *July/August 1996; the review of Robert Lecker's* Making It Real: The Canonization of English Canadian Literature *appeared in* Canadian Literature *152, Spring 1997.)*

I

Dennis Cooley is angry. He is also eloquent. He is engaging, and quite obstreperous. He is at times indulgent of his opposition, but never passive. He is inseparable from his writing. This is no disembodied temperate dispassionate critic of the old school. This is the Prairie critic, Dennis Cooley, poet, teacher, cultural entrepreneur, vital breathing thinking drinking real-life actual human being. We encounter Cooley in the text of *The Vernacular Muse* (1987) and respond as readers to the force of his personality, the thrust of his formidable intelligence, imagination, and commitment. And oh my God it's a joy to find someone alive in words. So often the language of literary criticism is like formaldehyde.

The principal argument in Cooley's collection of critical essays is straightforward. Let us restore life to literature, and literature to life. A simple, monumental, necessary, and curiously iconoclastic proposition. Anarchy in the groves of academe. Cooley's argument is at times familiar, as he marshals leading critical and cultural theorists to his cause, and at times quite strange. He has his own way of going, and his own way of being. He will make his case with reference to the Prairie world, to specifics of the particular cultural community he inhabits. He will hold this world to be intrinsically of value, worth writing into art. If The Great Tradition©, or the extended Cosmopolitan Tradition, cannot open to include and be enriched by, revitalized by, the local, colloquial, everyday reality of Prairie living, the miraculous thud of blood through human veins, then literature dies. Is dead. And Cooley's world is very much alive.

Discussion in the title essay, which is embedded at the book's centre, ranges from arcane to esoteric to extraordinarily ordinary. Cooley argues that established literature, what he describes as the received canon, determines the criteria of literary acceptability, proscribes the vital new. With distance between the written and spoken word in Canada ever increasing, this is disastrously stultifying. Orality falls victim to print; ingenuity, referentiality, ambiguity, and high-mindedness squelch the immediate, the local, the vernacular. Literature has become a self-contained, self-limiting discourse. With Michel Foucault at his side, joined occasionally by Terry Eagleton, Anthony Easthope, and especially Walter J. Ong, Cooley argues cultural legitimacy as the exercise of power which effectively disenfranchises all who express their lives in their own voices—what is not literary is allowed no place in literature.

This is a matter of language, not content; a matter of voice. Anything may be the subject of literature, so long as it is said in the appropriate manner. Listen to Cooley on Auden:

> When he introduced his radical politics into British poetry, the literary establishment had no difficulty in recognizing and admiring him as a poet. That's not surprising: Auden's voicing, for all its audacity, presented no deep affront to accepted discourse. Learned, intelligent, controlled, it bore all the signs of the literary. It used symbols, drew on myths (especially of pastoralism and of the apocalypse), observed (however sinuously) conventional prosody, spoke of serious things, inverted syntax, built to climaxes, marshalled its own metaphors, thickened with intricate binaries of meaning, fairly hummed with literary allusions. Its ironies could easily be forgiven.

Auden's voice is literary; therefore, his writing is literature. But many speak otherwise. Women. Native peoples. The working middle class. Most Canadians. Yet their voices occur in literature only parenthetically, with implicit condescension. Their voices in print remain "voices"—in quotation marks.

Cooley begins the title essay, "The Vernacular Muse in Prairie Poetry," with a reference to Elias L. Rivers' "Prolegomena Grammatologica: Literature as the Disembodiment of Speech," in which the signal differences in oral and written Latin during the Roman Empire are said to have sustained "a diglossic or bilingual world of cultural communication." We are not far from that, here, now. When John Metcalf can argue that the best models for Canadian writing are such very dead second-rank Englishmen as he encountered in his English childhood, and when a number of certifiably intelligent Canadian academics trip over their own credentials in the rush to agree, then it would seem we already live within a diglossic condition, and, in our own peculiar dissociation of sensibility, suffer the consequences. What we say and how we write are, to many, an incidentally coincident embarrassment.

'Accepted' Canadian writing is what David Arnason defines as the Tory tradition; it is written in what T.D. MacLulich calls the Tory mode. 'Accepted' writing is an expression of the bush-garden mentality; its critical elevation to canonical status, clear evidence of the colonized mind. But Arnason argues that we are not always under siege and summons up a syllabus of thematic Whiggery to prove it. MacLulich maintains that the barrier between garrison and landscape is language itself; specifically, the illusionary neutrality of high Tory style—neutral, because empowered culture invariably measures itself as the norm; illusionary, because, as Eagleton argues, objective disinterest in literary matters is a myth sustained by vested interests, in our case, by the "custodians of received culture," as Cooley describes the garrisoned establishment. Meanwhile, Canadians speak. Canadian-speak. But the establishment does not listen. It reads only with its eyes.

Using Ong's *Orality and Literacy* as a principal resource, and with passing deference to Jacques Derrida, Cooley makes an eloquent case for reinstating orality in the literary text. A good and reasonable suggestion. Cooley makes of it a ringing manifesto, arguing his case with passionate intelligence and powerful rhetoric. After providing a couple of poems in/of Prairie vernacular, and discussing their effectiveness with erudition bordering at times on parody, he leaps, inevitably, into a discussion of Robert Kroetsch. Non-literary texts, the vernacular, oral history, and a superb command of established literary convention combine in his title essay, with breathtaking aplomb. If there is a flaw, it is perhaps that Cooley risks treating Kroetsch as an authority, and his writing as authorized text. For a few brief paragraphs I had the feeling that all else in his essay was threatening to become a gloss on Kroetsch's remarkable achievement.

Still, in his thorough if idiosyncratic consideration of orality in literature, in his analysis of established opposition to the vernacular voice as both form and content, in his endnotes on imagination as a terminal condition in our academic institutions, and in his carefully modulated suggestions for change, reinforced by excellent appraisals of original work by Andy Suknaski, Dennis Gruending, and Kroetsch, Cooley has written an essay that matters, that changes things. Cooley's writing is so solidly 'placed,' and in 'time,' that even to disagree with him is an affirmation of your own being in the world, of being *here*.

The book's central argument is first articulated in the opening essay. In "Placing the Vernacular," Cooley plays the role of artful mediator. He draws an equation between what he calls 'eye' poetry and what he calls 'ear' poetry that makes them seem equivalent. Yet eye poetry is the traditional/conventional monologic page-poetry of literature. Ear poetry centres on the vernacular, dialogic word-spasms of actual speech. By examining both in the specific context of an essay on Saskatchewan poetics, Cooley gives the vernacular muse all the laurels of The Great Tradition© which somehow comes off in the comparison as epicene and alien. I'm not sure that Cooley illuminates greatly the characteristics of ear poetry in this essay, but he does make his reader recognize that the vernacular is a voice worth listening to. Marshalling John Stuart Mill (eloquence is heard; poetry overheard) on behalf of tradition, and Ong's "secondary orality" as the basis of ear poetry, he develops binaries of landscape against speech, originality against replication, and, of particular interest, male against female, which at the very least suggest there is more than one way to make a poet.

Cooley leads a sympathetic reader to realize how few people in this country actually write 'Canadian.' And what they're up against if they try. We in effect learn received literature only with our eyes and, in our writing, seldom show that we are listening to ourselves, our neighbours, speak. Much of our writing is done in what we call, with disheartening acquiescence, Canadian English. Cooley wants more—and this is where his argument runs into a bit of trouble. Canadian writers must not only speak Canadian in their writing, write the spoken word, they must reject the literary. Or, as Kroetsch does, subsume it. Now this can make good art. Witness *Seed Catalogue*. But it can also hold the world of beauty hostage to triviality and inconsequence. Drunk is not necessarily more profound than sober; boorishness, not necessarily more vital than grace; pettiness, more focused than perspicacity; the common, more redolent of the universal than the special, the inspired, the extraordinary. The voice of a Prairie baseball game is legitimate literature. But literature should no more be restricted to the ball diamond than to the ivory tower. Perhaps it is his rhetorical gusto that makes me feel at times as if Cooley's argument is more *against* tradition, influence, and the text than it is *for* orality and the vernacular muse.

The other essays in this collection speak to or for the central argument, all except what is probably the most brilliant, unusual, and entertaining essay on line endings in poetry that is ever likely to be written. "Breaking & Entering (thoughts on line breaks)" is a perfect expression of the vernacular critic's voice. With casual authority, Cooley identifies sixteen ways to break a line and offers a brief discussion of each, drawing into his discourse glancing references to the poetics of Douglas Barbour and John Keats, Al Purdy and William Carlos Williams, Phyllis Webb and Marianne Moore, and even Ogden Nash. He asks, "If we divvy up grammatical units, why not words themselves?" and the casual urgency of his words reminds me of games after school in Waterloo County, even as he opens onto the poetics of e.e. cummings. His essay is precisely what the title suggests, and it is very well done. It should be required reading for anyone teaching poetry still alive enough to resist burial.

Cooley writes long essays. I was not particularly interested in reading about Robert Duncan's "A Poem Beginning with a Line by Pindar," and yet as I progressed through the unhurried, humane, and highly informed discussion I became enthralled. It is exhilarating, even liberating, to share with a critic the process of thinking. Personally, I prefer the more free-wheeling theoretical debates, the rhetoric and the erudition, the charm, the anger. But even reading the relatively restrained essays on Dorothy Livesay's political poetry, on *The Stone Angel*, on Sinclair Ross's short stories, and on Ondaatje's *The Collected Works of Billy the Kid*, I found myself accepting Dennis Cooley as perhaps the most interesting and versatile critic writing in Canada today. Writing whatever, writing Canadian.

II

One measure of the worth of a literary essay is the extent of the margin notes it commands from the attentive reader. In my copy of Constance Rooke's *Fear of the Open Heart* (1989), the white spaces on the page are almost obliterated. From the very beginning, she engaged me in spirited debate, my share of which found its way into hen-scratched marginalia. In neatness, alone, she had the advantage. Otherwise, we carried on a fair dialogue to the last page, with its lovely declaration that reading, to her, "is not a solitary act. Whatever idle or auspicious day-dreaming it may entail, reading is also a response to another person's urgent speech."

Exactly. That's it exactly. Her book sanctions my presence as a reader in the discourse being written. Rooke invites the reader to relate directly, intimately, and openly to herself as writer, as she is revealed in the text. In doing so, her criticism is its own best argument in support of what she calls the "theory of intimacy." While she relates the fear of an open heart in Canada to rather archaic notions of garrison mentality, she posits it also as the barrier between reader and writer that comes of modernist conditioning, a barrier that denies the intimacies to be had among words.

The theory of intimacy that she expounds in the first of thirteen essays on Canadian literature argues for the personalization of text. It goes beyond basic semiotic principles of reader response to insist on the possibility of an interactive personal relationship between reader and writer, a personal encounter among words. It argues that the most valuable literary criticism is a public display of deep-reading, to enhance the reading experience rather than the text itself. Good criticism is an expression of the critic's capacity for intimacy, shared with other readers as an act of generosity arising out of aesthetic appreciation and intellectual discipline.

The title of Rooke's essay collection is somewhat ironic, for the author herself shows little fear of an open heart. Yet the title is aptly chosen because she is writing in and about a world where such fears persist. She sees Canada caught in the grip of emotional repression; her critical vision is of writers, especially women, struggling against this inheritance, towards openness and freedom.

Rooke's combination of revelation and rhetoric is quite unlike anything in Canadian letters since Margaret Atwood's broadside in *Survival*, published in the early seventies. There is a similar tendency in Rooke for generalizations to be offered as actuality, for opinion to become, a few pages later, proof. Her vision is not so grand as Atwood's, but she writes with a more sophisticated critical wit. Most significantly, she is not constrained, in the way of thematic criticism, to see art and society as worlds in parallel, reflecting one another but not interpenetrating. Thematic concerns of one era have become the cultural politics of another.

Inevitably, given the critical preoccupations of her particular personality, Rooke has favourites. For the most part they are women and writers of fiction—although her in-depth celebration of P.K. Page is one of the best essays on a single canon of poetry to have appeared in this country in some time. Perhaps ever. She writes with comfortable authority about works by Mavis Gallant, Sheila Watson, Margaret Laurence, and

Margaret Atwood. Included also are an exhaustive reading of Michael Ondaatje's *Coming through Slaughter* and two essays on peripheral fictions by John Metcalf.

There is a delightful arbitrariness to her approaches which invites her reader to wonder what she would do with texts not addressed. It would be interesting to know how she would treat Metcalf's principal work, *General Ludd*, or some of his better short stories ("Robert, Standing" comes to mind as among his best). I would be intrigued to read a more relaxed consideration of Ondaatje, and to read her on Ethel Wilson's *Swamp Angel*, or on the writings of Elizabeth Smart, Robert Kroetsch, or Daphne Marlatt. I know Rooke has published widely on a variety of subjects, but the critical personality so openly present in this book invites speculation on what she might say within the extended sphere of the reader's own interests, whose presence in the discourse she has so eloquently sanctioned.

Sometimes her approach seems narrow, but this is in part a rhetorical illusion. Her considerations of food in the fiction of Alice Munro and hands in the works of Margaret Atwood are disconcertingly single-minded. Yet the critical insights in such a process are illuminating. By seizing on food, hands, and the like, in the writing of others, she acquires structural motifs for her own writing. Around these she offers analysis and explication almost at random, or at least on her own agenda, not that of the text. And always, her reader is given access to more than it seems.

Perhaps the most satisfying of her criticism is on the work of Margaret Laurence, especially in the grandly named essay "Hagar's Old Age: *The Stone Angel* as *Vollendungsroman*." Here she pursues with passionate intensity her interests in the condition of women in a misogynist world and of the old in a world committed to the denial of aging. Rooke's reader is drawn into Laurence's text, as well as her own, by the force of character and critical analysis in easy harmony. Her commentary on the distance between immediacy and intimacy in Mavis Gallant is controlled and very clever, while her meticulously indulgent reading of Atwood's *The Handmaid's Tale* seems a little contrived. Both depend heavily on her theory of intimacy—but with Gallant personality offers revelation while in Atwood it comes closer to providing sanction for critical perversity.

Despite her openness, Rooke is not egalitarian. In coining a term like "vollendungsroman," for example, to describe novels of 'completion' or personal closure, Rooke signals her appeal to a limited readership. Her discussion of women in *The Double Hook* reads almost like an apology, and might seem rather arcane except to someone equally familiar with both Watson's novel and its extensive critical context. Her rather oblique insights into the fiction of Alice Munro confirm its continued refusal to yield graciously to critical inquiry, and for the more casual reader might seem exclusionary. The informed reader who is not entirely at home with critical theory or Canadian texts will sometimes be at a loss. Rooke's criticism demands knowledge on the part of her reader, and commitment, as well as an open heart.

Constance Rooke risks something rare among Canadian intellectuals. She thinks in public. It is this, her thinking in public rather than issuing the residue of private thought, that makes her work compelling, dynamic, and occasionally elusive. Sometimes she sways an argument in her favour simply by the force of personal preference. Several times she congratulates herself for critical acumen and, at one point, prides herself on being what she describes as an extremist critic. The effect is not of arrogance or condescension, however, but of self-assured humility, of engaging vulnerability. In opening herself to the reader almost as an act of critical grace, she re-creates the text as a context in which to find one another, and oneself, among words.

Already known as editor of the *Malahat Review*, as a short story writer, and among academics as chair of the Department of English at the University of Guelph, with *Fear of the Open Heart* Rooke joins company with Linda Hutcheon and Dennis

Cooley, among the best of our contemporary critics. Her writing in this book is sometimes eloquent, never pedestrian. It is intelligent and expresses a fine critical imagination. Sometimes radically innovative, it is often courageous, passionate, and humane. *Fear of the Open Heart* is a good book. It really is.

III

In 1974 Frank Davey delivered a scathing condemnation of thematic criticism, the title of which, "Surviving the Paraphrase," identifies *Survival*, Margaret Atwood's commentary on Canadian literature, as his principal target. His paper became a published essay in 1976 and, in 1983, part of a book, both with the same title. Davey went on to construct himself as a cultural edifice, while Atwood has soared in public esteem as a poet and novelist and woman of letters. She is an excellent recipient of honorary degrees, guaranteed to deliver a wickedly timely and witty address, irreverent enough to make even the most proper of academic hosts feel squishily daring.

An intriguing question is what would Davey do, now, if he were tempted to build a career on Atwood's recent Oxford publication, *Strange Things: The Malevolent North in Canadian Literature* (1995)? Possibly he would find a more worthy object of contempt; or possibly, a writer more vulnerable. Atwood's book is beneath the former and she, as a writer of iconic presence, beyond the latter. So much for Davey, but what about Atwood, what about *Strange Things*? Here is a book, the most significant aspect of which is that someone might take it seriously, as Davey did *Survival*, because of its author's formidable stature.

The title of *Strange Things* is taken from Robert Service, one of the author's main sources of image and opinion clusters in her free-wheeling discussion of the 'north' as anything in Canadian literature that is neither urban nor agrarian. In a text that gathers four lectures delivered at Oxford in 1991 under a histrionic and pandering subtitle, Atwood demeans the notion of Canada as a northern nation, affirms the careless generalization of A.J.M. Smith about nature evoking, in Canadians, stark terror, and lumps high art with low, truisms with the arcane, solely on the basis of content, without regard to historical, linguistic, or cultural context. The result could be dismissed as chatter but for the fact that the quality and reception of her other work lends authority even to the most banal of platitudinous assemblages. That is what makes this book dangerous.

Its astonishing co-opting of other texts is unsettling; the absolute lack of moral or aesthetic discrimination is disappointing; the adolescent whimsy as a substitute for reasonable argument is condescending; 'cute' as a rhetorical device, grating; and the effusion of social and literary generalizations is wrongheaded, foolish and destructive. One is annoyed to think that Atwood's British audience at Oxford would have had their every bias about the inchoate condition of Canadian culture confirmed, but one is—that is, I am—outraged that such nonsense is now lodged in print. Its relative permanence within the Atwood canon, in the Canadian tradition, and within English letters makes her book worth the discussion.

As someone associated with so-called thematic criticism of the seventies, I have a vested interest in seeing the iniquities of the approach exposed. *Strange Things* is a model of why thoughtful critics and readers moved on to other avenues of exploration in response to matters of literature and society. As a writer and traveller with a vested interest in things Canadian and northern, I am dismayed at Atwood's haphazard polemics and a little embarrassed to be commenting on them in public. Perhaps I am an inappropriate reader: Atwood has taken careful measure of her Oxford audience and declared herself outside the academic loop, a scholarly maverick, merely a writer, merely a woman at that, and there at Oxford only to amuse.

Perhaps her most disconcerting mode of amusement, even without querying her reliance on resources like Ogden Nash, John

Robert Colombo's *Windigo* anthology or *The Complete Poems of Robert Service*, is Atwood's devotion to paraphrasing. There was a time this seemed acceptable among Canadian critics—on the premise that one's audience might not know the texts under discussion. Several decades ago it became evident that intelligent critical commentary could bridge the gaps between audience ignorance and the speaker's argument while maintaining the integrity of the text or texts under discussion. To do so would take a breadth and depth of knowledge not usually associated with the thematic approach. The problem with paraphrase as rhetoric is not that facile generalizations become inevitable, but that they conceal authorial condescension behind a tangled hedge of borrowed narrative, defining the limits of a garrison that isn't there.

A full six pages, or twenty percent of "Linoleum Caves," the last of her four talks, is taken up by retelling an Ann Tracy novel, *Winter Hunger*, while five pages are devoted to a paraphrase of Marian Engel's *Bear*. Ethel Wilson's *Swamp Angel*, about a woman "escaping from her disgusting creep of a husband," is given two. In "Eyes of Blood, Heart of Ice," fifty-nine lines of George Bowering's poem "Windigo" find their way into the text, along with two and a half pages devoted to paraphrasing an execrable poem by W.H. Drummond. One-fifth of "The Grey Owl Syndrome" is taken up with a facile rendering of Robert Kroetsch's *Gone Indian*, while the opening talk is preoccupied with E.J. Pratt's poem *The Titanic* ("They also serve who only stand and sink"), which he wrote, says Atwood, when he might have been writing about the Franklin disaster but didn't. This is not criticism or critical commentary: it is connecting the dots.

Instead of pencil crayons, Atwood uses opinion. Her explanation of the wendigo, she says, with unusual logic, will illustrate "the extent to which Native motifs have infiltrated non-Native literature and thought." She declares with authority about Earle Birney's "Can. Lit," "This poem continues to be quoted as a still-accurate encapsulation of the flatness of the Canadian imagination." Such intellectual shabbiness becomes arrogance with the depthless observation that A.M. Klein situates the poet at the bottom of the sea, in "Portrait of the Poet as Landscape," because, "apparently, that's where Klein felt it appropriate to place him." This is something, she observes without further explanation, with which she is "intrigued." With similar condescension, she offers the following intertextual insight, given here in its entirety: "Nor do the final arctic scenes in *Frankenstein* provide any clue to the Wendigo's meaning."

It is important to discuss *Strange Things*. It will be read and much used as a resource for understanding 'the Canadian experience.' Its summer-camp prose and witty irreverence, its simplistic arguments and aphoristic rhetoric will enable it to endure any such judgement as mine—which might, I regret, seem northern malevolence, but is not. It is genuine dismay. At least, I am consoled, *Strange Things* has the redeeming feature of being brief.

IV

Robert Lecker is so wide-ranging an entrepreneur within the small but divisive economy of Canadian literary studies that a reviewer of anything he writes, particularly when it is published by someone other than himself, must necessarily declare a position in relation to his extensive field of influence. I have never done a book with his press nor an article in his journal, except when it has been guest edited. Although we spent a few memorable days together in southern Italy, where we ran on ancient roads through sun-drenched olive groves, we have never lunched. We share a publisher, Anansi; I was on his Ph.D. examination committee; I am mentioned with some ambivalence, or my writing is implied, quite often in his work; he once sent me a complimentary letter about my essay "Bushed in the Sacred Wood," a letter I value both for its unexpectedness and its critical acumen.

Position declared, I would argue there is much in *Making It Real: The Canonization of English-Canadian Literature* (1995) to rival the best that has yet been written on the politics of Canadian culture and literary studies. The first four essays are passionate, intelligent, and, if sometimes short on specific details, invariably provocative and intriguing. The rest, another six essays including a didactic epilogue, is an elaborate and sometimes inspired gloss on the opening argument(s).

Despite his subtitle, Lecker writes about more than the formation and manipulation of literary taste and the literary canon in English Canada. What he offers reader-critics is an elegant and highly persuasive polemic on the need for defining and meeting civic responsibilities, on the moral necessity in a Canadian context of acknowledging the presence of Canada in our literature, and of our literature in Canada. Using literary criticism as his principal field of discussion, with occasional references to fiction (from mainstream to arcane), and a very few to poetry, he argues that Canadian literary studies have become isolated, private, solipsistic, esoteric, proscriptive; we have left ourselves nothing to study but the studies themselves, or so it seems.

During what Lecker describes as the industrialization of Canadian literature, which he sets in an historical context between the Canadian Writers' Conference held at Queen's University in 1955 and the "Future Indicative" Conference at the University of Ottawa in 1986 (which I organized), with the 1978 Calgary Conference on the Canadian Novel as, perhaps, its moral nadir, a thematic hegemony articulated self-affirming canonical status to select texts, excluding unnamed others as marginal to the collective purpose. This in turn forced closure —the canon as garrison. Critical discourse not concerned with consolidation turned elsewhere, to the obfuscations and delights of critical theory, or to multiculturalism and marginality as a new frontier, the centreless centre.

Writing without the bitchiness that characterizes some of his periodical essays, Lecker the cultural critic shows an astute understanding of the historical imperatives informing canonization—while leaving Lecker the literary entrepreneur largely out of the equation. He describes with critical discretion his own position relative to his various enterprises, including ECW Press and *Essays on Canadian Writing*, and to other critics, especially Frank Davey (avoiding Davey's penchant for writing and rewriting himself into the shifting centre of Canadian cultural history). Such restraint curiously strengthens his position, enhances his insights. He knows what he is talking about and tries to sway the reader through argument based on research and rhetoric. Without compromising his own achievements, he is able constructively to critique the consequences of their impact.

He avoids Davey's sly assumption in "Surviving the Paraphrase" that the so-called thematic critics conspired in a sort of cultural vacuum to erect perimeters around critical discourse, and mounts a sophisticated plea for renewal, not of the values of those more ingenuous times, nor of the critical strategies and procedures, but of what might be termed their cultural self-consciousness. If Canada is no longer reasonably to be presumed a monolith, in which canonical texts are inseparable from the literary institution whose values they reflect, celebrate, and perpetuate, then still it is necessary for our cultural survival to imagine the country, the nation, as a collective fiction, to explore canonicity not as the limit of enclosure but as a field of inquiry in our ongoing discourse with ourselves. The alternative, Canada as merely an agglomeration of competing forces, and Canadian literature as Canadian only for academic convenience, anticipates the collapse of Canada as a cultural entity.

There is so much in the first half of *Making It Real* to argue with, for and against, it is difficult to imagine an informed reader who will not fill the margins with expletives, retorts, exceptions, notes, arguments, commentary verging almost on a parallel text or private subtext. It is equally difficult to imagine a wide readership, for the specialized knowledge necessary to engage in such a debate will exclude even the most literate non-

Canadianist, ironically undermining Lecker's valid arguments for a return to criticism as a public act.

The second half of the book, while certainly thoughtful and provocative, does not elicit the same complexities of response. Following a statistical analysis of anthologized short fiction that is far more valuable for its peripheral insights than its quasi-mathematical exactitudes, Lecker delivers a rather interesting excoriation of the New Canadian Library, especially the NCL marketing of so-called "classics." (To my lasting embarrassment, I was on the "Classics Advisory Committee," having been invited by Jack McClelland and Anna Porter in 1974 to take over the general editorship of NCL after Malcolm Ross's anticipated departure, an event the possibility of which outraged Ross so much that he held on for another decade or so, until he was eventually succeeded by a very patient David Staines, after McClelland and Porter had both moved on to other interests.) In the following essay, he isolates *As for Me and My House* as our most notable classic manqué. Then there are parallel essays on Northrop Frye and Frank Davey: the Frye essay is commendable for its reading of the Conclusion to *The Literary History of Canada* as a personal narrative; the Davey essay, taking the same tack, is devastating. Davey, as narrator, comes across as a clever opportunist, smug and manipulative; "Surviving the Paraphrase," as shallow, solipsistic, pseudo-subversive.

Lecker writes with edgy wit and a fair amount of bravado. He is better when he is contemplative, writing with passionate intensity, demanding reader response, insisting we attend to what he says, not to what he does, or has done. Canada matters; Canadian literature matters; critical activity in the field of Canadian literature has a cultural function, social responsibilities, historical relevance. If we as readers and critics find ourselves locked in a hall of mirrors, perhaps it's time, he argues, to break glass.

Works Cited

Atwood, Margaret. *Strange Things: The Malevolent North in Canadian Literature.* Oxford: Clarendon Press, 1995.

Cooley, Dennis. *The Vernacular Muse: The Eye and Ear in Contemporary Canadian Literature.* Winnipeg: Turnstone Press, 1987.

Lecker, Robert. *Making It Real: The Canonization of English-Canadian Literature.* Toronto: House of Anansi, 1995.

Rooke, Constance. *Fear of the Open Heart: Essays on Contemporary Canadian Writing.* Toronto: Coach House Press, 1989.

The Paradox of Meaning

(This essay was conceived as an aural text and, paradox notwithstanding, is meant to be read as such. By allowing resonant space between discrete segments of discourse, I had hoped in writing it to argue the necessity of moral engagement for the critic of Canadian letters without being righteous or proscriptive. In pushing the limits of what an essay can be, in counting on you, the auditor or reader, to hold its disparate parts in mind and let them coalesce in rhetorical patterns drawn as much from your personality as my own, I wanted to engage as poetry does, on the level of commitment. Parts of this project were delivered in Fredericton in April 1995, under the title "The Invisible Palimpsest," as the keynote address at a conference on "The Poetics of Self: The Art of Autobiography" held at the University of New Brunswick, and other parts in a faculty talk entitled "Critical Responsibilities" given at St. John's College, University of Manitoba, when I was for a brief time the visiting writer-scholar in residence, in September of the same year.)

> Works of art are of an infinite loneliness and with nothing to be so little appreciated as with criticism. Only love can grasp and hold and fairly judge them.
>
> —Rainer Maria Rilke

You have to wonder if Rilke had any idea what he was talking about. The romantic faux-muscularity, the Hallmark sentimentality, the rank elitism; the pretensions of his intellectual indulgence are an embarrassment, even more so because they seem plausible, reassuring, almost inevitable, coming as they do from an artist of established sensibility.

Works of art are of an infinite loneliness and with nothing to be so little appreciated as with criticism. Only love can grasp and hold and fairly judge them.

Look on the inside of the front cover of *Brick, A Literary Journal.* Rilke's words proliferate, copy by copy. Delivered to the minds of *Brick* subscribers, his words urge love on them so refined that not only should they grasp and hold works of art, but fairly judge them without benefit of thought. In the beauty of infinite loneliness, transposed by Rilke from the artist in the angst and ecstasy of creation to the work of art itself, the readers of *Brick* are offered licence, indeed sanction, to appreciate through ignorance, indolence, and the limitations of individual imagination.

In the first radio broadcast of *Superman,* the eponymous hero was modestly described as "able to leap one-eighth of a mile at a single bound." A Toronto foundling of the 1930s, Superman was cast out as an infant from a world where "men and women exactly like ourselves but advanced to the peak of human perfection" were consumed in a ball of fire. The same virulent quasi-science of eugenics that led to the Holocaust and Hiroshima gave birth to the greatest superhero of modern times. There is a relationship between culture and history; text and context. There are no men and women exactly like ourselves.

Bev asks me what I am writing about. I don't know, I say. What are you supposed to be writing about? she says in her reasonable way. I don't know, I say. It's for a talk. What do they want you to say? I don't know, I say, feeling imprisoned by the linearity of her inquiry. I'll know when it's written down—circularity is enervating; like voluntarily restricting yourself to solitary confinement. Why do you say talk about when you mean write; why say writing when you're using a computer; why written down, written up, written out; how can voice be passive; what are the semiotics of syntax; how can articulation precede thought, words precede meaning? She looked at me sympathetically, even though these last queries were cast into an appropriation of her voice for ironic effect. Beverley is a teacher; her own questioning leads to meaning; mine, it seems, invariably, to the edges of incomprehension. How does writing think? That's clearly me, not even pretending to be her anymore: there is freedom in evading the boundaries of gender, of personality. I am now in the courtyard, but still behind walls. How does thinking write? she might have said. Might have. It's not reasonable to worry, she says, in her rhetorical way. You admire thinking in public; all you need is discipline—using the word differently, of course; for closure. Not really, though, for the discipline of the critic and of criticism, of will and of convention, the writer being written, analyst exploring the self, comes to the same end, which is no end at all but another, yet another, beginning. Thanks, I say to her in the ongoing present tense I am assuming for rhetorical convenience. Pleased to have helped, she turns to other things; and I watch her leave the prison of my speculation from the guard tower, conjugal intercourse having realigned my perspective; now I can look outwards as well as in, as I stand watch.

The secret, I say to myself, to delivering a public address is never hold the pages off the lectern against the light; your audience will start counting them partway through, anticipating structural ends that have nothing to do with the architecture of your argument. Or if you must, then as each page is read, shuffle it to the bottom of the stack; the implication being, like a cartoon drawing itself, you could go on forever. And might.

Carol Shields' brilliant novel *The Stone Diaries* begs the reader to bring her own life, his own life, into the text. If each version, each take, on a life, on the many lives opened to us in Shields' narrative, is both authentic and incomplete, then my lives as a reader are sanctioned (sanctioned: isn't that a lovely word; as its own antonym, a universe complete in itself).

Flowers and stone. The fiction is brimming with flowers and stone. Shields' novel is really about life as a clear glass Mason jar on a shelf of preserves: if properly illuminated and you fill it with water and cut flowers, or with water and pebbles, or if it merely picks up the sheen from the jars around it, it may be of profound interest and yet it is only a glass jar after all. It is only as good as what is put into it, what is placed upon it, or where it is placed. It is only a vessel, after all; only a lifetime, shelved eventually, like Lycidas, mourned with a glycerin tear. My lives are sanctioned by the many voices of her text—

—as the words coalesce, I introduce an image of Mason jars from my grandmother's cold cellar; I conflate Milton with A.M. Klein and allude somewhat elliptically to Pablo Neruda. Memories of Carol reading, of small ceremonies and social happenstance, puncture pretensions of objectivity, of the critic as critic and not another thing. (I cannot escape T.S. Eliot; I am growing old.)

Criticism is a process of elimination. The mind rages against meaning; how many words can you make from the letters in Beethoven? The mind rages against the indiscriminate onslaught of knowledge and awareness. You sit at the computer, ravaged, you know too much. Carol Shields in *The Stone Diaries* eliminates all but the most telling of trivia and what is left is the life, are the lives, of her characters, of herself writing and of you, as you read.

There is no destination without a point of departure. Said another way, you don't know where you are going without knowing where you have been. Since I abjured the instruments of distance and direction, I may not always know where I am but I have never been lost.

To be a critic you must know yourself as receptacle. Yes. But surely Eliot was wrong if he said the mind of the poet, the creator, is a catalyst, unaffected, unmoved by the process of creation. And surely he was wrong when he insisted that the best critic is disengaged from art as the object created. You are a receptacle without which the art is merely a pile of dry pebbles in the dark, a cluster of cut flowers desiccating on the shelf. You provide the water that sustains the vital illusion; and as the critic you are the light, illuminating the scene. Do not let Eliot tell you otherwise. He is dead: you have the incontrovertible authority of being alive.

This is not a permanent condition. His is.

I am a gentle man, a Canadian grandfather, too young for The Last War by a dozen years. The only fight I was ever in was when I was nineteen and a guy at a dance in a Lion's Club Arena in London, for no reason that I could figure out, punched me in the face. I got up and, since I didn't know what the issue was, I apologized to him. There was a long pause. He thanked me. Sporting a necklace of blood across the front of my white shirt I partied on in mourning to the sounds of the late Buddy Holly, the late Richie Vallens, and the late Big Bopper, until my friends took me home to sleep it off.

London. Ontario. If I had meant England, I'd have said so.

When I was nineteen I used to make up stories about Edith Cavell. Sometimes she was a flying ace in World War I, her sex disguised, of course, under leather and silk. Sometimes she was a champion golfer whose career dissipated when the black-and-white newsreels showed her stride over the fairways to be a little too manly. I remember describing her as a brilliant actress in local little theatre who disappeared in Hollywood, when it was still run by New York speculators. Sometimes I said she was a legendary wrangler in the foothills, and sometimes a madam. I was driving a tour bus for Jasper Park Lodge that summer and it was my responsibility to entertain my passengers. Most of my routes took me up or alongside Mount Edith Cavell. Since I had never been to Alberta before, and names like Edith Cavell meant nothing to me, I made up the landscape as I went along. The scenery was there for all to see but I imposed stories on it with reckless innocence, to be amusing, for tips, and because to give any mountain a human name, even that of a battlefield nurse, seemed a profound imposition. One day Randolph Scott told me he thought he remembered Edith Cavell from her Hollywood days as an extra in one of his earliest movies, before he became a cowboy star.

The paradox of meaning comes down to this: we are driven by the structures of our culture, by our history, by our innate desire for emotional coherence and intellectual order, towards meaning, but as we approach meaning we discover it renders us meaningless. The knowledge of paradise makes a mockery of our mortal experience; the achievement of wisdom makes the procedures to enlightenment trivial; the attainment of artistic perfection makes art irrelevant; mastery of language drowns out the silence of illimitable discourse; meaning makes meaning redundant. The critic must confront meaning as a moral issue and, morally bound, must abjure the temptations it offers. This is not an argument for ignorance, but rather for engagement. The critic who has ceased to listen, who has answers not questions, who has displaced emotion, displaced thinking, with thought, is no longer a critic.

On CTV W5 Repeat, July Fourth, 1995, America's birthday, number two hundred and something, Sheila Finestone challenges: What is Canadian culture; could you define that? Sheila Finestone is the Minister of Multiculturalism for Canada, and Secretary of State for the Status of Women. Asked to clarify, Sheila Finestone clarifies: Canada has no national culture.

Works of art are of an infinite loneliness. Sheila Finestone as the Secretary of State for the Status of Women is not a permanent condition of collective reality. She is already on the way to being lost among words, lacunal, a noun-phrase of inconsequence among strategies of rhetorical design.

The treachery of words is not always lovely. And that's where the critic comes in—as the curtain falls on the last act, between ending and closure, darkness and the applause as the lights go up.

On March 19, 1994, Dr. Jared Diamond, a professor of physiology at California State University discussing on the CBC program *Quirks and Quarks* a book ominously called *The Third Chimpanzee*, noted that Pygmies may be defined as people whose average height is under 5'2". The women are under 4'11".

And this: due to better nutrition we in North America are on the average taller than our fathers. Women are taller than their mothers.

You nearly miss the terrorist subversion of his language. But with the sure flight of a well-aimed bullet, an arrow from a crossbow flung free to pierce the flesh and smash the ribs and shred the viscera of an unsatisfactory wife, the assumptions of his language do not miss their target. The holocaust of women's history is sustained by an offhand set of mind, by the casual displacement of alternate realities, by science built on disproportionate binaries in which mankind is man and women are the material source and effluent of his numinosity. If God were not male in the Western tradition he would never have been allowed to be a god. 'Man' is a word continuous with men; 'woman,' within our language, an attenuated modifier. The syntax of a culture perpetuates its informing bias.

During a stopover in Madrid recently, on a flight from the Canary Islands where I had been lecturing on Arctic narrative, to Ottawa where I earn my living, I encountered an errant copy of Margaret Atwood's *Surfacing*. It was lying unattended on a bench near a neatly folded Spanish newspaper. Surrounded by the comings and goings of strangers, I did not pick it up immediately. It was enough for a while to contemplate the small and intimate surprise at this confluence of traveller and book. But of course I did pick it up, gingerly at first, turning the pages with prophylactic fingertips.

I also picked up the newspaper beside it, as if it were mine, tucked the book inside, and walked across to an opposing row of seats and sat where I could see if someone returned, searching for the lost book. Eventually a young woman wearing a backpack, emblazoned with a Canadian flag the size of a pocket, walked by, looking for something. When I approached her she feigned an inability to speak English and walked away quickly towards Departures. Feeling now that somehow the book belonged to me by right of forfeiture, I opened it to the title page, as I usually do an unfamiliar work, to explore the particulars of publication. Then: the familiar exhilaration, thumbing through to get a feel for paragraphing, the extent of dialogue, chapter lengths, the density of print and, of course, the tactile experience of the book as book; its sounds, its smell. No computer will ever replicate the sibilant hush, the musty chemistry. I like to have some sense of the geography of a text before entering, committing myself to its various causes.

My acquired copy of *Surfacing* has written on the inside of the front cover in faded lettering, "S J, Calgary, summer, 1974. My Book." This particular copy of this particular book has been knocking around airports for twenty years. Works of art are of an infinite loneliness and with nothing to be so little appreciated as with criticism.

Since the formulation of my own *Enduring Dreams* as a book, I have come to see the word 'book' as a functional literary term, a legitimate part of the critical lexicon. There was a time when to call a book a book was the mark of sophomoric inelegance. People may write books, manufacture books, arrange books in libraries, but in critical consideration, the book had no presence, was of no consequence. Instead, we spoke of the text according to genre and convention: the assumption was that 'book' was merely a delivery system; and 'text,' quite separable from the particularities of its manifestation in print.

If we do not understand this, however—that we read paper and ink, the font, layout, smudges, curled corners, coffee stains, each copy differing from every other copy, different on each holding, each reading, so that no computer could contain their infinite difference—then books will become only artifacts, museumed remainders, reminders that literacy did not begin as an electronic idiom. We will deny ourselves as readers, people reading.

Robert Lecker has written a book on Canadian culture called *Making It Real.*
Like all books of the dead it tells how to be dead
While there is still time to think about it.

Robert Lecker's words have never been so compromised
As when, having lost my sleeping mat on northern Baffin Island,
In my tent in a storm on a Clyde River esker,
I alternated between reading his book, propped against a fold
In my down-filled sleeping bag, text lit by the midnight sun,
And lying on top of it, pages spread-eagled under my bum,
Something of substance between me and the permafrost ground.

Running through the ancient groves of southern Italy: it is April 1991, the sun is brilliant, the wind soft, and I should be in Ottawa at a symposium on Sinclair Ross. Instead I am running between low stone walls on packed-earth roads, hardened by the traffic of a hundred thousand journeys. I organized the Ross conference and will edit a book of the proceedings, to be called *From the Heart of the Heartland*, to be published eventually in 1992. I am running inland north of Brindisi and I can taste the salt of the Adriatic merge with the salt of my own sweat, can feel it sting my eyes. And beside me, breathing the same rhythm, holding the same pace, sharing the comfortable silence of friends, a friend here whom at home I only know in passing, Robert Lecker and I run together through the thick and dazzling heat of that country. Sometimes we slow a little and then we talk, say things so personal of love, death, parents, they would not bear repeating; intimacy, in the sustained convergence of effort and being in a country not our own. The Ross book will not be out for another year; Robert will give his talk tomorrow on Ross's *As for Me and My House*, espousing concerns about canonicity, a subject that will eventually inform his invaluable book with the Kroetschean title, *Making It Real*—

—wherein Lecker offers reader-critics an elegant and highly persuasive polemic on the need for defining and meeting civic responsibilities, on the moral necessity in a Canadian context of acknowledging the presence of Canada in our literature, and of our literature in Canada
—wherein Lecker the cultural critic shows an astute understanding of the historical imperatives informing canonization, avoiding shallow assumptions that the so-called thematic critics, of which I was one, conspired in a sort of cultural vacuum to erect perimeters around critical discourse
—wherein he mounts a sophisticated plea for renewal, not of the values of those more ingenuous times, nor of their critical strategies and procedures, but of what might be termed their cultural self-consciousness. (If Canada is no longer reasonably to be presumed a monolith, in which canonical texts are inseparable from the literary institution whose values they reflect, celebrate, and perpetuate, then, still, it is necessary for our cultural survival to imagine the country, the nation, as a collective fiction, to explore canonicity not as the limit of enclosure but as a field of inquiry in our ongoing discourse with ourselves. The alternative, Canada as merely an agglomeration of competing forces, and Canadian literature as Canadian only for academic convenience, anticipates the collapse of Canada as a cultural entity.)—

—the irony being, of course, that even as we run among olive trees and cypresses, past the trulli domes, cylindrical wedges of piled stones, water-shed roofs impervious to time on a human scale, Sinclair Ross is being further locked into a critical pattern by our colleagues at home, at the symposium I organized and am missing because I had a chance to come to southern Italy, run with Robert through foreign landscape, and speak on narrative design.

The New Canadian Library edition of Margaret Laurence's *The Diviners*, a lovely sprawling saga of the self-as-national-paradigm, has an Afterword written by Timothy Findley, her friend and cohort in what Margaret called the writing tribe. Findley writes his commentary as a writer, and by that I mean novelist, an artist in prose, about the work of a peer. He begins: "Maybe it would be best not to read this until *The Diviners* has had a chance to sigh and to settle; until you, yourself, have had a chance to sigh and to settle." He continues: "the people here [and by that he means characters] ask of life and one another nothing more and nothing less than we would ask if we were written on these pages." He proceeds from solipsism to the following proscriptive manifesto:

> Books as seemingly different as *One Hundred Years of Solitude* and *Madame Bovary* (now there's a pairing), as *Lady with a Lapdog* and *The Moons of Jupiter* all speak of one condition: of being alive, and of the subtle horror we all experience of being trapped in human flesh when what we want—and long for—is something only the spirit can attain. I know this—and you know this. We all know this, at heart. But it takes a Marquez, a Flaubert, a Chekhov, a Munro, a Laurence to articulate it. Why?
>
> Don't ask.
>
> Be glad.

Do you not find condescension enervating? Aren't you as a reader put off by the fascist tyranny of the writer as critic-manqué? Findley, like the editors of *Brick*, like Rilke, says: this is art, keep your distance; honour what you are given with appropriate humility; submit to the authority of incomprehension; complexity of response is irrelevant; don't think. Don't be. Like shades of the sixties, that fitful end of the modern era, just let what happens happen.

Findley concludes:

> What means *the strength of conviction*?
> Perhaps, when you have let *The Diviners* sigh and let it settle, you will know.

Tiff, I would mutter, if Findley and I were friends, if you don't have anything to say, it would be better not to say anything.

Imagine listening to the radio. The ingratiating voice of professional iconoclast Rex Murphy. *Cross-Country Check-Up.* April 24, 1995. You have to imagine listening to the radio; it is not a passive medium. The subject of the day is the Oklahoma City bombing; what do you think of it? What do you think? Rex has some very strong and safe opinions that he articulates with vehement conviction in his preamble and between calls. He usually addresses male callers as 'Mister.' Women are called by their first names. To a Catherine or Kathleen he says he hopes she doesn't mind the informality, but he has to . . . he doesn't say what or why. Sometimes he calls male callers 'Sir.'

My two great-aunts, Ruth and Elizabeth, like so many women of their generation in Canada, never married. The Great War took away their lovers and their dreams. The Aunts, as we knew them, lived on a generous legacy from their father. They had a part-time gardener called Mr. Bendes; a housekeeper called Mrs. Mesmer. As the class strategies of their Victorian childhood crumbled they maintained decorum through an inverted formality of address. I can hear them calling: Mr. Bendes, there's a dog in the garden. Could you please get it out. Mrs. Mesmer, if you wouldn't mind we'll take our tea outside if Mr. Bendes can do something about the dog. The children will have orange juice please, Mrs. Mesmer. Yes, Miss Elizabeth. Yes, Miss Ruth.

To many of their generation in Canada people of colour, any colour but white, were Darkies; Jews were called Jews. The Aunts were not insensitive. They were good people who felt sympathy for the various adversaries their mighty God smote and drowned and otherwise trounced through the pages of the Old Testament, as they felt pity for the souls of the damned who did not take the New Testament to heart. Nor did they object when their church at the corner of Queen and Eagle Streets committed itself heavily to the purchase of a Gestetner machine for the Anglican mission in Old Crow, Yukon Territory. In my childhood I thought a Gestetner had about it an aura of divine providence.

Rex Murphy, like my Aunts, is innocent. We cannot blame them for the tragedies of this century. Some of us are inherently better than others, says the language, say their words, say the deeds their language encodes, sanctions, delivers. At such a notion, the Aunts shudder in their graves; Rex Murphy splutters into the microphone something about pipsqueak intellectuals. It's only words, they say, just a habit. The habits of this century have seen a billion human beings dead through slaughter, as many as have lived in all the centuries preceding. If you piled their corpses in St. Peter's Square, they would form a column so high, were you to perch atop the most recently deceased, you could see almost to the edges of Christendom.

Words are merciless. As writer the critic is accountable for only the impact of words on the page; likewise as reader the critic responds to the page as invisible palimpsest, text superimposed on language, or language on text. But the critic as critic is engaged in the meeting of minds, the brief synaptical marriages that constitute receipt of the delivered text, and has moral responsibilities, of no interest to writer or reader alone, without which both writer and reader are at single and singular disadvantage; the parson attendant on infinite unions, the quantum mechanic in a semiotic universe.

It is difficult for the critic to position herself between the past and the future, to find himself between book and the text. After being refined nearly out of existence, we indeed find works of art of an infinite loneliness, so long have we denied ourselves as readers implied by the printed word, denied our existence beyond reading.

I buy books, especially the books of colleagues—David Jeffrey's *A Dictionary of Biblical Tradition in English Literature*, Irene Makaryk's *Encyclopedia of Contemporary Literary Theory*, about $120 for these two alone. In David's book there are somewhat over one million words. In my *Enduring Dreams*, which came out in roughly the same time frame, there are well under a hundred thousand. Since my book sells at $16.95, or .01 cent per word, the values are roughly comparable. David and Irene edited their books, while I enjoy the illusion I wrote mine, which I do not think my colleagues buy. I mention this not because I begrudge the expense or covet the sales, but I am struck by the absence of curiosity that would prevent people whose careers are devoted to literature from embracing with excitement the words of an acquaintance, words not enshrined in the parallel worlds of Biblical tradition and critical theory, worlds that, personally, I find pale reflections of the one where human beings dwell. Perhaps my colleagues read books such as mine in secret.

(With the advent of writing came history: religion made absolutes out of dream and memory; literature happened.) In the beginning, after the word was written down, every other word was a commentary on the first: thence all literature is parody; and religion, typology. Until reading became a differentiating attribute of Western culture, writing was a sacred trust, both binding us to paradise and keeping us apart from it. We lived in a singular world, and we were at its centre, with gods or God conveniently above and other animals below. We presumed our medial status on the scale—for, as Aquinas said, "The light of faith makes us see what we believe," and (it is important to acknowledge this) we saw ourselves dead centre.

Before universal literacy, literature was not just another art form but, rather, the way in which language expressed our conceptions of a unified reality. As reading shaped the general imagination, empirical experience to the contrary, we maintained the concept of unity as an article of faith, an attribute of aesthetics, and the mark of an open mind. From Voltaire to Shaw, we had our dissenters. Still, as Frye's great code insists, the continuity of our interior, anterior, external, and prospective worlds continued through symbol and metaphor, syntax and myth. We could celebrate one thing, believe another, and do yet another. Difference was arbitrary.

I look at human bodies bulldozed into rubble in telefootage from Africa, from Oklahoma City, film-clips from Bergen-Belsen, and hear in the name of Jesus prayers uttered in thanks that this child was spared, that that agency received funds, and that our side won the struggle. "Man," said Donne, "... is not a piece of the world, but the world itself; and next to the glory of God, the reason why there is a world." "Without man," wrote Kant, "the whole of creation would be a mere wilderness, a thing in vain, and have no final purpose."

Perhaps many of us in the Western world now share the unease of Voltaire's celestial strangers over the incontrovertible menace of human progress, if not their inextinguishable alien laughter at the vanity of human wishes. Yet we pray, many of us, to the gods of our creation, take refuge in the religious expression of our desire to understand, our fear at being alone, our terror at being, through consciousness, responsible for everything. We have learned to live simultaneously in the parallel universes of urgent actuality and blind religiosity. We can lift a dying child above a mass of human corpses and say "thank God."

You think I am not talking about literature, here. I am talking about literature.

History is a part of literature, just as philosophy and the speculative sciences are a part of religion. From Aristotle's assumptions of natural coherence, that ontology and epistemology are coeval, to Stephen Hawking grasping at a unified theory to bring quantum mechanics and Newtonian physics into harmony, Western thought has maintained the human mind, our human presence, at the merging point of the large and small, past and future, the shaped white blur on the printed page, elision of space, breath pause between syllables, where the microcosm of word, macrocosm of meaning, meet. We are at the intercelestial nexus. Listen, you can hear the urgency echoing through silence, our need to witness—intransitive—our need: to witness.

In the March 27th issue of *Maclean's*, 1995, Allan Fotheringham comments obliquely on the multiple charges of rape and sexual harassment brought against Gerald Regan, former premier of Nova Scotia and one-time federal cabinet minister: "Every doxy who can find a lawyer can suddenly remember a pinched bum on the elevator." In these absurd times, he writes, his contempt unconcealed, "Secretaries with long memories bring down statesmen." In the Oklahoma City bombing issue, Fotheringham describes Conservative ministers in John Major's government "falling out of bed with doxies, popsies, tarts and other politicians' wives." The assumption that ministers and politicians are by definition male is stupid; the limp-wit characterization of women, dangerous. Only a few months earlier Frank Davey, the Carl Klinck Professor of Canadian Literature at the University of Western Ontario, came out with a book, *Karla's Web*, playing games with his title, embedding the Homolka/Bernardo murders in a literary construct, reducing the deaths of Leslie Mahaffy, Kristen French, and Tammy Homolka to figures in a playful allusion. Rilke, only a brief few decades before, wrote: "Works of art are of an infinite loneliness and with nothing to be so little appreciated as with criticism. Only love can grasp and hold and fairly judge them."

With print came the collapse of human consciousness as the measure of time and of space. This led to acceptance of separate and parallel structures, discrete worlds of life, and of art, and of religion; and, most frightening, acceptance that life is informed by art and religion, not the other way around. Consciousness is separable from point of view. If we abjure responsibility for our presence, assigning it to God, or gods, to Art, or the aesthetic structures that contain us, we are in danger, literally, of our own annihilation on this small planet, our theoretical perspective on the world.

To put it another way, our species has existed for no more than a flash in the life of our universe, and our universe is just one in an endless cosmos, so we should not be proud in our religions, yet take illimitable pride in our privilege as witness, DNA self-conscious of its own design. Literature is literature and not another thing, to echo Eliot. And religion, religion. Threatened by common sense, Eliot avoided dealing with life itself. The function of the critic-writer was increasingly, from Coleridge to Eliot and beyond, to transliterate actuality to art, and then abjure the actual as ephemeral; to treat religion as an aesthetic, aesthetics as religion, and avoid real life. The end was to elevate the artist to prophet, the priest to poet, and the life of the reader to the margins of heaven and hell, where their own lives mattered not a bit. This is no longer acceptable. We count. We must.

April 17, 1995. Lying flat on my back on the pavement, a cordoned-off segment of Copley Square in front of the Boston Public Library. It is 3:45 p.m. Life is a metaphor for running. During three hours, thirty-four minutes and three seconds, time that came to an end about ten minutes ago, I became what I was doing; ran out of my name, no longer a noun, nor pronoun, a verb, for a while, yes, a verb, a participle, by Heartbreak Hill, adverbial. And on the long last five-mile stretch of the Boston Marathon from Boston College, the long five hundred metres down Boylston Avenue to the finish, synaptical collapse, the vocabulary of a lifetime refused syntax, refused meaning, turned cellular; between body and mind was absolute zero; time and space were indivisible. I had become language itself; and as I edged through the finishers' chute beside the Boston Public Library, all the books reached through the yellow brick walls, grasping at the infinite possibilities my exhaustion embodied, to share in the mystery of such splendid unnecessary chaos; but hunched under a laurel of sweat, I picked up my finishers' medallion, a drink and a doughnut, and as the acid pooled in my muscles I lay prostrate on the cool pavement; and after a while I started thinking; and that was the end of adventure. Language falls into line, the library books relax. I have to plan a symposium on Arctic narrative in Ottawa, a paper on the poetics of self in Fredericton, a talk on iconicity in Winnipeg. Running a marathon, like reading a book, falls into a different perspective when it's over.

The function of critic as autobiographer is a moral necessity in a post-religious world. Literary criticism as an auto-graphic act (the critic engaged with his life, her life-time experience, in the text, with the book) is an obligation inseparable from our human will to persist, to endure the chaos of our own freed minds, to pleasure ourselves in the joy of bearing witness to the cosmology of our own perceptions, our own narrative design, and the wondrously indifferent cosmos beyond.

THE LANGUAGE OF CANADIAN POETRY

Landscape, Untitled

(How do you make English Canadian? How do you relate to the world when your soul frets in the shadow of a language that paradoxically is your own and yet alien? This essay confronts what has become recognized as a postcolonial condition: it explores procedures through which Canadian poets gradually accommodated English to fit experience for which it was ill-prepared by tradition or usage, in an often subtle revolution that has given to us, finally, a voice of our own. Written as part of a festschrift for Clara Thomas, published by Essays on Canadian Writing, *Summer 1984, early drafts were delivered as lectures at the Modern Languages Association conference in Erie, Pennsylvania and at the Universities of York and Birmingham, all in 1983. It was meant from the beginning to be a companion piece with the next essay in this collection, "Invisible in the House of Mirrors." Many of the poetry quotations in both essays are from a single anthology. I would like to think this was a result of my conviction that critical consideration of poetry can be only as accessible as the poetry it contemplates. It might also, however, relate to the fact that much of the writing and virtually all checking of citations were done out of the country, where Canadian poetry texts were in short supply.)*

I

Naming is a primary function of poetry. Adam was the first poet, and, to use A.M. Klein's phrase, each poet in his or her turn is "the nth Adam."[1] In naming, the poet does more than label and take inventory. The poet assumes imaginative control of the world. Through words the poet merges the experience of things and things themselves; defines through words both the centre and the limits of consciousness. If appropriate language is not at the poet's command, then the world from his or her perspective and for those who share it is quite literally beyond comprehension. Such is the case in a colonial context where the poet is bound to use words that are rendered inadequate by geographical transposition.

A language such as English that has served the colonial enterprise so well on a practical or instrumental level can still, in worlds away from its origin, confound the literary sensibility and set the literary imagination askew. The colonial literature of Canada provides ample examples of words simply not up to the demands made upon them in the new environment. The inherent weakness of colonial poetry is not so much a question of poets who, removed from their informing culture, are inadequate to the resources of the language, but rather the reverse. No amount of talent can domesticate alien words that, through a colonial set of mind, are not even recognized as alien. This dissociation between mind and environment is self-perpetuating. But gradually names and the named become reconciled through an arduous reinvention of the language, word by word. Gradually the new place falls under imaginative control. Then, as in Canada, indigenous poetry becomes possible. Then, as poetry, Canada becomes possible.

The nineteenth-century English gentlewoman Susanna Moodie, as Margaret Atwood re-creates her, responds to the New World on disembarking at Quebec with a plaintive declaration:

> I am a word
> in a foreign language.[2]

Before leaving home, Moodie may have thought Canada a foreign word. But as first experienced, she finds Canada so substantial and unaccommodating that consciousness itself seems alien, and her own character, so far removed from its originating context, the creation of consciousness. Atwood's conceit is no metaphor: English that has crossed an ocean in Moodie's mind has become in Canada a foreign language; and Moodie, far from being the reservoir of language she was before leaving, has become merely an element within it, a word, herself.

Atwood is one of the few Canadian poets both to recognize and to resolve into poetry the discrepancy between language born of one place and the reality of another. In "Progressive Insanities of a Pioneer" she articulates the disorienting predicament of consciousness in a strange milieu:

> Things
> refused to name themselves; refused
> to let him name them.[3]

Again, she does not speak in metaphor, but literally. Without naming, there is no "tension / between subject and object." The mind, without shape or circumference, collapses.

Atwood seldom writes in metaphor. Her tropes are more subtle and more aggressive, particularly when she is trying to make language the bridge between experience or perception and the world experienced or perceived. When she writes of sinking through stone to the knee, or being a mirror, or being a pool ("Think about pools"[4]), she means quite literally what she says—that is the way it is, or 'seems,' which is another way of saying 'is.' Often, apparent metaphors are in fact image-equations for an emotional state, particulary in poems where the mind in the presence of landscape is forced into confrontation with itself. Language is literal; it is consciousness that is figurative.

Perhaps it is inevitable that a poet who stretches the literal possibilities of language to its limits should be so aware of its limitations. Specifically, Atwood recognizes in her poetry that there are times when language does not fit the experience of things perceived and must be forced, sometimes nearly to the point of incoherence. And when the language simply does not fit, when it remains steadfastly alien, then there is only madness or silence.

Early Canadian writers, bound to use a language ill-suited to conditions in the so-called 'New World,' inadvertently discovered another option: they wrote bad poetry. What the colonial mind, virtually by definition, could not comprehend was that language itself was the problem. It is one thing for Atwood from a present perspective to have the fictional Moodie recognize words as a barrier between subjective and objective realities; it is quite another to suppose the historical Moodie could have recognized the same. From the perspective of the historical Moodie, colonial dissociation was not the result of a language depleted and distorted by transposition to a new place; colonial dissociation would more likely have been regarded as the cause itself of verbal misprision, if such had been recognized at all.

Words in a discrete verbal language grow out of the customs and culture, the history and sociology, of people in a particular place. They define and reflect the community by providing what for non-literate peoples is a mystical bond between themselves and the conditions of the landscape that shape their lives. Words are inseparable from the geography in which they have come into common usage. But they are also inseparable from the consciousness that has come into being *through* their usage. When they are transported in the mind, they carry the conditions of their origin with them. This makes them useful instrumentally, for ordinary discourse, and yet virtually assures that they will be inappropriate in bringing a new world under imaginative control.

Simply knowing the denotative value of a word does not guarantee that it accurately conveys meaning. The word 'snow' provides a good example of how English in Canada was, and to an extent continues to be, merely an historically expedient lingua franca. On a January day in Canada one may look outside and say, "It is very cold out there and the snow is deep." What one might mean, however, is only that it is the normal temperature outside for a Canadian January, and the snow is of normal depth for this particular part of the world. Yet we feel obliged to say "cold" and to say "deep." The Inuit have dozens of words for snow; the English have only one. Canadians have none. Without modifiers, Canadian use of the word 'snow' is obtuse and obscure. Adjectives must compensate for the word's Teutonic origin and its evolution into modern usage in a moderate climate.

To put the case on a broader base, consider a line from the nineteenth-century poem "Acadia" by Joseph Howe:

> For ages thus, the Micmac trod our soil.[5]

The glaring and inadvertent irony of the line, proclaiming prior possession of the land by virtue of race, nearly obscures the ineptitude of Howe's language. Not only does "our" dispossess the native people of their heritage and history, but it asserts against their concept of coexistence with the land the alien and overwhelming principle of land ownership. Their very name in this context is subverted, for Micmac means 'the people' and here its meaning is virtually reversed to stand for an exotic faction. Furthermore, the opening words of the line cast over the aboriginal existence the net of European time: "thus," through the cycles of "our" history, "for ages," they lived in this place. And how so? They "trod our soil." But one treads European byways, English meadows, the streets of London. In the wildness of early Acadia, the geography was not passive, not to be "trod" upon. It was, and in good part still is, active, complex, aggressive. One encounters, experiences, endures, surmounts, submits to, exalts in, lives with the Acadian landscape. One does not tread its soil. "Soil" itself is an odd and inappropriate synecdoche, suggesting the rich, turned fields of an English countryside.

Joseph Howe was not a poet by trade, but as a journalist and politician he was a professional in the use of words, very much at home with the English language. The language he was born to, however, like the sentiments he expressed, was founded in a different place. Reading "Acadia" one reads in fact of an England strangely transformed, not of a particular Canadian region, despite the poem's unmitigated 'New World' chauvinism.

Everywhere that English travelled as the language of colonization, people shared Howe's problem. Generations after settlement took place, consciousness and sensibility continued to be shaped by words and by syntax that sustained the dissociated colonial set of mind. The genius of Twain and Whitman was their revolutionary re-creation of the English language as an American idiom; but it should be remembered that their contributions only came about many decades after the American War of Independence. In Canada, a similar process, without benefit of an ideological base, has extended through more than two centuries, accomplished for the most part by poets whose intentions outreached their achievements, and it is not yet complete.

Ineptitude early in the Canadian tradition was inadvertent, and therefore difficult to counter, although evidence suggests that one or two poets tried to turn an awareness of their limitations to advantage. Archibald Lampman, for example, is one of the best Canadian poets of the past century. With rare sensitivity, he allows language to be the expression of his experience with landscape, rather than using it in an effort to make the land submit. Yet even he, upon occasion, loses out in the struggle towards poetic coherence. The following mixture of awkward personification, inflated rhetoric, and comically inappropriate words is the opening stanza of his 1888 poem "Storm."

Out of the gray northwest, where many a day gone by
  Ye tugged and howled in your tempestuous grot,
And evermore the huge frost giants lie,
  Your wizard guards in vigilance unforgot,
Out of the gray northwest, for now the bonds are riven,
On wide white wings your thongless flight is driven,
  That lulls but resteth not.[6]

In a grot, unforgot. Thongless. Such awkwardness is unusual in Lampman's poetry, an aberration. There are poetasters in the Canadian tradition, however, who never rise above such doggerel. Consider the images and conceits in the following excerpt from an 1842 poem by the Canadian (as opposed to his Irish namesake) Standish O'Grady:

> In winter here, where all alike contrive,
> And still withal few animals survive,
> Till summer's heat, so potent and so quick,
> Enough to make the *Crocodile grow sick*;
> With vile mosquitoes, lord deliver us,
> Whose stings could *blister a Rhinoceros.*
> If on the living insects are thus fed,
> How ill must fare the worms when we are dead![7]

O'Grady died before his poem saw print, which may have been a critical judgement.

Being aware of a problem does not necessarily mean the solution is at hand. In the following, a sonnet by Wilfred Campbell published in 1893, the poet seems to recognize that the only way he can get into the picture—that is, find language that will effectively merge consciousness with the landscape—is quite literally to climb in. The effect is bizarre, and only a little redeemed from the ridiculous by the wistful supposition that his irony is intentional:

> I sit me moanless in the sombre fields,
> The cows come with large udders down the dusk,
> One cudless, the other chewing of a husk,
> Her eye askance, for that athwart her heels,
> Flea-haunted and rib-cavernous, there steals
> The yelping farmer-dog. An old hen sits
> And blinks her eyes. (Now I must rack my wits
> To find a rhyme, while all this landscape reels.)
> Yes! I forgot the sky. The stars are out,
> There being no clouds; and then the pensive maid!
> Of course she comes with tin-pail up the lane.
> Mosquitoes hum and June bugs are about.
> (That line hath "quality" of loftiest grade.)
> And I have eased my soul of its sweet pain.[8]

Sometimes the line between catharsis and a laxative is rather fine. The next excerpt, from an 1894 poem by Bliss Carman, shows no regard at all for the function of language in the poetic merging of self with natural process. The result is disconcerting:

> Only make me over, April
> When the sap begins to stir!
> Make me man or make me woman,
> Make me oaf or ape or human,
> Cup of flower or cone of fir;
> Make me anything but neuter
> When the sap begins to stir![9]

According to *OED*, the meaning of sap as a 'simpleton' was long established before Carman used it here.

Bliss Carman wrote some memorable lines of poetry. He is widely regarded as a major Canadian poet. He also wrote some very bad lines, abusing both language and the landscape, in his effort to express a discursive sensibility in what he took to be a unified world. Poets somewhat more responsive to the problems inherent in the poetic use of English in a Canadian context had no better solutions. As early as 1825, the Canadian Oliver Goldsmith published in *The Rising Village* a spirited celebration of British North America in which he rather crudely acknowledges the need for episodic stimulation to make the lyric aspects of his poem take root. Thus he inserts the maudlin story of Albert and Flora into what is otherwise a hybrid pastoral-epic-chronicle-vision. Most of the descriptive passages in the poem are given narrative quality through extensive use of personification, but this only makes the awkwardness of his descriptive language seem more graphic when it falters.

At his best, Goldsmith delivers such innocuous lines as the following with aplomb:

> And where the forest once its foliage spread,
> The golden corn triumphant waves its head.[10]

To this couplet, the poet appended a note which rather ponderously explains that the process of clearing land is actually a good deal more difficult than his verse allows. He does not add that by corn he really means grain, for then as now corn in the North American sense of the word is Indian maize and in the field at harvest is not golden but a deep luxuriant green. His image, then, is literary, metaphoric, though it pretends to be descriptive. The incipient metaphor, in any case, on close analysis itself collapses in confusion. If head of corn can wave triumphantly, then by virtue of parallel syntax the forest must literally "spread" its foliage—possibly as tribute in anticipation of the corn's bravado.

Howe, in "Acadia" a generation later, uses similar personification in an attempt to vitalize language that otherwise renders the Canadian landscape virtually opaque. He makes the Indians an extension of the land, then explosively transforms both into myth through a graphic depiction of the slaughter of innocents —that is, of English settlers. He also catalogues, naming tree types, for example; he surveys and documents, naming the qualities of a flower, lamenting the expulsion of the French from their Acadian homeland; he spins tales, brief and timeworn stories, to give the place a life of its own. Instead of using words to define the Canadian landscape, perhaps through naïveté Howe reverses the procedure, using characteristics of place to rework the language, to make it pliable, plausible, if not quite new. In this, he anticipates the best and most revolutionary aspects of poetry by Charles G.D. Roberts, Archibald Lampman, and Isabella Valancy Crawford in the next generation. Without seeming to recognize the extent to which language itself stood between imagination and the world he wished it to convey in his poetry, Howe left us with work the best of which seems eccentric and the rest simply not very good.

To his credit, or perhaps because he was a closet poet, Howe avoided the tendency among his contemporaries to reduce language in their poetry to literary artifact, especially in the description of a landscape that seemed to elude or refuse definition. The result of this tendency was poetry that for the most part was mediocre and derivative. As Daniel Wilson suggests in an 1858 review of Charles Sangster's *The St. Lawrence and the Saguenay*, that particular poem suffers because it "more frequently re-echoes the songs that are to be gathered amid the leaves of the library shelf, than under those with which the wind sports among the branches whereon songbirds warble their nuptial lays."[11] Ironically, Wilson commits the very offence for which he rightly admonishes Sangster. As the 'poetical' enters his prose, the words seem estranged from their Canadian context. Wilson's recognition that the path to success for the poet of the 'New World' lies not in the direction of 'literariness' does not guarantee that he knows a better route himself.

II

There are worlds of difference between English words in the poetry of Charles Sangster, Joseph Howe, Wilfred Campbell, Standish O'Grady, and Oliver Goldsmith and those same words, Canadian words, in poetry by Margaret Atwood, George Bowering, Robert Kroetsch, and their contemporaries, writing now. The process by which English is becoming a Canadian language is infinitely complex. It might be illuminated, though, by the series of brief passages that follow, arranged not to develop an argument but to reveal idiosyncrasies in the changing function of language as the process occurs. Each quotation is accompanied by a brief commentary. The quotations are in chronological sequence, dated, and identified by author. They are otherwise set free of context to avoid formal or thematic intrusions on a consideration of the word as word, image as image, trope as trope. Most are taken from the 1974 edition of Klinck and Watters' *Canadian Anthology*—affirmation that they have been drawn from the mainstream. All passages, as a concession to orderliness, are based on a single and quintessentially Canadian motif—winter.

*

though around thy shore
Is heard the stormy wind's terrific roar;
Though round thee Winter binds his icy chain,
And his rude tempests sweep along thy plain,
Still Summer comes, and decorates thy land
With fruits and flowers from her luxuriant hand;
—Oliver Goldsmith, 1825[12]

The words are nonspecific—innocuously opaque. The images are cosmetic jewellery. Generalization is made concrete through arbitrary personification. However, metaphoric activity is jarringly aligned with image rather than personality. The result is somewhat obscene: if Winter holds the place as a *being* in chains, then the parallel structure of the trope suggests that what he is doing, sweeping her plain, is indeed, as the poem says, quite "rude." One-half of a conceit cannot reasonably insist on place as a person while the other half limits it to geography.

*

> Thou barren waste; unprofitable strand,
> Where hemlocks brood on unproductive land,
> Where frozen air on one bleak winter's night
> Can metamorphose *dark brown hares to white!*
> —Standish O'Grady, 1842[13]

Words in the first two lines are charged with emotions to chill a speculator's heart; but the landscape is generalized beyond recognition. The sentiment is quite in keeping with the hyperbole of the second two lines, though not with the wit. The poet's lack of restraint has led him to at least one memorable image, "frozen air," in which a single word is virtually redefined by the conditions it describes. "Frozen" air is Canadian English.

*

> We worship the spirit that walks unseen
> Though our land of ice and snow:
> —Thomas D'Arcy McGee, 1858[14]

Words in the second line are nearly emptied of meaning, so much are they a cliché; yet cliché becomes metaphor. "Land of ice and snow" is not Canada—it is a trope that stands for Canada. George Orwell has written of metaphors that in a state of exhaustion cease to be metaphors, but here we have the opposite, a generalization so vapid it can only have meaning as metaphor.

*

> What though the northern winds that o'er thee blow
> Borrow fresh coolness from thy hills of snow,
> and icy Winter, in his rudest form,
> Breathes through thy vallies many a chilling storm
> —Joseph Howe, 1874[15]

Again, imprecision, personification, gender stereotypes, and again, the vulgarity of Winter, this time rudely blowing his cold breath along Acadia's valleys. To his credit, the poet tries to make the imagery conform somewhat to actuality, but the closer his images come to the lyric, to a descriptive function, the more inadequate seem his words. A "chilling" storm is commonplace and redundant; a winter storm in Canada could hardly be otherwise. The idea in the first two lines that wind draws cold from snow is diminished by the word "coolness" from clever insight to quaint conceit. Neither sentiment nor syntax is strong enough to transform the word "coolness" to make it new. It lingers inappropriately, undermining both the lyric and narrative values of its immediate context.

*

From his far wigwam sprang the strong North Wind
And rush'd with war-cry down the steep ravines,
And wrestl'd with the giants of the woods;
And with his ice-club beat the swelling crests
Of the deep watercourses into death,
And with his chill foot froze the whirling leaves
Of dun and gold and fire in icy banks;
And smote the tall reeds to the harden'd earth;
And sent his whistling arrows o'er the plains,
Scatt'ring the ling'ring herds—

—Isabella Valancy Crawford, 1884[16]

How vivid the plain here, and real, compared to Goldsmith's. Mythic rather than generalized personification fuses image with metaphor so powerfully that the language itself is wonderfully precise, even when the landscape is occasionally a bit diffuse.

*

Never a bud of spring, never a laugh of summer,
Never a dream of love, never a song of bird;
But only the silence and white, the shores that grow chiller and dumber,
Wherever the ice-winds sob, and the griefs of winter are heard.

—Wilfred Campbell, 1889[17]

Personification for description and mood alone. The generalization here is not in the description, but *of* the described: bud of spring, laugh of summer, dream of love, song of bird. These are flaccid things, generic images, good words reduced to inadequacy through evasion. And the shores, what shores? How silent, if winds and winter "sob" against them? These are only words, words that draw meaning not from the landscape that the poet wishes to describe, nor obliquely from the resources of language, but from common usage; dictionary words.

*

Here by the gray north sea,
In the wintry heart of the wild,
—Bliss Carman, 1893[18]

This is winter from a nice warm study, a literary convenience, image transformed into a metaphor—honest perhaps to emotion but a distortion nonetheless. If "wintry" and "heart" have literal meaning at all, then the opening line, "by the gray north sea," must not; or conversely, if the poem is set close by the sea, then it cannot on the same literal level also be set in the "heart of the wild." If one line is taken to be metaphor and the other literal, then the image will serve. The landscape, however, has then been reduced to poetic device.

*

I sat in the midst of a plain on my snowshoes with bended knee
Where the thin wind stung my cheeks,
And the hard snow ran in little ripples and peaks,
Like the fretted floor of a white and petrified sea.
—Archibald Lampman, 1893[19]

The plain—as real as being there. The perspective is participatory; poetic consciousness is a presence within the landscape. What happens, what is felt, what is seen, what it is like—these are fused into a wholeness of 'what is' by the consciousness that contains them, by the poem itself. Consciousness and text are virtually one and the same. The effect on language is spectacular. The simple authenticity of the first line, the striking precision of the last, both descriptions of stillness although one is purely narrative and the other a lyric trope, contain between them, like parentheses, the simplest of images in the simplest of language and lend each word new and vital meaning. "Thin" and "hard," in particular, have been remade through resolutely Canadian usage. "Thin" wind is what stings the cheeks of any winter traveller, who would be still in contemplation at that place, in that moment of time. "Hard" snow runs in "little" ripples on the frozen surface of the winter. 'Thin' and 'hard' have become Canadian words.

*

The following passages are from a poem by a poet whose best work fuses language and landscape as no other had before him. The originality and quiet splendour of his diction, however, sometimes provide in the early work of Charles G.D. Roberts a licence to err (while the best of his later poetry seems merely imitation of himself). The following are excerpts from "The Skater," taken in sequence:

> My glad feet shod with the glittering steel
> I was the god of the winged heel.
> . . .
> And the woods hung hushed in their long white dream
> By the ghostly, glimmering, ice-blue stream.
> . . .
> A spinning whisper, a sibilant twang,
> As the stroke of the steel on the tense ice rang;
> . . .
> And I turned and fled, like a soul pursued,
> From the white, inviolate solitude.
>
> —Sir Charles G.D. Roberts, 1896[20]

Apart from the mildly awkward metonymy of "glad feet," these couplets read well and carry with them an aura of authenticity. "Ice-blue" stream, on reflection, seems more poetic than actual, but the sounds of steel on ice are convincing, and the fearsome intensity of winter isolation is real enough. But! When, ever, in Canada or elsewhere, is it possible to have deep drifts of snow, woods hushed in snow, and a stream of open ice to skate upon? If the ice is clear, then the snow has yet to come. Every outdoor skater knows that with snow come shovels. The words seem authentic, but the scene is a fake.

*

All the lake-surface
Streamed with the hissing
Of millions of iceflakes
Hurled by the wind;
. . .
Then on the third great night there came thronging and thronging
Millions of snowflakes out of a windless cloud;
They covered her close with a beautiful crystal shroud,
Covered her deep and silent.
—Duncan Campbell Scott, 1905[21]

Descriptive precision combines with narrative intensity to create a very effective dramatic scene. Snow lying like a crystal shroud is a beautiful image, though more authentic for its metaphoric value than its descriptive accuracy.

*

If our eyes we'd close, then the lashes froze, till sometimes we couldn't see;
It wasn't much fun, but the only one to whimper was Sam McGee
—Robert Service, 1907[22]

Winter here is solely a setting for narrative action; it has neither lyric nor metaphoric value. The snow is Styrofoam; the cold, a dramatic necessity.

*

Now the old folded snow
Shrinks from black earth.
Now is thrust forth
Heavy and still
The field's dark furrow.
—F.R. Scott, 1936[23]

The diction is simple and direct, the images precise. Only in the peculiar dynamism of the verbs is there a hint of personification which suggests this passage might be part of a larger metaphor.

*

What of the winter? Half the year is winter.
—E.J. Pratt, 1940[24]

Winter: reduced and simplified; narrative exposition.

*

and the voice draws their pencil
like a sled across snow;
—P.K. Page, 1946[25]

Winter is a fact of life; snow itself has become the metaphor.

*

till the chilled nail shrinks in the wall
and pistols the brittle air
—Earle Birney, 1949[26]

Old words, here, made new. 'Chilled' has never before meant what the poet makes of it in these two lines; 'pistols' and 'brittle' have been remade entirely. Other meanings of these words have not been abandoned but, rather, subsumed. Each key word in these brief lines makes every other a new and different word. The chilled nail shrinks; it pistols the brittle air. A dictionary could not explain what here explains itself.

*

I would take words
As crisp and as white
As our snow;
—A.J.M. Smith, 1954[27]

A commonplace image made extraordinary through a logical inversion; snow may be routinely described as crisp and white, but it is entirely new that words should be described that way. The metaphor takes the nature of snow for granted, especially of "our" snow, but turns familiarity to wonder through its precision in defining a particular quality of language, of 'words.' A sort of self-fufilling prophecy, this passage is a fine example in itself of the concept it seems meant to convey:

I would take words
As crisp and as white
As our snow;

*

after a while wind
blows down the tent and snow
begins to cover him
—Al Purdy, 1968[28]

Snow is snow; it is what it is, does what it does. *Word and element* are one.

*

the rustle of the snow
. . .
thistles bright with sleet
. . .
At night the house crackled.
—Margaret Atwood, 1970[29]

No metaphors. Images precise, striking, authentic. Consciousness re-creates the language. The house does crack, the snow does rustle, and thistles sometimes are bright with sleet in the Canadian winter. *Words and the experience* are one.

*

We took the storm windows/off
the south side of the house
and put them on the hotbed.
Then it was spring. Or, no:
then winter was ending.
. . .
No trees
around the house.
Only the wind.
Only the January snow.
Only the summer sun.
—Robert Kroetsch, 1977[30]

Pure meaning. No modifiers; no metaphors. Winter is a season defined by the experience of the people the poem addresses; the snow of January is self-explanatory, a condition familiar in the experience the poem addresses. This is a Canadian poem. The words are regional, substantial, authentic. They are inseparable ultimately from experience or consciousness; accessible, ultimately, to anyone, and, once grasped, they carry the potential of universal significance.

III

Canada is a word (think about words).

POSTSCRIPT

There is a whole area of language as deep and secret as the psyche that to date has gone largely unexplored. No one looks at the word that *seems* to mean the same from place to place, speaker to speaker, that might have the same lexical definition, yet means differently—sometimes radically and profoundly so. 'Queen,' for example, to the American, the Canadian, the English: fairy-tale romance, constitutional ambiguity, tradition. There are other meanings, besides, which extend beyond cultural boundaries, related to being in drag, to chess, to apiary, to bed size. But Queen with a capital *Q* means differently to Americans, Canadians, and English.

Studies in dialect and idiom tend to quantify the obvious. Cross-cultural studies dwell on functional communication or on idiosyncrasy. Linguistic, semantic, and semiotic studies deal with relationships. Systems prevail. Lévi-Strauss, building on Saussurean principles of verbal structure, recognized the profound impact of language on the development of the individual within society. Lacan, rather violently imposing Lévi-Strauss and Saussure on a hapless Freud, deduces the importance of language on the development of the individual within the species. Chomsky discounts to a large extent the experience of the individual in the acquisition of language, and Steiner, likewise, in the imposition of silence. The function of language in relation to consciousness and to the world is a matter of considerable interest and much theorizing. Yet theory for the most part attends to structures, to syntax, to planes of meaning, linear and spacial, and pays little attention to the discrepancies of meaning *within* the words themselves, discrepancies that may arise due to the very structures of language and consciousness that they sustain.

It is just because language is system, and meaning is systemically determined, that words can evade or subvert lexical and allusive meaning, can render speech or writing a secret code perhaps inimical with and perhaps in service to the speaker/writer's desire to say. A number of feminist writers have recognized language itself as a source of repression and not just through Lacanian syntactical and symbolic ordering but within, deep within, the words themselves. Sadly, however, in the verse preceding entry into Judy Chicago's symbolically extravagant feminist oeuvre, *The Dinner Party*, she writes that "Lo," when women are heard and recognized at last, our species will return to "Eden."[31] Could she have used words less appropriate, resounding as they do with both literary and theological traditions of female subjugation? Yet Simone de Beauvoir in 1949 called her inquiry *The Second Sex* (*Le deuxième sexe*) with obvious confidence, knowing that the meaning of words would be determined, or redetermined, by awareness of their source: 'second' is historically accurate, temporal acknowledgement of an ordered primacy; but second is also emphatically an ironic rejection and, with more subtle irony, second alludes to the future, the new chance to get things right, the end of practice, of God's first and failed experiment, were there a God. If de Beauvoir's title had been on a book by Norman Mailer, the words would have meant quite differently. Used as it is, it usurps linguistic misogyny.

Another French writer, in words reminiscent of Atwood's Moodie, declares that her language, "although it is mine, is foreign to me." Asserting the feminist necessity to reinvent language without rejecting it, without receding into incoherence or silence, Madeleine Gagnon declares: "I am a foreigner to myself in my own language and I translate myself by quoting all the others."[32]

A half century earlier, James Joyce acknowledged in *A Portrait of the Artist as a Young Man* much the same problem from an Irish perspective. His response within context is an ironically naïve declaration of passionate commitment, and beyond text, in subsequent texts, it is the reclamation of language not through passion but erudition. In *Portrait*, Stephen is in a discussion of words with the dean of studies:

> He felt with a smart of dejection that the man to whom he was speaking was a countryman of Ben Jonson. He thought:
>
> —The language in which we are speaking is his before it is mine. How different are the words *home, Christ, ale, master* on his lips and on mine! I cannot speak or write these words without unrest of spirit. His language, so familiar and so foreign, will always be for me an acquired speech. I have not made or accepted its words. My voice holds them at bay. My soul frets in the shadow of his language.[33]

Joyce in the shadow of his given language; woman, as Julia Kristeva says, "estranged from language"[34] or, as Gagnon might say, "foreign to it"; theorists enthralled with its apparent and elusive systems; Canadian poets like Kroetsch and Atwood, George Bowering and bp Nichol, forcing upon old words new and radically unequivocal ambiguities; all demand of us a reassessment of the language we use so casually to comprehend our relations in and with the world and ourselves.

If we have not the words, then we are estranged from every one and every thing. In the preceding sequence of Canadian poetic images, this estrangement, at least from the landscape, is seen to diminish as language is reinvented by the poets, reassessed by the readers. As presented, this procedure may seem to ape through exaggeration developments in the major tradition that, arguably, constitute neither improvement nor deterioration. The gradual shift from ornamentation and metaphoric analogy to the unadorned metonymic representation that characterizes so much of the best contemporary poetry is, however, empirically and emphatically an improvement in the Canadian context.

Especially in the twentieth century, arguments have been put forth which parallel and reflect the development towards possession of an alien and only language by some who think we all—not only women, Irish, working class, Canadians, other neo- or post-colonials, all who are bound to use contemporary language for more than diversion and the exchange of goods—we all find soul and psyche more alienated than appeased by what language has become, by what words imprisoned in syntactical structure and rigid traditions have become. Through much of her life, Gertrude Stein argued that writers must work back in the English language to the "excitingness of pure being," where word and thing were virtually one.[35] In her own writing, as William H. Gass describes it, words become things, are in effect real, on their own, "as physical as statuary."[36] Stein and Gass argue for, and in their own writing offer by example, words that are artifact and object and conceptual presence all at once, complete in themselves and yet, discontinuous from context, hint of other worlds, other things. Along with Robert Kroetsch, the most articulate and aware speaker in Canada of his own adventures with language in literature, they urge that language move away from vapid cliché and from the indulgence of idiosyncratic originality. Meaning will no longer be conveyed by image or vision, by complex analogical construct; meanings will accrue, rather, amid the discontinuities of word-things, through shared experience between writer and reader of the possibilities provided by text.

Kroetsch's lines—

> Only the January snow.
> Only the summer sun.

—are real. The words are real, the poem, the snow and sun are real. January, the summer, only, only, the—are real.

Notes and Works Cited

1. A.M. Klein, "Portrait of the Poet as Landscape," in *Canadian Anthology*, ed. Carl F. Klinck and Reginald E. Watters, 3rd ed. (Toronto: Gage, 1974), p. 347.
2. Margaret Atwood, "Disembarking at Quebec," in *The Journals of Susanna Moodie* (Toronto: Oxford University Press), 1970, p. 11.
3. Margaret Atwood, "Progressive Insanities of a Pioneer," in *The Animals in That Country* (Toronto: Oxford University Press, 1968), p. 39.
4. Margaret Atwood, "Tricks with Mirrors," in *You Are Happy* (Toronto: Oxford University Press, 1974), p. 27.
5. Joseph Howe, "Acadia," in *Nineteenth Century Narrative Poems*, ed. David Sinclair (Toronto: McClelland and Stewart, 1972), p. 25. At least Howe acknowledges a native population. As recently as 1954 a poet as sensitive to social issues as F.R. Scott could write of Canada before white settlement being "empty as paper," the landscape just waiting for the "language of life," "the full culture of occupation," to "turn this rock into children" (F.R. Scott, "Laurentian Shield," in *Canadian Anthology*, pp. 276-77). Less surprising, both Catharine Parr Traill and her sister, Susanna Moodie, a century before Scott, erased indigenous culture from the landscape, even if they begrudgingly admitted the spectral presence of the people themselves.
6. Archibald Lampman, "Storm," in *Canadian Anthology*, p. 124.
7. Standish O'Grady, "The Emigrant," in *Canadian Anthology*, p. 29.
8. Wilfred Campbell, "At Even," in *Canadian Anthology*, p. 96.
9. Bliss Carman, "Spring Song," in *Canadian Anthology*, p. 113.
10. Oliver Goldsmith, "The Rising Village," in *Nineteenth Century Narrative Poems*, p. 3.
11. Daniel Wilson, "Review of Sangster's *The St. Lawrence and the Saguenay*," in *Canadian Anthology*, p. 70.
12. Goldsmith,"The Rising Village," p. 25.
13. O'Grady, "The Emigrant," p. 28.
14. Thomas D'Arcy McGee, "The Arctic Indian's Faith," in *Canadian Anthology*, p. 61.
15. Howe, "Acadia," p. 19.
16. Isabella Valancy Crawford, "Malcolm's Katie," in *Canadian Anthology*, pp. 88-89.
17. Wilfred Campbell, "The Winter Lakes," in *Canadian Anthology*, p. 94.

18. Bliss Carman, "A Northern Vigil," in *Canadian Anthology*, p. 110.
19. Archibald Lampman, "Winter Solitude," in *Canadian Anthology*, p. 135.
20. Sir Charles G.D. Roberts, "The Skater," in *Canadian Anthology*, p. 104.
21. Duncan Campbell Scott, "The Forsaken," in *Canadian Anthology*, pp. 152-53.
22. Robert Service, "The Cremation of Sam McGee," in *Canadian Anthology*, p. 208.
23. F.R. Scott, "March Field," in *Canadian Anthology*, p. 261.
24. E.J. Pratt, "Brébeuf and His Brethren," in *Canadian Anthology*, p. 236.
25. P.K. Page, "The Stenographers," in *Canadian Anthology*, p. 435.
26. Earle Birney, "Man Is a Snow," in *Canadian Anthology*, p. 299.
27. A.J.M. Smith, "To Hold in a Poem," in *Canadian Anthology*, p. 273.
28. Al Purdy, "Lament for the Dorsets," in *Canadian Anthology*, p. 465.
29. Margaret Atwood, *The Journals of Susanna Moodie*. The first two lines are from "Resurrection," p. 58; the third is from "Thoughts from Underground," p. 54.
30. Robert Kroetsch, *Seed Catalogue* (Winnipeg: Turnstone Press, 1977), pp. 11, 13.
31. Judy Chicago's *The Dinner Party* was on exhibition at the Art Gallery of Ontario, Toronto, May 22–July 4, 1982.
32. Madeleine Gagnon, "Corps I," trans. Isabelle de Courtivron, in *New French Feminisms: An Anthology*, ed. Elaine Marks and Isabelle de Courtivron (Amherst: University of Massachusetts Press, 1980), p. 179.
33. James Joyce. *A Portrait of the Artist as a Young Man* (London: Jonathan Cape, 1952), p. 194.
34. Julia Kristeva, "Oscillation du 'pouvoir' au refus," interview by Xaviére Gauthier, trans. Marilyn A. August, in *New French Feminisms: An Anthology*, p. 166.
35. Gertrude Stein, *Four in America* (New Haven: Yale University Press, 1947), pp. v-vi.
36. William H. Gass, *Fiction and the Figures of Life* (New York: Knopf, 1970), p. 90.

Invisible in the House of Mirrors

(This essay on language and poetry in a Canadian context reflects enthusiasm for theoretical concepts that may now seem relatively commonplace to specialists in the field. I think my direction at the time was well taken, however, and remains in retrospect a worthwhile course. Commentaries on the poetics of Robert Kroetsch, Daphne Marlatt, and George Bowering, in the latter half of the essay, hold up particularly well. This essay follows closely on "Landscape, Untitled," which immediately precedes it in this collection. It was written during the spring and autumn of 1983, while I was an exchange professor at the University of Hull and Visiting Professor of Commonwealth Literature at the University of Leeds, to be delivered as a public lecture at Canada House in London, November 9, 1983. It was published as a monograph by the Canadian High Commission to the United Kingdom in the same year, Number 21 in the Canada House Lecture Series.)

I

Language is of course Borgesian, a labyrinth of labyrinths. Words are reflecting surfaces within a closed, enclosing system. They offer an illusion of depth. The infinite possibilities of their syntactical arrangement are a maze of corridors, each giving way to another and another. Words reflect words, refract and repeat without limit, within the fixed walls of the finite structure. This is not a metaphor. There are no metaphors inside a labyrinth. Imagine yourself surrounded by mirrors. Imagine yourself, like Dracula, with no reflection. You search for yourself among the mirrored planes—but you are nowhere to be found. Knowing you are there is not enough. Descartes was wrong. When Adam named the world on our behalf, he placed himself, and us, his heirs, apart from it. He became the words he spoke, and set poets forever-after the task of transcending the limitations of language to assert the reality of their own existence and, by implication, ours as well.

Poetry is the perverse and necessary art by which language is turned upon itself to yield up the very presence in the world of the substantial self that it denies. In Canada, poets in English must use a language that evolved into a coherent system in some other place than our own, through time upon the surface of which we float, the jetsam of an alien history. The sense of individual being within the Canadian landscape can sometimes be so ephemeral as to make the place, our place, seem virtually uninhabited. Consequently, many Canadian poets show a special interest in the Adamic function of naming the 'New World,' each as if for the first time. Their poetry yearns to fuse consciousness with the landscape, words with things, with the object-world; their poetry yearns to affirm their being, our being, to make us be.

A few, most notably Margaret Atwood, recognize apparent futility in the attempt to re-create ourselves in a place that seems intrinsically opposed to our presence, through language that belongs somewhere else, words that won't fit, word arrangements that render us mute. "Our flag," she says in "Two-Headed Poems," "has been silence, / which was mistaken for no flag." Later in the same poem she argues:

> You can't live here without breathing
> someone else's air,
> air that has been used to shape
> these hidden words that are not yours.[1]

So acutely aware is she of the problem we share, Atwood seems at times acquiescent. Yet she makes of our absence, and her own, fine and haunting poems.

Others, Robert Kroetsch, Daphne Marlatt, George Bowering foremost among them, refuse both invisibility and silence. They reinvent the language; one word at a time, they make it ours. They do not struggle with words to define the landscape and thereby somehow take possession of it, as other poets have so often tried to do, and so often failed. Rather, it is the land they use to redefine the language. Their experiences of and in the world, their consciousness of the landscape within which they find themselves, translate in their poetry, through the force of their poetic bravado, into words so substantial as objects, inseparable from the things they signify, that we, among them, reading the poem, reading and reading, become equally as substantial. Through words, we become ourselves; become real.

It was only towards the middle of this century that Canadian poets discovered that their inability to establish a lyric presence within the Canadian landscape had more to do with the nature of language than with the natural world or the authenticity of their experience within it. Our early poets personified the land—unable to infuse it with consciousness in the manner of their Romantic counterparts, they gave it personality on its own, sometimes using Indians as its embodiment, more often simply turning it into an unwieldy concatenation of improbable giants. Sometimes they reduced the land to the stuff of documentary, in prolix passages that seemed meant by their density to prove that it existed at all.

One or two of the best, later in the last century, did manage to fuse the landscape with self through the sheer lucid precision of their poetry. Few poets have captured the existential condition of being in winter with words more evocative than Archibald Lampman's, in such phrasing as "frost that stings like fire," "winds that touch like steel."[2] Not, however, until A.M. Klein's magnificent poem of 1948, "Portrait of the Poet as Landscape," did a Canadian poet acknowledge through poetry the importance of words themselves in the relationship between being and the world:

> For to praise
> the world—he, solitary man—is breath
> to him. Until it has been praised, that part
> has not been. Item by exciting item—
> air to his lungs, and pressured blood to his heart—
> they are pulsated, and breathed, until they map,
> not the world's, but his own body's chart![3]

"Look," he says of the poet, earlier in the same poem, "he is / the nth Adam . . . / in a world but scarcely uttered, naming, praising. . . ." It is by words the poet becomes real, each poet in his turn.

In her 1960 poem "Butterfly Bones," Margaret Avison shows the limitations of language evident in poetic usage, moved as it is "towards final stiffness" within the forms of literary convention.[4] The real and vital world of words that is our natural heritage, what she calls "Adam's lexicon," is "locked in the mind." We no longer have access to words that once spoke for the living relationship between self and other, Adam and the world he named. Whether this is due to the seemingly fixed nature of literary forms (the alternate title for the poem is "Sonnet against Sonnets") or because literature draws attention to our loss in a world that we impale with words in order to comprehend is, in the poem, indeterminate. But Avison is a poet, writing, not mute; the very existence of her poem suggests our problem originates not so much in poetry as in language itself.

Many other Canadian poets of the last quarter century or so have written about words, made words and the problems of words for the poet, for all of us, the subject of their poetry. Adam appears time and again: the original Canadian. Sometimes, as in Jay Macpherson's casually serious poem "The Fisherman," he seems to embody the role of language in separating us from the better world. Naming is simultaneous with the Fall from Eden:

> Old Adam on the naming day
> Blessed each and let it slip away.[5]

David Helwig, in a whimsically haunting poem, "The Bugbear," relates language to the Fall into mortality—that, with a Heideggerian twist, is what makes things real. Of the child-scaring bugbear he rather ironically intones:

> A hundred times
> we wish that Adam
> had named him
> so that he might be real and die.[6]

If each poet is the nth Adam, Adam is the algebraic root of n, the primal poet.

It is as a failed Adam that Atwood's prototypic Canadian in "Progressive Insanities of a Pioneer" is overwhelmed, in a place where consciousness and the landscape were (are) mutually impenetrable, where

> Things
> refused to name themselves; refused
> to let him name them.[7]

Words for Atwood may be as solid as flesh or a flight of stones. They thicken the tongue, swell "with other words, with blood,"[8] fall away from the bone, make spells, make poems, but most important of all they provide an environment in which to live, the palpable dimensions of our lives. When they will neither adhere to the world nor become it, the object-world where we have our object-being, then we in effect live in two worlds—and always with the risk that we may fall into the abyss between, which is madness or silence.

Atwood's concern for words and the paradox of language, especially in this/that place named Canada, is shared by so many that it seems endemic. Words about words. Certainly all poetry is in some measure, as Irving Layton has said, about poetry; art, like language, is self-referential. "Each art," writes Konrad Fielder, "expresses only itself."[9] But in so doing, art, and in particular poetry, uses divers worlds to make its presence known and felt. And, curiously, in Canada Mallarmé's assertion that poems are not made of ideas but words has a special and literal relevance, for it is words themselves, not language with its unlimited syntactical possibilities, but words as words, that so often provide the subject and rhetorical objective of Canadian poetry.

A.J.M. Smith wrote in "To Hold in a Poem," in 1954:

> I would take words
> As crisp and white
> As our snow; as our birds
> Swift and sure in their flight.[10]

And for four more stanzas of a single sentence he hangs all the weight of words and place on that opening phrase: I would. I would take words, I would hold in verse, austere. I would; a yearning for what exceeds his grasp, escapes his capacity to achieve. His poem, a deconstructionist's delight: its genius in the impossibility of its intent and the unlimited indeterminacy of its significance as it plays with lingual and literary conventions towards that end, to hold in a poem the spirit of a place when its physical presence refuses still to be named.

John Newlove, another generation, Atwood's generation, evokes in "The Pride" a vision of how the land itself will come to us, but not through the stories we tell of it, not until the words are right:

> Those are all stories;
> the pride, the grand poem
> of our land, of the earth itself,
> will come, welcome, and
> sought for, and found,
> in a line of running verse,
> sweating, our pride;
>
> we seize on what has happened before.
> one line only
> will be enough
> a single line and
> then the sunlight image suddenly
> floods us
> with understanding, shocks our
> attentions, and all desire
> stops, stands alone;
> we stand alone

> we are no longer lonely
> but have roots,
> and the rooted words
> recur in the mind, mirror, so that
> we dwell on nothing else, in nothing else,
> touched, repeating them,
> at home freely
> at last, in amazement.[11]

In what could be a quotation from Wittgenstein, at least in poetic transliteration, Newlove says: when the right words spring "upon us, / out of our own mouths, / unconsidered, overwhelming," then we have roots; "we dwell on nothing else, in nothing else, / . . . at home freely / at last." What for Wittgenstein is a truth, however burdensome, in Canada is only a possibility. Wittgenstein never envisioned our invisibility in the house of mirrors, but then he was not born into a language that belonged somewhere else.

Language precedes our presence in the world. It is a public place, a communal place within which we live with others of the same family. But the words—words are different. We share them and yet they are personal and sometimes private; inseparable of course from language, they are also inseparable from self. Language and consciousness are not co-extensive, for language contains consciousness. But collectively they coexist—for language can no more be, without consciousness, than consciousness can be (in the Husserlian sense of awareness of being aware), without language. Words, however, ground consciousness in the world, as Husserl insists. Words can have substance as real as the landscape they signify, as the mind that holds them within. Even as language seems to keep us separate from the world, words have the capacity to join us to it—or also, as we in Canada must sooner or later acknowledge, the capacity to render us insubstantial, not transcendent but invisible, unreal.

To be an individual in the world is to be conscious of oneself within language, separate from the world. Jacques Lacan argues that early language acquisition and the child's sense of otherness are coincident. As we grow into language we become ourselves. But language is a given, while our relationship with words, and the relationship our being in the world sustains between words and the things they signify, are very much open to change. Thus a poet like Newlove envisions the people of Canada coming alive in the land not through the radical transformation of our whole language but through the as-yet-unachieved precision of just a few words, a perfect brilliant line or image or unyielding phrase. And Atwood in her poetic projections of 'Canadian' response to the land, especially in the early volumes *The Animals in That Country* and *The Journals of Susanna Moodie*, and in "Two-Headed Poems," similarly relates our problems of language to words themselves, the refusal of individual words to merge with the things they are meant to signify. We remain apart from the landscape because the words by which we know ourselves do not fit it, and the landscape remains outside of us because our words will not contain it. We live within language and we live within landscape, but the two refuse to coincide.

Atwood ensures that what might be of only parochial interest is given in her poetry universal dimension. The divided self and alienation from the world, both in consequence of *being* as a condition of consciousness, which in turn is the creation of language, although endemic in Canada are by no means indigenous to it. In much of her poetry, it is the function of words in relation to private being, more than to public, that dominates, and of course nothing is of more far-reaching significance to the reader than the nature of individual existence.

Gwendolyn MacEwen, contemporary with Atwood and Newlove, writes, at times with an eerie passion, to illuminate the paradoxical function of naming in relation to being, usually without reference to a Canadian context. In fact, in what could easily be taken as an analogue for the alien nature of language in her own country, she writes most effectively in what might be a transcultural idiom, as an outsider among the rooted cultures of Greece and the Arab world or as an observer within the imagined splendour of ancient Egypt. In the 1966 "Poems in Braille," MacEwen creates a disconcerting dialectic out of the relationship between words and the substantial world of things. For the 'you' of the poem, words precede individual presence:

> all your hands are verbs,
> now you touch worlds and feel their names—
> . . .
> the chair and table and book
> extend from your fingers;
> all your movements
> command these things back to their
> places; a fight against familiarity
> makes me resume my distance.[12]

For 'you,' words are a bond with the world and the means by which you bring it under imaginative control; but for the fearful 'I' of the poem, it is only things that precede presence, not words—words come *between* self and the world. The world has substance and self is an image drawn from it like the print from a cast, and is ephemeral and may perish. The real art is in the stone, not the print.

In a particularly resonant set of lines, MacEwen sums up the relationship between 'I' and the object world:

> I name all the things in my room
> and they rehearse their names

Two sides of a schism. In the first line the personal pronoun predominates; in the second, personality has been annihilated. Things, differentiated, seize control of the sentence as they struggle to accommodate names that are not in their nature, not yet. The 'I' could almost be Canada, and 'you' the embodiment of a relationship with language we must 'become' if we are to endure.

MacEwen argues a thing's true name is to be discovered, not given. The image, then, is more to be trusted than the word; an image reveals more than it says, while words may be concealed or obscured by the thing itself. The most enigmatic image, one that recurs often in MacEwen's work, the hieroglyph. MacEwen recognizes that images offer a mode of transcending the limitations of words, and the hieroglyph in this sense is inherently the most satisfying; the image as object as word—a word that literally contains its own meaning.

The relationship in poetry between word and image is infinitely intriguing. An image is more than its constituent words; it uses words to create an analogue with the object world, and as words contribute to an image they become merely properties of a complex aesthetic construct. Yet an image is also less than its words, for an image works by defining limitations, while words reach always beyond a particular context, participating in each instance with the whole of language. An image may be given a specific interpretation but its words will inevitably confound any particular fixed and finite meaning.

In "The Pride," John Newlove creates disturbingly authentic images of the landscape, alive with the Indian past. But those are all stories; only stories. When the exact right words come to us—then, then we will *become* the Indians and they us, and the land will be ours and we its living voice. For the Indian, word and image, place and self, were fused. It is they, then, who Newlove says are "our true forbears,"[13] waiting to be.

In a more private vision, Margaret Atwood shows an abiding concern for the destructive discrepancies between images and the lived-in world, between images and words as we struggle to sustain our individual presence within the world. This is a major motif running through her poetry and one of the informing principles in the play between linguistic structuralism and existential phenomenology in her very fine novel *Surfacing*. In "This is a Photograph of Me," she gives it a disconcerting twist. The poem opens onto a landscape in a blurred snapshot. There, in the background, the voice describing it says, under the lake, is her own drowned self. If you look long enough, you will see.[14]

Again: a deconstructing poem. It is, of course, absurd to think she has drowned; and yet, if we accept as real the image of the photograph within the poem, and the image within the image, then how can we not accept that same voice when it declares the image illusory, incomplete? The mind swarms with indeterminate possibilities, the dispossessed queen at the swarm's dead centre.

Seldom has personal absence in the landscape been revealed so graphically. Yet the concept embodied seems almost too readily to account for certain peculiarities of Canadian poetry.

Could the legendary wanderlust of Earle Birney and Al Purdy, George Bowering and Gwendolyn MacEwen be argued as the quest for places in the world to fit their given language better than home? Interestingly, little of their work or travel includes England, where their language originates. Could the penchant by Canadian poets for documentary form, noted by Dorothy Livesay, relate to their need to ground experience in the factual, experience that refuses to be rooted in the language they are bound to use? Facts; to compensate for the absence of reality? Could the splendid achievement of contemporary Canadian poets be the result of their confrontation with invisibility and silence? Atwood makes poetry of doubt. Bowering makes poetry out of his cheerful and lonely refusal to fade out or be mute.

It is paradoxically fascinating to consider the implications of living within an alien language, bound by habit and usage to words that deny our being in the world. Even the music of our poetry, the often discordant and sometimes melodic rhythms, could be taken in many instances as an expression not of the inarticulable truth but of inarticulability itself. "Anglosaxon Street," a 1940s poem by Earle Birney, imitates the structures and syntax, the assonance and aural dialect, of Old English poetry in order, it seems, to draw ironic contrast between displaced English slum-dwellers and both their Canadian context and their cultural heritage. Beyond that, Birney's rhythms make the point that the language he the poet must use is also alien, drawn like these people out of its own place and the culture that made it. These people, in Canada: "soaking bleakly in beer, skittleless."[15]

James Reaney makes much the same point about language with more disarming clarity in one particular quatrain of his poem "The Bicycle," which leaps from its fluid context in a lovely imitative jouncing, under the duress of suddenly ragged syntax and rhythm:

> The March wind blows me ruts over,
>   Puddles past, under red maple buds,
> Over culvert of streamling, under
>   White clouds and beside bluebirds.[16]

The echoes of Anglo-Saxon, of language used in such a way as to affirm its alien origin, poetry made from the awkwardness of words—all this conveys the exhilaration of adolescence which is what the bicycle means, in the life of the poem.

All of this, the speculation, the fascination, derives from the fact that when a language is taken from its place of origin to another place, it ceases to be the same language. Although the words may seem to be the same, even the relationship of the language to those who use it becomes quite different. Just as the culture of the Old World transported from abroad ceases to be an environment and becomes an instrument of nostalgia by which a lost world is kept alive, so too does language, transported, change from environment to instrument. We use it, but we have trouble living within it, recognizing ourselves among its words and conventions. English in North America crossed over with the founding settlers and was the established language awaiting everyone who followed.

In England, English and the civilization it expresses, as colour is the expression of pigment, are inextricably related. While language and race are not synonymous, a history of the English language illuminates the history of English civilization and the English people. A history of the English language in Wales, Ireland, and Scotland as surely illuminates the history of the Welsh, Irish, and Scots, for whom the language superimposed on their own is no less rooted in the lost Indo-European dialect that is their common ancestor. But a history of English in Canada is necessarily little more than an account of linguistic peculiarities, and in the United States a survey of variant usage. It was not superimposed but transplanted; otherwise, there were only Indian dialects, which were incomprehensible, or a vast silence. In India and Africa a history of English might somewhat more closely relate to a history of the peoples involved, but then surely to their oppression, to the collapse of civilizations, not to their development. Throughout the English-speaking world, outside of Britain, people share in common not so much a language, which varies remarkably from place to place, but the condition of living with a language that is not in any true sense their own.

Language is the expression of a particular people through

time in a particular place. In each word of a language, as a casual reading of the *Oxford English Dictionary* will reveal, there are history and geography, culture and the complex origins of a civilization. This holds true as much for prepositions and articles as for verbs and nouns. Each word on its own, amplified by its syntactical potential, speaks history, articulates the landscape, the place and the times of its emergence into common usage, whether the speaker is aware or not of its freighted implications.

An example which, for a bit of needed irony, I will draw from Canadian language, not English, will serve as a model for what I mean. In my part of southeastern Ontario, settled through land grants issued to demobilized soldiers after our war with the Americans in 1814, English is thoroughly entrenched as the only language. Yet the village we live in is called, on old maps, Belle Roche as well as Bell Rock and Bellrock; on some old maps the Depot River appears as Deep Eau—a lingual compromise! But the word I am coming to is far more historically complex. Locally, people refer to the scrubland with which the district abounds as 'brulie.' It is not a word they hear in school or in town, or are ever likely to see in print; but it is a word they grow up with, a part of the local topography, inseparable in their minds from the landscape it signifies. Its origin seems to be French, probably from the fur traders, many of them *bois-brûlés*, who travelled the area for two centuries before settlement. I assume it is derived from the French although its origin is obscured in usage, and in usage its origin is irrelevant. Yet when the farm people around Bellrock speak of 'brulie,' the past and present converge. However unwittingly, in a single word they are expressing their rootedness in the place they no doubt never questioned might be their own, and real.

Now, consider that every word in the English language is equally as laden with the history of a people in a particular place. Every single word. Without exception.

Walking in the English countryside, as surely as one walks amidst the history, one walks among words.

Reading English poetry, it is impossible to separate language from the social and historical traditions, the geography and the people, the language contains.

In Canada, this then is what our poetry yearns for: words so right for us they become ours, inseparable in consciousness from the world with which they will merge.

> We wanted to describe the snow
> the snow here, at the corner
> of the house and orchard
> in a language so precise
> and secret it was not even
> a code, it was snow,
> there could be no translation.[17]

The alternative, in this poem by Margaret Atwood, is silence: "Our other dream: to be mute."[18] To be dumb, free from the tyranny of language that holds us apart from the world; or mute, masters of language so *precise*, *effortless* and *vital* that it ceases to obtrude as a separate entity between us and the world—words, unspoken, in which we and the landscape are one.

Confronted by silence, Atwood retreats in her poetry into a medley of wit and despair. Refusing when it happens the perfect beauty of her words, she dwells instead on the absence they reveal. On the other side of silence, however, other poets wrench language to make it fit their worlds; "so precise / and secret . . . / there could be no translation." Bowering, Kroetsch, Marlatt; their words become things, a landscape to live within.

Daphne Marlatt has talked of the capacity for language to provide an environment in poetry so palpable and compelling that we and the poet are re-created together within it. In the prefatory remarks to *What Matters* she states it this way:

> . . . i was writing poems, both short- & long-line, composing out of a poetic that taught me language, its 'drift,' could ground my experience in the turn of a line as tense, as double-edged, *as being felt.* In the oscillation of a pun, or a rhyming return, i sensed a narrative that wasn't only mine, though i participated in its telling & was thereby told. Caught up in it, connected, in the body of language where we also live.[19]

To live within the body of language!

The effect of words: *as being felt.* What a beautifully concentrated and irresolvably ambiguous phrase. Being: verb and noun. Words, *being* felt. And in the condition of being, as *felt*, through words. Here, as in her poetry, ambiguity struts and stutters with more substance than mere coherence could possibly muster.

Marlatt, Bowering, and Kroetsch all write to make words things, as-being-felt. But Marlatt, especially, also insists that words on the page are things in themselves, discrete objects, fully two-dimensional in the two-dimensioned world of print: not as the concrete poet, who builds flat sculptures out of the alphabet; but like Mallarmé, to control, break from the linear tyranny of syntax and logical meaning, to make of the unyielding word an act of initiation, leading into a vision at once private and liberating. While Bowering and Kroetsch also attend to the impact of print in the reader's eye, their poetry shows more concern for what Christopher Fry has called "the intervening landscape between me and you," poet and reader.[20] The word as object is in their poetry, to continue with Fry, "a coil spring of energy within an architectural shape," released within the reader's consciousness, while reading.

In Kroetsch's poetry, the Husserlian principle to which all three implicitly subscribe, of word and object interpenetrating, intertwined within consciousness, finds its purest and most playful expression. But Kroetsch differentiates between the fusion of word *and* thing, and the equation of word *with* thing in practical usage. The latter denies the possibility of poetry, the existence of the poet.

In the following passages from the delightful and unsettling sequence of poems called "Seed Catalogue," Kroetsch rather sardonically puts forth the case against himself, what he as a growing young poet was up against in the illusory practical world where the landscape was presumed to be shaped by a few measures of wire, and words were a distraction from the real work at hand, subduing the land, making it yield. But, as with everything Kroetsch writes, things are not quite what they seem. Almost in spite of itself this passage shows, by a brilliant deployment of unadorned language, how the poet ultimately prevails. Despite the equation by his father in the poem, separating word from thing ("Son, this is a crowbar"), the poem itself insists, not this is a crowbar, but crowbar, the thing, is a crowbar; as fencepost is fencepost. While identifying the problem, in words that apparently deny imaginative presence, Kroetsch offers its resolution—for the words he uses insist on their own substantiality, word-things that admit the poet as a real presence among them. And us, too.

> Son, this is a crowbar.
> This is a willow fencepost.
> This is a sledge.
> This is a roll of barbed wire.
> This is a bag of staples.
> This is a claw hammer.
> We give form to this land by running
> a series of posts and three strands
> of barbed wire around a quarter-section.
> First off I want you to take that
> crowbar and drive 1,156 holes
> into that gumbo,
> And the next time you want to
> write a poem
> we'll start the haying.
> *How do you grow a poet?*[21]

In this country of Kroetsch's childhood—with difficulty. But after the haying is done, after there's no one left to do the haying, the poem remains, the story, the song. After the fenceposts have rotted away, and the claw hammer has been lost, perhaps for a poet to find someday, the words remain, connecting the mind that made them and the mind that reads, connecting both with a whole list of things and with the people who used them, connecting people to the land. Even in denial there is affirmation, if the words are right.

As Bowering says, in a sentence that is a poem on its own:

> To name is
> to begin
> to admit.[22]

II

As the prelude to what follows, which is less argument than demonstration, a marvellously conflated line by Irving Layton will serve as a pivotal conceit. The line:

> Whatever else poetry is freedom.[23]

The precondition of freedom is to be, and Layton in his poetry speaks with honesty and absolute passion from the depths of being. But it is a persona we read, in his poems—the lover, the rabbi, the clown; an intriguing, appealing, obstreperous, sensitive, joyful, outrageous and angry poetic device. He comes alive for us *through* language, not within it. A poet of his own generation, his poetry expresses himself, exposes himself, but refines the living consciousness of the poet himself, as Joyce might have said, right out of existence. He was the source or, perhaps, catalyst—but to find a poet at the centre, being-within-words, one must look to the aggressive postmodernism of writers such as Bowering and Kroetsch and Marlatt, whose poetry makes of absence a presence, of lack a plentitude, whose words in poetry are more substantial than anything they might be interpreted to mean.

Influenced by American poets more than most of their contemporaries (open, then, to a kind of English that Americans since Whitman have resolutely determined to be their own), apparently far more responsive than younger poets in Canada to the philosophical bases of postmodernist thought and aesthetic theory, these three are at the centre, alive in their poems, within words, among words. Sometimes with infuriating disregard for coherence, sometimes with delightful candour, they tempt or invite or demand their reader's presence there as well.

The essence of their anti-romantic exploitation of self is both argued and illuminated in a stanza from the poem "Farewell" by Frank Davey:

> The only process
> is moving now onward. Causing breath
> to follow breathing. I walk naked
> within my clothes, within

> this hostile air. I write these words
> that someone, will remember me,
> or at least finding me here
> poisond, burnd, loved, unloved, will see words
> moving.[24]

This all but brings tears to the eyes. As the reader is made conscious of reading by the poem's art, the words in effect become conscious of being read. They move. And in their movement the reader and the process of reading, the writer and the process of writing, are merged, as lively as atoms in a renegade molecule.

The reader reading the reader reading writing written the writer writing wrote the reader reading. And the writer, perhaps, lives on or again.

In the following discussion, passages are given without reference to context. Where whole brief poems are quoted, form and meaning are disregarded except specifically in relation to individual words on the page. Interpretation, explication, *explication de text*, reduces such poetry to an aesthetic arrangement of signs—of no more significance than speculations on where the nude descending Marcel Duschamps' staircase might have left her clothes.

Dance is more than a body in motion to music.

George Bowering might easily be the invention of his own writing. He seems perpetually to be drawing himself into splendid existence through the sheer force of words on paper; sharing with boundless generosity the experience of being with readers. Being together, in words. Especially in his poetry, Bowering comes alive not so much through words as among them, sly and vivacious among words—not personality but a vital presence, which the reader shares. His poetry is never *about* himself, but about *being*. Consider the following poem, "The Frost":

> But the morning
> hoar frost
> the breath of cold birds
> on trees

the metal of January
in this place.
The crystal, white
hanging from the iron handrail
cold to fingers
sweet to taste.[25]

At first it seems the reader has stumbled into a winter scene by William Carlos Williams. So solid do things appear, they might be Paterson, New Jersey. But this is a landscape alive with more than the breath of cold birds. It is alive with the shifting values of language and the literal presence of the poet's mind. This is no scene, but a drama. The words are precise, specific. There are no verbs in the poem (unless you count 'hanging,' a participle). The nouns are things (except January which is adjectival). An arrangement of things: made exact by concrete adjectives. The nouns and adjectives are reciprocal, qualifying each other in tight solid clusters, each pair hinting at narrative. In the first three couplets, personality is elusive, implied by attitude and perspective. In the last two, crystals, the handrail, are cold, sweet, conditions of being, to fingers, to taste. Being is a definite presence, not individuated but sentient and dynamic. Cold and sweet become verbal: that is what crystals and metal *do*, in this place, in January.

In an excerpt from another winter poem, "The Snow," Bowering transforms words into experience. Despite the syntactical simplicity of the passage, the simple precision of the words taken separately, he goes beyond evoking response, he brings the reader to life within the scene, the scene and the words inseparable in the reader's experience from perception itself:

The snow
does not clasp

it falls away
from foot steps

a light spray
of energy, soundless

as the crackling
of the sun.[26]

The poem rises from passivity into palpable action. The observing consciousness that notes the snow "does not clasp / it falls away" is represented in the poem only by an adjectival foot, an absence, the shape of imprints. And yet, out of this an image gathers force, then overwhelms. Each word means, in itself, and clear syntax draws the words forward in a sequence, the music building, towards completion. But with a slight shift, suddenly the image surges out of control—it transforms from an image of the landscape, the external world, into one of perception, of the senses fused:

> a light spray
> of energy, soundless
>
> as the crackling
> of the sun

A brilliant dazzling witty image: not of sight or sound but an implosion of the senses through words, an experience of oneself experiencing, beyond the capacity of words to describe. Bowering exploits a created tension between conventional and contextual meaning, turning words upon themselves, to re-create in the reader's mind an instantaneous and inarticulable experience as if it were happening, as it is read (and it is); the reader alive in the *poem's* world (rather than in the *poet's* world, as with Layton).

In the following poem from *Between the Sheets*, Bowering attends explicitly to the capacity for words to reduce 'personality' to inconsequence, while simultaneously rendering things real and the self substantial.

> Against description
>
> I went to the blackberries
> on the vine
>
> They were blackberries
> on the vine
>
> They were
> blackberries
>
> Black
> berries.[27]

To begin: a rather simple lyric, beginning with "I"; a singular action of no significance. I went to. But "they," they had substance, they were blackberries. And they were alive. This is their distinguishing characteristic: they were "on the vine." They "were" what they were, blackberries being blackberries. Past tense. Past tense, at least, until the irrepressible poet sneaks in; asserts himself. "Black / berries." Two lines. A perception; insight. Black. Berries.

As things change in the poem from objects of description to word-objects, being-in-words, the poet is transformed from an ephemeral "I," a pronoun, into the very act of perceiving, a verbal presence—as much there, in the final couplet, as black/berries themselves.

Robert Kroetsch writes poetry, it seems, to be free of words. In a good-natured sort of way his poetry follows the austere architectural dictum of Mies van der Rohe and Le Corbusier that "less is more." The fewest words, placed perfectly, reach farther, touch more, probe deeper, transcend language, become experience, more so than a flood of words enhanced by the most fluent orchestration, articulate in the extreme. As we are contained by language, to be most truly ourselves we must struggle to be free of the limitations it imposes upon us, upon our consciousness of self and the world, self in the world. This, the poet might achieve by shaping words on the page, the way sculpture shapes air. Through the space among words—freedom from the tyranny of their limitations.

It is as much by the spacial arrangement of words as things, as by their temporal flow, that we and the poet are freed, to become real. If words remain words, they are only words. But Kroetsch demands that poet and reader and poem are one, fused for the time of the poem in a unity of being. The poem frees us from words, to be. In-the-world. *Dasein.*

Consider: the entire fourth stanza in a poem from the sequence "The Criminal Intensities of Love as Paradise" (surely there is a complete and vast poem in that title alone). The poem is called "Standing Near a Waterfall":

bent & the break
and then comes
after after
the reaching sea.[28]

Forcefully, and with such panache of vital obscurity, Kroetsch acknowledges that we the readers are alive in the world. We are not creatures of the poet's imagination as Layton would have it. We have seen waterfalls. We exist. Listen: words, and a waterfall . . .

bent & the break
and then comes
after after
the reaching sea.

The water is bent. We know that from our own experience with waterfalls. The flat surface arcs away from the horizontal; heavy, inexorable. It doesn't drop or plummet; it is bent—"& the break," its smoothness shatters. The solid substantial plane of water breaks. Between bent and the break, not even an 'and.' Only an ampersand. Break is not a consequence of bent, in our perception of the scene, to be aligned in a sequence of causality by a coordinating conjunction. Bent and break are visually part of the same action, inseparable. The visual ampersand, a non-word, confounds the linearity of syntax; allows for the simultaneity of events.

But the second line of the stanza begins with "and." Now, from the waterfall, "then comes"—and Kroetsch's readers have all seen for themselves the water roiling in heaving pools below, and in consequence of, a waterfall. Water gathering power and form, moving away. And suddenly, in the refusal of image, our minds fill with images—as "after after" gathers divers landscapes into simultaneous presence: after, after, until the water joins "the reaching sea." The sea reaching in, beyond the landscape of after and after, to the water breaking from the fall; the sea reaching out, the broad reach of the sea bent over the surface of the earth.

In reading such lines, one becomes aware that most poetry describes landscape as if readers were blind.

Kroetsch assumes we have seen waterfalls, and uses our experience in the world to play with us among the words, to affirm that we are as real as the words and the world they contain. He does not summon an imaginary waterfall into our presence, but us into a world where waterfalls are real.

Compare this modest celebration of the reader's authenticity to the second half of A.J.M. Smith's 1943 poem "Sea Cliff," which, I suspect, it intentionally echoes. After he introduces austere images virtually stripped of implication in the first stanza, Smith the modernist cannot resist meaning. The poem is about this, as much as it is about rocks and water, and renewal born of the strength to endure:

> after—
> after the ebb-flow,
> wet rock,
> high—
> high over the slapping green,
> water sliding away
> and the rock abiding,
> new rock riding
> out of the spray.[29]

The stuttering of the first few lines conveys the paradoxical conviction that pure imagery, so much to be desired, must inevitably give way to explication. In Kroetsch's "after after," the words are what they describe. In Smith's "after— / after," they are a declaration of the inadequacies inherent in language to convey without mediation. Unlike Kroetsch, Smith imagines the real world of experience must necessarily submit to the poet's art, the poem's artifice, thereby declaring the reader to be not part of the world but separate from it, observing through the poet's eyes and, if the poem is good enough, through the poet's transfigured soul.

The following, also in Kroetsch's "The Criminal Intensities of Love as Paradise," is a four-line stanza from the poem " 'And Dreamers, Even Then, if Dreaming.' "

> eerie & enter
> if
> & the pale garden
> chill as white.[30]

Bowering has described literature as "*telling* the story as it happens": the immediacy of Kroetsch's lines as a process, virtually committing the reader to participate in creation as the words struggle towards coherence, the poem not in the words but in the struggle—literature is *here*, literature is *reading* the story as it happens. And the story is happening not just while, but because, it is being read. In the haunting narrative born of these four lines, the reader's dream and the poet's merge:

eerie

Without a capital, eerie, vulnerable to the margin; isolated by blank space and an ampersand; a story on its own, a word trembling with stories. The sound alone, a story.

& enter

The soft *e* drawn out to an abrupt halt. A command: enter. The inexorability of action in a dream. Or an invitation: the eerie draws inwards; enter.

if

On a line alone. Unadorned with capital or punctuation. Following hard on the previous line, followed by space. If becomes verbal, the beginning and the centre of a maelstrom of possibilities. If . . .

& the pale garden

No matter what, at the end of if, a garden. Paradise regained? Pale! Death. Pale garden; not of growing things; spectral, frozen—

chill as white

The refusal of chill to be a part of speech! Insistence on white as a noun, a thing!

Words, forcing confrontation with the dream-horror they cannot express. Words, making the story happen within us. Our story; the poem as story. Consciousness struggling towards coherence while paradoxically the words move towards disturbing ambiguity and the extinction of personality. An anomaly within a dream. If dreaming.

Kroetsch, too, picks up the poetic possibilities of blackberries, crediting his interest to the French poet Francis Ponge (on whose work Marlatt did an M.A. dissertation).

> . . . If blackberries can be
> blackberries, I reasoned, by a kind of analogy,
> lemons can, I would suppose, be lemons.
>
> Such was not the case.[31]

With characteristically self-deprecating good humour, Kroetsch is apparently overwhelmed by words, reduced to inanity, a causality of thought, of thinking.

"Blackberries." Things and word: inseparable. Blackberries are blackberries are blackberries. Echoes of Gertrude Stein. Real language. But the reasoning "I," witty, speculating, intrudes. Lemons, objects of speculation, separate from the word, the tentative poet between. "Lemons" is only a word, and the poet, now, is lost in the emptiness of such/was/not/the/case. Yet the creating consciousness that shaped all the words upon the page and plays among them, especially among the empty ones, is undeniably a presence in the poem, as are we, who share his sport.

In a beautiful poem called "Daphne Marlatt," George Bowering suggests development in the impact of Marlatt's poetry. He is driven to metaphor:

> I always thought the words snapt from
> her one by one, twigs the birds rested
> on & when they flew someone snapt them
> off.
>
> . . .
>
> how could you follow them without breaking
> your tongue.

> Even then no one knew she was pisst off,
> she didnt know because women didnt really
> know & she made poems that were questions
> stretcht out in space, ready to be snapt off.
> Now you should hear her shout. It
> is as if a stick had come alive in your hand.[32]

Hearing some of Daphne Marlatt's short-line poems aloud is like reading the script for a mime show. The experience may be interesting but it is incomplete. To know really what is going on, we must see the words played out on the page. Marlatt insists that words are literally spacial—not merely a visual cue as to how they might be heard (as by convention poetry generally appears in written form: pause, breathe, stress; the music of meaning), but spacial, things upon paper. And the words sometimes skitter about, among the commas and slashes and dashes. And sometimes they remain utterly enigmatic, objects on a stage around which the action takes place, shapers of the action by their presence but as bereft of singular meaning as an unexplained column of stone or a shaft of silk reaching the stage from high in the flies.

This does not mean Marlatt is unaware of the music; as she explained to Bowering in an interview published in *Open Letter:*

> Any word is a physical body. Its body is sound, so it has that absolute literal quality that sound has, which connects it up with sounds around it. And then, it has that other aspect, which is meaning. . . . You move out from the word to a shape, which is the whole poem.[33]

You move out from the word. It is the sound of words, as the eye hears, that gives them a third dimension, a physical body, in the reader's mind.

Consider: the stanza of words opening her poem called "ardour's."

> fire light
> livd in from
> within[34]

The arrangement of words does not confound their sequential meaning, but it draws each word out of context in its turn, lets it be an object, almost a poem in itself. The weight of each word is felt. Normally, the weight of words is severely modified by syntax and contextual meaning: firelight / lived in / from within. But here, Marlatt separates "fire" and "light" on the first line, giving them equal value. Instead of one word qualifying and limiting the other, she allows each to stand for a variety of possibilities limited only by the reader's experience and imagination. Fire. Light. Two phenomena, forced into a relationship by their isolation following the poem's title (which, however, as a superscript, keeps drawing at the poem, drawing the word "fire" away from literal meaning into a syntactical context: ardour's fire [is] light lived in from within. Fire as metaphor. But arranged as it is in the poem, the fire is real, a burning.)

The second line curiously gives each word, livd/in/from, equal weight and value. Dropping the *e* from "livd," Marlatt allows a hint of the word 'livid' to enter, but of far more consequence she forces attention onto the ascending l-v-d, soft-to-hard, aural presence of the word, and separates it decisively from "in." Sense, in turn, demands caesura after "in" and before "from." Being on a line of its own, in spite of following the word "from," "within" is forced to maintain a prepositional value. From within, where "within" takes on the value of a noun, suggests merely a location, more or less anatomical. But "from/within," paired prepositions, opens towards opposing possibilities. And "in/from/within," which by the spacial arrangement we are forced to read separately, each word a presence on its own, suggests experience without limit. Again:

> ardour's
>
> fire light
> livd in from
> within

Marlatt demands our presence within the poem. She shapes the world; we enter and take on substance the way we might when enthralled with a painting by Jackson Pollock.

In the following few lines from the opening of a poem called “largely sea,” the words clash at first in a dissonance of meaning, syntax, and sound, then settle into a strange and haunting coherence before breaking again into discord:

at, eye
cloud your
silence casts

a light
spray sea
islands us
out of the waves’
crash we stand

stranded.[35]

Following the title, “largely sea,” the first six words in the first three lines seem to dart about in a manic rush going nowhere. Hints of meaning generated by the proximity of the words are shrewdly shattered by their syntactical discontinuity:

at, eye
cloud your
silence casts

The words try to mean but they cannot quite connect. Then suddenly, “a light.” The mind circles—“your / silence casts / a light.” “At”: direction/place. “Eye”: perception, a mood received. But a light in the poem also leads, anticipates: “a light / spray.” The spray, the “sea,” it “islands us,” we stand “out of the waves’ ” reach, “crash we stand, / stranded.”

Coherence is only an illusion. Yet listen to the music of this second part as it builds towards substance:

a light
spray sea
islands us
out of the waves’
crash we stand

stranded.

The near-rhyme solidifies: islands, stand, stranded. The consonants harden; and the sibilants harden too, from the long sigh of spray and sea, through the dying hiss of waves'/crash, they gather into the stark complaint, stand/stranded. But the music is also due to syntactical distortion—"islands us," for example; both words have different sound values here than grammatical convention would normally grant them.

And to the eye—poems within the poem. The eye makes a poem of the isolated elusive enigmatic title; and a poem from the spacial pairing of "a light /. . . stranded."

What at first might seem self-indulgent in Marlatt's poetry, so fiercely does it sometimes resist our efforts to penetrate the surface, will eventually be felt as we enter the poem, become the poem with all of our senses working, the result of her determination to create a theatre of words on the deep white spaces of the page.

Berry-picking must seem a Canadian obsession, when you think of how often it appears in Canadian poems. The best-known example of the type probably is Irving Layton's, on himself as the poet-victim while his beloved picks on, real in the real world, her lips "redder than the raspberries." Marlatt's contribution to the genre, the first lines of a poem she names "to, carry thru," is characteristically more difficult to paraphrase. The poem begins:

> to/
> go pick black
> berries & raz
> berries,
>
>   she sd the
> contact high in
> vites rambles well.[36]

"To/." Everything follows as a consequence of "to." A directional preposition, or, more likely, the first half of an open infinitive. "Go." The completion of the infinitive, or an imperative, or even a plea for sharing. Then: words spaced as objects tumble forward in a sequence of animation and meaning—briefly. Movement is halted abruptly with the drop in a line and the disintegration of sense. Each word in the last two lines is a sound-rune, separate from others, an object on its own—relating only through inference, through conjecture; the way objects in a field relate to one another only in the consciousness that perceives them. A tree, a stone, a road.

And then there is space, and the eye leaps back for reference, something to root the mind in, a structure of simultaneous meanings that will yield coherence. Instead, syntax breaks apart and the word-objects lie scattered on their own, each as real in the field of consciousness as the others: "black" as real and substantial as "pick" or "berries."

In her long-line poems, Marlatt creates an illusion of greater coherence, but the same austere integrity is at work. The poem is not a text of meaning, nor convoluted metaphor. It is an arrangement of possibilities. It must be entered, experienced from within, as we, reading, become the poem that she was, writing it.

> Words, vacuous as
> kites. Race the air currents tug at strings for opening
> mouths, gulp, air tails are laid in. As i'm jealous of her,
> she-fish, her ease. Myself divests of aches, pain, Rain's
>
> a festival the way it gentles us now. We bend in to see
> the sky's immense racks of rainwear,
>
> Naked our skins swim
> this element, those kites, paper, shouting the wet air.[37]

Marlatt makes poems in which to lose and find yourself, reading them.

It is possible, then, for Bowering, for Kroetsch, for Marlatt to write the poems they write. All three share the common influence of certain American poets, but even more so they share a concern for the reader as a participating presence within their poetry, which lends to their work an air of distinctively Canadian postmodernism. William Carlos Williams has taught them all a literal precision, through words unobscured by metaphor or metaphysics, through which things occupy space in imagination. The three of them as a matter of course accept in their poetry Charles Olson's ideas of composition by field, where word-objects on the page shape in the mind a landscape as real as the world around us. But they also write directly out of their experience of themselves in the world as Canadians. They make it possible to live within the Canadian landscape, "in a language so precise . . . there could be no translation." To be, in the world; Canadian.

Notes and Works Cited

1. Margaret Atwood, "Two-Headed Poems," in *Two-Headed Poems* (Toronto: Oxford University Press, 1978); iv, p. 6; ix, p. 70.
2. Archibald Lampman in *Canadian Anthology*, ed. Carl F. Klinck and Reginald E. Watters, 3rd ed. (Toronto: Gage Educational Publishing, 1974); "Winter uplands," p. 133; "Winter Evening," p. 132.
3. A.M. Klein, "Portrait of the Poet as Landscape," vi, in *Canadian Anthology*, pp. 347-48.
4. Margaret Avison, "Butterfly Bones; or Sonnet against Sonnets," in *Canadian Anthology*, p. 449.
5. Jay Macpherson, "The Fisherman," in *Canadian Anthology*, p. 518.
6. David Helwig, "The Bugbear," in *Canadian Anthology*, p. 557.
7. Margaret Atwood, "Progressive Insanities of a Pioneer," in *The Animals in That Country* (Toronto, Oxford University Press, 1968), p. 39.
8. Atwood, "Two-Headed Poems," vi, p. 67.
9. Konrad Fielder, quoted by Sheila Watson in "Gertrude Stein: The Style is the Machine," in *Shiela Watson: A Collection, Open Letter*, 3rd ser., no. 1 (winter 1974-75), p. 170.
10. A.J.M. Smith, "To Hold in a Poem," in *Canadian Anthology*, p. 273.
11. John Newlove, "The Pride," vi, vii, in *Canadian Anthology*, p. 562.
12. Gwendolyn MacEwen, "Poems in Braille," i, v, in *Canadian Anthology*, p. 572.
13. Newlove, "The Pride," p. 563.
14. Margaret Atwood, "This is a Photograph of Me," in *Canadian*

Anthology, pp. 364-65.
15. Earle Birney, "Anglosaxon Street," in *Canadian Anthology*, p. 296.
16. James Reaney, "The Bicycle," in *Canadian Anthology*, p. 499.
17. Atwood, "Two-Headed Poems," v, p. 65.
18. Atwood, "Two-Headed Poems," xi, p. 75.
19. Daphne Marlatt, prefatory note to *What Matters: Writing 1968-70* (Toronto: Coach House Press, 1980).
20. Christopher Fry, "Looking for a Language," address at Great St. Mary's Church, Cambridge, Eng., November 20, 1983.
21. Robert Kroetsch, "Seed Catalogue," 6, in *Field Notes* (Don Mills: General Publishing, 1981), p. 58.
22. I credit Bowering with the words but their arrangement is mine, a sort of found-poem I lifted from I'm not sure where.
23. Irving Layton, "Whatever Else Poetry is Freedom," in *Canadian Anthology*, p. 394.
24. Frank Davey, "Farewell," in *Selected Poems: The Arches* (Vancouver: Talonbooks, 1980), p. 76.
25. George Bowering, "The Frost," in *Touch/selected poems 1960-70* (Toronto: McClelland and Stewart, 1971), p. 44.
26. George Bowering, "The Snow," in *Touch*, p. 32.
27. George Bowering, "Against Description," in *West Window* (Toronto: General Publishing, 1982), p. 135.
28. Robert Kroetsch, "Standing Near a Waterfall," in the sequence "The Criminal Intensities of Love as Paradise," in *Field Notes*, p. 124.
29. A.J.M. Smith, "Sea Cliff," in *Canadian Anthology*, p. 282.
30. Robert Kroetsch, "'And Dreamers, Even Then, if Dreaming,'" in "Criminal Intensities," p. 144.
31. Robert Kroetsch, "Sketches of a Lemon," in *Field Notes*, p. 124.
32. George Bowering, "Daphne Marlatt," in *West Window*, p. 43.
33. Daphne Marlatt, interviewed by George Bowering in "Given this Body," in *Open Letter*, 4th ser., no. 3 (spring 1979), pp. 69-70.
34. Daphne Marlatt, "ardour's" in *Net Work Selected Writings* (Vancouver: Talonbooks, 1980), p. 85.
35. Daphne Marlatt, "largely sea," in *Net Work*, p. 79.
36. Daphne Marlatt, "to, carry thru," in *Net Work*, p. 32.
37. Daphne Marlatt, "Getting there," in *Net Work*, p. 81.

HOW FICTION WORKS

HIMMLER'S GOT THE KING LOCKED UP IN THE TOWER OF LONDON: AN ESSAY ON *BADLANDS* AND *BURNING WATER*

(How do we believe what we read? What is it in the coming together of language and consciousness, as we apprehend narrative, that permits us to suspend disbelief? This essay examines how narrative works in relation to language, and how language works within narrative, while exploring distinctions between modernist conventions of realism, born out of humanism, and the vital extravagance of postmodernism. The moderate discontinuities in the essay suggest a struggle against linear constraints; perhaps influenced by Kroetsch and Bowering, I was finding expositional formalism more and more suffocating in my desire to articulate creative as well as critical responses to language, experience, and particular texts. This was written while I was Visiting Professor of Commonwealth Literature at the University of Leeds in the fall of 1983 and delivered at a conference there on April 27, 1984, the proceedings of which were published in 1985 by the University of Leeds Press in a book called Re-Visions of Canadian Literature, *edited by Shirley Chew. It also appeared in* Present Tense, *published by NC Press in 1985.)*

DEIGHTON, LEN. *SS-GB*. St. Albans: Triad Panther, 1980. " 'Himmler's got the King locked up in the Tower of London,' said Harry Woods." The opening sentence of Deighton's novel says everything he has to say. The rest is anticlimax, the explication of a premise. Yet many readers read the rest.

IN THE MODE of existential realism adopted by most writers of 'male adventure' from Dashiell Hammett to John Le Carré, by most novelists in fact of the twentieth century, Deighton exploits the actuality of language, the factuality of words. His writing is based on the assumption that he can say virtually anything he wants in print, so long as he says it with reasonable decorum. Words on the page are apparently more reliable, and even more real, than the time-tossed moment of our separate lives. Insofar as the reader reads, there is no reality but what is being read. That is the illusion, the fallacy and the largesse of literary modernism.

" 'HIMMLER'S GOT THE KING locked up in the Tower of London,' said Harry Woods."

HOW IS IT POSSIBLE to arouse not merely the willing suspension of disbelief, but to inspire reader complicity in the suppression of contrary knowledge? For Deighton's statement to work at all, the reader must be aware of the historical implications which render it absurd. However, in written narrative, words are the only facts, logic is the logic of grammatical structure, limits in all respects are determined by language. Within a declaration sanctioned by Harry's apparent disinterest, everything connects. Each naming word is a nexus of historical possibilities; the verbal phrase suggests plausible action among them. Harry, whose statement in the present tense contains the historical and therefore establishes his priority over it, speaks in the narrative past, as the action is happening. This then is the truth that counts, because it is immediate, past and irrefutable. The other, what we think we know, is only hearsay, an extratextual rumour. History is remade, as always, in order to make the present instance inevitable.

Why irrefutable? Because grammar is absolute. Even when it sustains enigma or anomaly, as is often the case in a poem, for example, it is the precision by which the terms of the contraries are arranged that allows articulation beyond words, which is the genius of poetry. Verb tense and grammatical alliance in Deighton's sentence are open to neither ambiguity nor paradox. Meaning is no more irrelevant here than in poetry, but it follows the dictates of grammar—it does not determine them. Each part of speech relates to all the others in a relationship that ultimately is shaped into coherence as a clause subordinate to the fact-in-action, Harry Woods, speaking, or having spoken. There is nothing to refute. In the closed world of Deighton's opening sentence, and sustained throughout his novel, a separate reality prevails. Himmler's got the King!

POSSIBLY IT IS BECAUSE print occupies space in order to give language a temporal presence that it fosters the illusion of time and place being subject to the rules of grammar. Syntax, like gravity, apparently governs all. It has no substance and no duration, but time and the substantial world are utterly at its disposal. In ideogrammatic languages, syntax is relative, governed by proximity and implication: grammar is determined by meaning. But in phonetic print, the rules precede meaning. Perhaps the cumulative dynamics of syntax follow from alphabetical necessity (the word 'alphabet' itself declares sequence). Perhaps the exacting structure of syntax derives from a print form in which the letters bear no intrinsic relationship to the words they articulate. Without words, syntax has no relevance, like gravity in a vacuum. Yet paradoxically a phonetic word only exists as a potential of meaning, without syntax to place it in relation to time and space. The smallest self-contained phonetic unit is a sentence. The ideogram, say in Chinese, for 'chair' is a spacial concept, a thing in itself. But the word 'chair' in phonetic print awaits the linear context of a coherent grammatical construct to have meaning. Otherwise, it is simply a familiar arrangement of letters. Waiting.

READING IN A NARRATIVE world where the limits of consciousness and of knowledge and experience are established by the principles of grammar, the reader enlivens a reality more coherent and sound than his or her own—probably more exciting, since anything can happen there, if it is said right. We are apparently alive, reading realistic fiction, the way we never are in living life. Creation, it seems, is no match for Len Deighton's world of words.

But of course the opposite is true. Far from allowing us to live in a parallel reality, as it were, the success of such reading depends on the denial of self. The syntactically structured world only works at the expense of personality. A confrontation between reader and text or the critic and herself, a violation of absolute distance between the writer and text, threaten to collapse the illusion of narrative reality. If one approaches the fiction sufficiently informed, then nothing of matter will matter, least of all personal being. The highest achievement of such art, which is the essence of modernism, is to make life irrelevant: syntactical realism refines both the real world and the reader right out of existence.

FICTION IN THE MODERNIST mode is the ultimate solipsism. There is no life beyond art. Therefore to be is to be fiction, a figure in the narrative ground, a word. As George Bowering's ironic conception of his namesake, George Vancouver, is described in *Burning Water:* "He wanted to be a famous story very much (62)," and so "he wrote all over the globe (63)." His cartographical expedition was "a fact factory (186)," writing the world down on maps to make it real. To make nowhere into something, a text, and to place himself within it, Vancouver is obliged to name the world, and then become "the name they thought of first (100)," to become, in short, a word. Bowering's

Vancouver is simultaneously an example and a parody of the ironic questing hero, in search of himself. Dawe in Robert Kroetsch's *Badlands* likewise yearns to be a word, to have his name pinned to an assemblage of bones, the Daweosaurus. Not the man but his desire is what Kroetsch burlesques. William Dawe struggles towards immortality and when he discovers that it is not conditional on his personal presence, he lets himself die.

Both Kroetsch and Bowering confound the heirs to New Criticism who take the illusions of realism for reality itself. The existential quest of the protagonist in these two fictions is conveyed in language and a context that insists such a venture is arbitrary and of dubious significance, either inside the narrative or without. The conventions of realism prove to be its undoing. The more we doubt the verity of Bowering's ridiculous Vancouver, the more engaging he becomes. And Kroetsch's Dawe, his story told, is ultimately declared, like the view of life his life embodies, radically incomplete.

It seems more inevitable than peculiar that characters in modern fiction should quest for meaning to their lives through language, meaning which experience of the world has increasingly denied. Even Sartre, ever suspicious of the word, called his autobiography *Words*; and Barthes wrote *Barthes par Barthes*. Both of them tried to make the phenomenon of personal being comprehensible; not to liberate or re-create it, but literally to make it real, the subject as object. But perhaps language all along has only been a metaphor. Perhaps it offers nothing more than illusory compensation for our bereaved condition; or only distraction from it.

In this sudden age of ours, which we sometimes call postmodern, it is equally as inevitable, perhaps, that the desire to be, through language, should be contained in a narrative design that not so much refutes or ridicules the existential quest as incorporates it into a more elastic and exacting vision. Kroetsch and Bowering often in quite different ways demand their readers *be*, but don't make *being* easy. Kroetsch reconstructs the deconstructed universe, with us inside. In Bowering, time and again, the word-world wobbles on its written axis, gravity for an instant dissipates, and we are flung back into 'reality' for brief and disconcerting encounters with ourselves, reading.

Badlands insists there is reality beyond the text, only by implication; Bowering's world, however, sometimes quite aggressively interpenetrates with our own. The differences between the closed re-conceived world of Kroetsch and the defiantly open are evident in the different uses of language to expose the arbitrary and limiting nature of conventional narrative. Bowering delights in using proper syntax to convey the sheerest nonsense, in forcing the reader to accept as narrative reality what is patently absurd. He is adroit at deflating or violating expectations with a turn of phrase that makes the solemn suddenly obscene, or the bizarre tenderly affecting, or the outrageously fake for an instant authentic. One whole chapter, devoted in lurid detail to a sexual encounter, careens away from us when in the last line we discover the intimacies were experienced not by whom we had assumed but by another couple entirely, the incorporeal word-name Banks and his incorporeal wife. It is a jarring moment for the reader, who is stuck with trying to assimilate a retroactively extraneous response.

Kroetsch in a more subtle violation of expectations, consistent with the narrative illusion that must be sustained if he is in the end to declare it null, if not void, uses words to play response against meaning. The following allusion to a murder is effectively contrary:

> And Web's innocence would light the room. As it lit the dark that night, years before, when he burned his own father's shack to the ground. And used the light of that burning to make his way. (163)

Web's father was inside the shack at the time! One is exhilarated by the image, however, as much as horrified by the action. The word "innocence" is turned inside out and brilliantly illuminated. Kroetsch's language not only distracts from a conventional response to the event but evokes its nearly lyrical opposite.

Not that Kroetsch is always subtle in matters of language,

especially where Web is concerned. Web probably swears better, with more verve and obscene affection, than most readers are likely to have encountered before, in print or on the street. But such innovative use of words, as with the shack fire and elsewhere, draws attention to elements within the narrative and not away from it. Essential to Kroetsch's novel, the illusion of narrative reality must remain intact. Where the quirks of language in *Burning Water* reach with frequency beyond the text, intentionally violating narrative perimeters, Kroetsch's shore them up.

In the structure of *Badlands*, wherein Dawe makes field notes which through his daughter blossom into narrative, while Anna tells a story of herself, with another Anna, in which her father's notes are something of a talisman and ultimately as ephemeral, two distinctly separate versions of reality are held simultaneously present. They must be equally convincing if each is to prove the undoing of the other. As the novel draws towards completion, the women's transformational vision which contains the male linear quest proves as incomplete as the contrived experience of the man. But the closed system that contains and nurtures both, which is the novel itself, insists they are complementary and, together, form a whole. The two Annas at the end, resolutely free of time, walk off arm in arm singing a lusty song which commits them to its flow, in spite of themselves. We the readers walk between them.

The tremendous vitality Kroetsch gives to Dawe's story and to his daughter Anna's, and the intriguing tension he sustains between them, comes, ironically, in good part from the extent to which he taunts the reader's credulity. Just as the misdirections and excesses of language lead not away from the fiction but deeper into it, so too with the plethora of ironies, conceits, motifs and thematic contrivances. The reader is repeatedly confronted in Dawe's narrative with such improbabilities as Grimlich's perpetual toiling beneath Drumheller, with such incongruities as Sinnott's car parked in the middle of the river, with such absurdities as Web's mid-air encounter with Anna Yellowbird and their subsequent discovery of the Daweosaurus. What is amazing is that the narrative sustains it all: it is all part of the story, episodes and adventures in the meaningful quest.

Anna's world, although different, is no less a strain on the reader's imaginative benevolence. There are two Annas, many Billys, a lot of gin, a reversal of the river quest ending at the source, and a defecating bear suspended from the air, its genitals exposed. Yet the reader accedes without even realizing it. The patterns and transitions seem appropriate, even inevitable, in context.

Each version of reality works, yet they would seem to cancel each other out. If the male quest for meaning has narrative legitimacy, then the female remains Penelope on the sidelines. If the female transformation is convincing, then the male has properly been discarded. The reader, who has conspired to make both versions work, is caught in the middle, caught reading. The novel, of course, subsumes both into a single version, one reality. The reader then is inside, looking out.

Bowering's *Burning Water* more directly involves the reader in the procedures of its unfolding narrative. In a brilliant series of deflations, Bowering uses the reader's vulnerability to the realist mode to highlight its fallacies. Many of his premises and postulations are more outlandish than anything Len Deighton could muster, but whereas Deighton's creation is deadly earnest, as modernist realism essentially must be, even the gothic, romantic and comic varieties, Bowering demands that his readers have fun—extratextually as well as within the narrative. He insists there is a world beyond the text at every turn, and adroitly makes it, too, a part of the fiction, as fiction is part of it. And each time we, or one, or you and I, catch a glimpse of ourselves in the shards of interpenetrating realities that are strewn along the way, the possibility of the objective reader, the reliability of the dispassionate critic, both dissipate. There is no place for the bloodless, except in the boneyard of yesterday's prose.

Bowering is as determined to expose the illusory nature of narrative reality as Kroetsch in *Badlands* is to maintain it—both for much the same ends, to break down the artificial and the arbitrary barriers between life and printed word, to break through the walls of the labyrinth which language has built around us and in which we too readily find ourselves lost. Not surprisingly, Bowering's principal tool in the constructive demolition he undertakes is language itself. This he mercilessly deploys to flaunt our apparently obsessive will to accept the unacceptable. Words, phrases, clauses, sentences, paragraphs, in *Burning Water*, all fall into place according to grammatical convention. And if they baffle, mislead, or confuse, if they amuse, infuriate, or impress, so much the better.

Instead of rejecting narrative reality when forced to confront ourselves responding to it, we make allowances for its idiosyncrasies. If a passage with Vancouver vomiting, after trying to quell his desire for a taste of the remnants of Captain Cook's flesh that have been retrieved from the cannibals, concludes on the entirely irrelevant note by Mr. Menzies that the sea is also a garden (126), well why not? That is what happens to be on his mind. The breach of linearity makes him absurdly more real, not less. And if Vancouver occasionally contemplates the "reassembled body of his old teacher" (189), that too is possible. Vancouver and Menzies are real inventions, after all, and if their behaviour is anachronistic or bizarre, or the focus on them is somewhat oblique, that in no way discredits their narrative validity. It only means that we must work at a more frenzied pace to suppress our disbelief, drawn to do so by the irresistible pull of imagination at the mercy of syntactical coherence.

On one occasion, with dazzling silly irony, syntax itself becomes the joke. Captain Vancouver interrogates some Indians:

> "You have been a great distance inland?" asked the stout sailor of all the world's seas.
>
> "It is a relative question," said the first Indian. . . .
>
> Vancouver couldn't wait for the interpreter now. He leaned forward, his short wig slipping a little on his head. He addressed the young barbarian directly, in a rough estimation of the Nootka tongue.
>
> "How through forest it days with canoes many is?"
>
> Years later Benjamin Wharf would be built where this aching query was put. (143)

Even here, Bowering cannot resist the historical follow-through which, in context, is a jarring *non-sequitor*. To continue for a moment in Latin, however, *post hoc ergo propter hoc*. Everything connects; perhaps not always because print is a linear medium.

Grammatical convention in *Burning Water* sustains the illusions of narrative logic and progress, even when the language itself, what it says, denies both. Consider the following, in which the language struts and sprawls like a lexical Mick Jagger—patently fake, ingenuous, aggressively trite. As narrative it works—while simultaneously declaring itself absurd. The passage has to do with missing knives, table knives:

> . . . one evening, just when the orange and red sun was falling into the edge of the ocean like a polychrome postcard, an alarm went up from the gallery, and a dark-visaged man raced by the guard and dived with less grace than dispatch into the darkening brine. He just missed two canoes on entry, and was halfway to shore on egress from the water.
>
> "That thief has five of our best *coltelli*," hollered Mr. Gransell, who was under the impression that he had uttered a French plural, and thought that the occasional such borrowing gave class to his gallery.
>
> "Hang it, the Old Man will be hotter than last night's fireworks," said the watchman.
>
> "I am already heated fair to well," said Captain Vancouver, who had hied himself to the position upon first hearing the cook's shouts. He had been a bundle of nerves all day, and now he was glad that some action seemed called for.
>
> "You'll be wanting the cutter, sir?" suggested the sailor, anxious to deflect attention from his inevitable failure.
>
> "Of course, we shall employ our one cutter to retrieve our other five," said Vancouver, flushing with excitement and anger in the red light.
>
> "Droll," said Menzies. (68)

Droll, and much else besides.

IT IS EXCITING to speculate on the relationship between print and time. To what extent does the predilection of our culture with linear time and with causality derive from the sequential nature of phonetic construction? One of a finite number of letters must follow another, and they must be followed by another, in what may be infinite progression, as letters become words and the words, sentences, and the pattern of sentences, a text. Could there be a determining relationship between the linearity of phonetic print and our various mythologies of origin and ultimate ends? Or between the reduction of world to a sequence of letters and the abiding cult of progress in Western civilization which presently goes by the name of Science but has been in the past called Reason, Faith, Destiny? Could the structure of the printed word itself bear responsibility for our obsessive conception of history as a forward flow or as the lengthening shadow at our feet? What is not recorded as history, we call pre-history; that which happened before the text. Perhaps time begins with the printed word; and all else that we conceive as cultural absolutes are the consequence of phonetic design.

WHILE PRINT WAS STILL the medium of an elite, perhaps myth, history, and religion were shaped by alphabetical construction. But human consciousness must have remained essentially what it had been when language first invaded it and took dominion. From Gutenberg to McLuhan, however, print might be seen to have increasingly determined not only what was thought but how we thought about it. The very nature of consciousness we have willingly, even willfully, submitted to the tyranny of syntax and the printed word. Now, Bowering and Kroetsch demand we wrestle free of print, the false and narrow dictates of narrative reality. Their fiction means to jar us out of the modernist fallacy (the fallacy of existential realism) wherein we have come to accept words as facts and syntax as sense; where we have come to think of reality as a text. Both Kroetsch and Bowering are determined, it would seem, to break us free of linear time and our obsession with the present moment as the culmination of an historical sequence, as if, again, reality were a text.

Bowering's ambition in *Burning Water* obviously extends beyond a revisionist history of Captain George Vancouver—although it may well include a revision of what history is. To force the collapse of time as an ordered sequence in the reader's mind, Bowering does nothing so crude as to violate chronology—that would merely replace one questionable structure with another.

Rather, through word games of occasionally outrageous proportion but sometimes with the subtlety of needles, he makes the very notion of historical time both arbitrary and irrelevant. By fusing variants of a present-day idiom with blatant fakery of an idiom of the past, his prose insists that time has no dimension at all, that everything is *now*. So wary does his reader become of language that even hints at historicity that excerpts from the real Vancouver's journals seem a sham, a narrative trick (if the note of acknowledgement can be trusted and they are, indeed, Vancouver's words). It is as likely that Vancouver and Captain Quadra have interludes in one another's arms as that Vancouver is shot by his Scots botanist, the one with the "glittering eye" who also bags an albatross which in this version skids into the deck on its chin, virtually at the same moment that Coleridge, halfway around the globe, is envisioning his poem "The Ancient Mariner" on a like motif, and that Blake is being put upon by philistines for confounding the linearity of print and carving picture poems, but of course is bound thereby even more to linearity as each line is painstakingly etched upon a copper plate, or that coastal Indians of the late eighteenth century debate middle-class values in the talk-show idiom of the educated modern masses ("There you go, speaking out of some habitual framework of guilt" [92], says one to another), or that Vancouver's men survive on sauerkraut (and perhaps they do: it is impossible to know exactly where imagination has given way to fancy—but it is a curious culinary oddity that Bowering has them cook the sauerkraut and soak it down with vinegar rather than ferment it), or that Vancouver shares with Quadra, as well as tender moments, the occasional cup of Blue Mountain–brand coffee. All this is as likely as not.

Historical linearity is an illusion which Bowering's zany sense of the absurd finds most accommodating. To be violated, conventions must be effectively present. The conventions of historical time, of sequence, coherence, and causality, are so thoroughly ingrained in the reader's consciousness that nothing is too bizarre, if placed in the proper context; nothing is too silly, if surrounded by the pomp and circumstance of history. Language used against sense, words that violate authenticity, these do not impede the narrative flow. Events are related in the past tense, after they have happened, so no quirk of language, farce of words, will alter them—they exist prior to the immediacy of text, which is present experience in the reader's mind. History is what we make of it; whatever we will.

Kroetsch's demolition of historical time in *Badlands* is not so much through ridicule as it is in *Burning Water*. Kroetsch does not play grammatical inevitability against absurd language and incidents. Consistent with the closed form of *Badlands*, time is not collapsed through reader response, but rather its nature is reinvented as an integral part of the narrative and the novel's structural form.

Kroetsch attacks conceptions of time in the Western world with a superabundance of irony. The form of his novel is ironic. The journey in search of immortality, the quest to defeat time, to become a word, is linear, a river journey. But the story comes to us through Anna—she does not so much tell it as mediate between it and our world outside the text. The words are not hers, they are a separate domain, narrative reality. Anna's own story, which is not linear but transformational as she moves through phases of drunken illumination towards an independent and separate self, contains her father's. The ironic tension between the two is sustained throughout the novel: historical time is the expression of one man's fear and desire; it is related through a woman's loneliness, which is its legacy, and finally dismissed as irrelevant. But in letting her father's story snap like an elastic into another perspective, Anna implicitly acknowledges it as a source. It ends but it does not end. With Tune's death Dawe's chance for surrogate immortality expires (ironically, beneath the very clay that contains the bones on which Dawe rests his bid for the immortality of fame). And Anna is not his son. But he is her father (she being the result of one of his forays east); and she subsumes him, his story, into her own.

Irony runs deep, through Dawe's narrative especially. The ironies of Anna's world are primarily in relation to what we know of her father's. But everything about Dawe is couched in irony. He is the questing hunchbacked shaman on a journey into deadland, in pursuit of forever. While a World War rages in the distant background, he searches among bones for lasting life for himself. He digs among pre-historic remnants, the detritus of an era discarded by time, for a place in history. His search to defeat the linear flow of his life is sequential, an episodic narrative. Dawe is the ironic embodiment of Western man; he searches in death for meaning. He mounts history as if it were an aging whore, and rides it into oblivion. He dies of his own success.

IN HIS IMPORTANT ESSAY on Noam Chomsky's theories of generative and transformational grammar, originally published in *The New Yorker* and reprinted in *Extraterritoriality* in 1971 with footnote responses by Chomsky, George Steiner argues that a universal grammar and innate deep structures as determinants of language acquisition and usage would lead to only one or a few languages whereas, he declares, there are over four thousand in current use and these are likely the remnants of an even larger number. Chomsky argues that multiplicity of language is the result of specific adjustments necessary for cooperative survival among separable groups. Steiner insists that such diversity is contrary to the Darwinian principles of competitive progress.

They are, of course, speaking of the spoken word—language as an oral medium. They are speaking of an epoch preceding rapid travel of the masses, when language was a garrison to protect the interests of a participating segment of the species. Steiner is rhetorical and Chomsky didactic; but both argue that language is the expression of a people, defines them, provides the limits of their consciousness, and is the repository of their collective experience with the world. Whatever the implications as to origin and evolution, the relationship between syntactical arrangements of the spoken word and humankind's enduring presence on the planet has undeniably been intimate. And the relationship between separate languages and subsections of the species seems in terms of anthropology an absolute, a magical or religious bond.

Perhaps print changed everything, but so subtly we hardly realized. The garrison became a weapon, the weapon a vehicle, the vehicle a prison; and the prison has become the labyrinth of our present lives.

IN THE BEGINNING, before the word was written, reality could be conceived, perhaps, as female. Language and the consciousness it sustained occurred in the perpetual present, each word a timeless moment, each sentence an expression of the speaker's presence in the world. Continuity was through repetition, through rebirth, and language was magic. But after print, when the word became substance, language came to be the mediator between consciousness and the world, and reality became male. Magic gave way to reason; circles to lines; rebirth to renewal; timelessness to chronology; patterns to fact. History began.

Now we live among atomic particles and microchips, on the edge of an absolute night; and time means nothing again.

Perhaps language is only a metaphor. Perhaps another reality, integrated or even androgynous, is in the offing and history, finally and mercifully, has come to an end.

KROETSCH AND BOWERING both use language and the narrative text in efforts to effect a change between consciousness and the nature of reality. In their small immodest ways they aspire to alter not only how we perceive reality through print, but our conception of what it is. These are not mean ambitions, and if only partially realized it is perhaps because their objective is inseparable from the medium they are bound to use to achieve it.

Bowering's concern in *Burning Water* is primarily with perception; with how we read the world to be. With a lovely sense of paradox, the collapse of historical time is related through incidents that affirm the primacy of language over historical process. Languages that once held diverse peoples separate, at some point turned into the implement of collective aggrandizement. Captain George Vancouver sails "sixty-five thousand English miles" across the surface of the earth on behalf of the British Crown (240). He uses language to turn the unknown world, from a British perspective, into historical and geographical facts, in the service of national interest. Blood dropping from an English tongue spreads over half the globe: Empire is founded and sustained on the written word.

But with even greater irony, George Vancouver inhabits a world written for him by a fictional George Bowering. The world he claims for England and for the sake of his immortal name is just a fiction within another fiction. His story and all the facts that it contains are only the made-up project of a writer in search of himself in a story. Poor George. The poor Georges. One is merely an historical remnant, a word reinvented, and the other is an author who travels the globe in pursuit of the words that are already inside him. It is essential to note that the Vancouver who is written by the *fictional* George Bowering is intended as an authentic historical reconstruction. The benighted author of the dust-jacket copy apparently mistook this for the novel's intent. But the George outside the text, in control of the Georges within, of course insists that the quest of the textual Bowering for meaning and completion through narrative patterns is equally as absurd.

The two Georges are locked to a common destiny by patterns and affinities that derive in fact from accidents of language —Vancouver, a place and person; George, a word they both inhabit. The connections are not spacial (the fictional author flits about the globe with little reference to the subject at hand); and not temporal (the fictional author is convinced of the time that stands between them); and certainly not in deference to logic. Yet their lives eventually merge. When Vancouver at last weeps for himself "utterly and perfectly . . . alone" (249), he transcends words to become a fiction inseparable from his fictional author. He dies, and that version of Bowering disappears into the words of his death.

The character, Bowering, has been the reader's persona as well, the reader inside the text, for whom the narrative worked, likewise, as a real created world. But for the writer writing and the reader reading outside the text, that same reality is impossible, an illusion of words sustained by the most arbitrary of patterns, derived solely from language itself. *Burning Water* reduces the word-world to words and restores to the reader a sense of the real beyond text, of reality as a context in which all time may be present, all places here, a context in which even books may be real.

In *Badlands* the conception of reality rather than its perception is the object of the narrative's implicit discourse. Kroetsch establishes within the text two distinct versions of reality: one is linear, an existential adventure, which Kroetsch associates with the male quest for continuity and significance, a quest for renewal that is ultimately bound to failure; the other is transformational, a structuralist reality of patterned repetition, associated with the female, with rebirth. Dawe's whole existence is contained within the story nurtured by his daughter into being, transliterated from his field notes into narrative simply by virtue of her being aware of them. But the female yearning for completion is no less illusory than the male's for continuity. Had there been no Dawe, there would be no one to tell his story.

The triumph that Kroetsch allows the two Annas at the end is not the destruction of linearity and the existential conception of reality—merely its deflation. Authentic reality, the text insists, is a story told in two ways, each of which may deny the other but which are mutually dependent on the other's presence. The concept of reality as a text has been reduced to metaphor.

IN HER NOVEL *Surfacing*, Margaret Atwood displaces the existential quest of the female narrator with transformational descent into the primal source of human being. The image of her mother guides the narrator back through all the selves that have preceded her; but the image of her father snaps her into time again, and leaves her there.

In *Green Water, Green Sky*, Mavis Gallant breaks narrative linearity by boxing a vapid central character within four largely discontinuous accounts, and draws a sad and squandered soul into substantial presence as the heir to familial patterns that make her ultimate demise inevitable. This is a narrative world informed not by Heidegger and Sartre but Lévi-Strauss.

In *Badlands*, Kroetsch insists: reality, despite the narrative flow, is not an existential treatise; nor, despite narrative displacement, is it a structuralist design. It simply is; and therefore so are we.

FOR CONSCIOUSNESS GOVERNED by the printed word, the world of experience is derivative and ephemeral. Criticism has long been the diversion of a colonized mind. But the conception of reality as a text, and the conviction that text is reality, no longer hold. Novels like *Badlands* and *Burning Water* challenge the logical structures of conventional modernist inquiry, which deny uncertainties born of the text or from prior knowledge. For myself, I would choose at this point to be guided by Wittgenstein's fragmentary and cumulative model or McLuhan's field approach, in which the tension between antinomies might well convey more than their resolution. How much that we mean, I wonder, has been lost in trying to be understood?

WORKS CITED

Bowering, George. *Burning Water.* Don Mills: Musson, 1980.
Kroetsch, Robert. *Badlands.* Toronto: New Press, 1975.

RESPONSIBILITIES OF THE POSTMODERN MIND: THE FICTIONS OF GEORGE BOWERING

(The first time I read George Bowering's Burning Water, *I didn't like it very much. I wrote a brief descriptive analysis about the discrete fictional reality of the text, despite Bowering's insistence within the novel that the edges of a text are arbitrary and the notion of separate realities a dangerous illusion. At a conference in Thunder Bay, with comic immodesty the non-textual George took me to task for letting him down. I reread the novel, reread the rest of his fiction, and tumbled, like Alice, into a hole of wondrous absurdity, stepped, like Alice, into a world of delightfully logical implausibilities. This essay began as a sort of penance, but as I contemplated the very serious subtext of Bowering's exhilarating and exhausting experimentations, it came to seem a moral responsibility. The postmodern text is in many ways affirmation in defiance of existential despair. I wanted to capture something of that. This essay was first published as "Life/Story" in a special issue of* Essays on Canadian Writing *devoted to Bowering, edited by Ken Norris, Summer 1989.)*

TALKING ABOUT GEORGE BOWERING'S postmodern fiction is a tall order, if the intent is to make sense of your own responses or to resolve the anomalies, the contrarieties, the improprieties in regard to tradition, convention, or narrative coherence. You could get lost in a single story and never get out again. That's the beauty of it. Once into a Bowering fiction, one of the really good ones, you never do get out. When you read Bowering, you and the text exist by mutual consent. But in the refusal of text to submit to the criteria of logical causality or narrative order, your place in the rational world is subverted. You as reader are brought quite literally to consciousness of yourself in the fiction, even, paradoxically, while your presence outside the text is being affirmed. You are haunted in a Bowering fiction by image fragments of yourself at play in the mirrored walls surrounding you. And yet the pleasures of your confusion are poignant reminders of your being in the world, in time.

Such play as Bowering offers can be a serious affair. What his fiction does is to counter the argument of George Steiner that art bears no responsibility for being. The symphony at Auschwitz resounds no less than in a concert hall. Suffering and moral outrage might render listeners deaf, but not the music mute. To endorse the proscription that there can be no poetry after Auschwitz is to miss the point. Words and language are still there, so long as consciousness survives. The moral question is, can they be redeemed from servitude, can they again be used or heard to aesthetic effect when their most splendid sound has risen unperturbed through human smoke? The answer must be yes, but only through a profound change in the relationship between art and life, through the demolition of barriers between the two—so that the experience of art and the experience of life are not somehow discrete and different, but interpenetrating aspects of individual consciousness. It is necessary now, Bowering's fiction would argue, or I would argue on behalf of his and other fiction in the postmodern affirmative, that art acknowledge our presence in the world as individuals, separable from the collective. As individuals we survive and perish. It is when art and language gather us in groups, deny our individual presence, that we make concentration camps and die in them.

To bring art and life together, that is the not inconsiderable postmodernist task undertaken by Bowering's fictions. Here we move a long way from the ideological representations of Northrop Frye or of T.S. Eliot—to bring art and life together involves a radical change in the nature of art itself. Art must be different in kind from what it has been. This is not merely a matter of altering our perceptions, overriding our acquiescence to the notion of art as art and not another thing. Art as a cultural and aesthetic artifact is irrelevant, can even be dangerous. Art must command presence, and not only in terms of apprehension. Forget about art as object or objective correlative, the reader, receiver, as receptacle, the critic as catalyst. Knowledge and appreciation are no longer enough. Art can never be complete; closure is impossible so long as we are alive in the text. Participation is the only way out of the moral silence that threatens to close around us. Art for our time must affirm being over meaning, and that is a clamorous affair. It must insist on the receiver as subject, assert the vitality of presence over the moral exhaustion of transcendence. Meaning in itself is meaningless.

Two things come immediately to mind from this manifesto: first, most contemporary writers of fiction, especially in Canada, seem unaware of this change in necessity, perhaps because Canada is such a safe place in the world that we can afford to be righteous; and second, the moral intention of art has little to do with morality itself. A considerable body of Canadian fiction sustains moral awareness of one sort or another, offering a particular moral vision as a kind of subtext throughout or culminating in a specific moral conclusion which can be extrapolated for critical analysis, or ignored. But there is little that involves the reader directly in moral experience—not moral experience as a complement to aesthetic effect, but, rather, moral experience inseparable from aesthetic effect, from the experience of the work itself. There is precious little writing in Canada that argues for art, itself, as a moral activity.

A notable exception is Margaret Atwood's *The Handmaid's Tale*. Morality is an inevitable element in dystopian fiction, and this novel involves the reader with explosive force in the moral complexity of its world. But reading *The Handmaid's Tale* is in itself a moral experience. We not only learn through the novel that morality can be confusing; we are genuinely confused. What Atwood gives the reader to think about is often at odds with what the narrative demands we feel. We find ourselves within the text, unable to sort out the contraries. And outside the text we find ourselves reading. The relationship between reading, the novel, and the author whose personality informs the work, inhabits the text, and shares with us her deepest and most whimsical fears, refuses closure. Atwood's postscripted academic retrospective at the novel's end, while ironically appropriate as a soulless deconstruction of the primary text, is unnecessary. We have already found ourselves horrifically enthralled with the absence of moral coherence by the time we get that far.

Bowering is more subtle and more obvious. He assumes postmodern responsibilities of the text with manic intensity, Miltonic immodesty. He wants nothing less than to give his reader life; and to give himself in the process—to give himself life, give himself to the text, give himself as a gift to the reader. This is what his fiction says: let's meet in the text for a while, free among words to be ourselves. It was inevitable, perhaps, following Husserl, following Saussure, Heidegger, Hitler, Goebbels, following Barthes, following Derrida, inevitable that realities beyond the text and within would eventually merge, that writers like Bowering would conceive fiction as the interpenetration of personalities, art as a context for being, and being, the context of art.

IN "FOUR CALIFORNIA DEATHS" Bowering turns a narrative labyrinth inside out. We cannot find our way in, yet we cannot escape. A seemly paradox in the contemporary world. "Four California Deaths" is a wonderful story. The narrator in the frame story is right, though. The story he tells is not properly a story at all. Nor is the story he occupies. Nor are the two of them together, the frame and the narrative quartet it contains. Not stories, not properly. And yet, "Four California Deaths" is quite wonderful.

The story, properly, occurs inside the reader's head. In the act of reading, we give Bowering room to play. It must be understood this is not a quaint description of imaginative response to aesthetic stimuli, not description by analogy of what happens when we read conventional narratives of writers from Renaissance to Holocaust who dream-create alternative realities in which to become lost. It is a literal account. The text is only the beginning. The story, properly, is what occurs to us within the text, while we are there. In mind, we complete the narrative. With personality, our own personalities, we participate to make it whole.

Recreation becomes re-creation. Reading "Four California Deaths," I make the story happen by actively participating as an individual human being holding all its disparate parts in mind and building from them a coherent experience of my own which may or may not have anything to do with someone else's story.

Consider what Bowering gives us: a frame story related by a Bowering persona, and four brief accounts of death by misadventure. The reason I describe the narrating persona as Bowering is that a whole network of connections is established between the person speaking in the text and a person, more complex and enigmatic, outside the text. Whether or not the prior or originating personality is truly Bowering is, of course, relevant only to Bowering. What is important is the extent to which the frame is an expression of consciousness. The narrator is there as he tells it, and what he tells is this: he has made love with the woman who will be and, as the frame closes, has been his reader. His own behaviour he finds mildly ridiculous—as lover, as writer asking to be read, as writer being read. He banters with her about themes and purpose, about sex and death, mystery and puzzle. He thinks, while with her, about writing and nakedness and the time it will take her and does take her to read what he has written. She, his reader-lover, whom he has promised a salad afterwards, has "gorgeous long legs," he says, "as important to me as the air now filling my lungs." Now: as he is writing; now, as you read.

But leave the frame, with its whimsicality and high seriousness, its inconclusive affirmation of life, art, sex, and salads, its canny celebration of the writer's relations with the reader, this writer who won't just leave off, "turn over and go to sleep, like a normal man," and refine himself out of existence, but insists in the end on asking if the reader-lover "got it"—and although *we* did not, cannot, *she*, our representative, says she did. Look instead to his four brief narratives linked by an absurd web of incidentals and a network of common themes. Each tells of the death of a celebrated personage: Jean Harlow, Babe Ruth, Albert Einstein, and Tom Mix. Each celebrity is a fixture in the popular imagination, each has become an archetype. Their deaths here are absurd—there is no connection with the actual demise of the person behind the personage. Yet the accounts are presented in clinical detail—or, perhaps, "with reportorial dispatch" would be a more appropriate turn of phrase. And each death is a joke, relative to the world outside the text.

Harlow dies naked in a tattoo parlour; the Sultan of Swat dies in the minor leagues; Einstein suffocates in a high-school chemistry lab; and Tom Mix is squashed to death by Tony, the Wonder Horse, who has been bowled over by a 1937 DeSoto. All die within the jurisdiction of the San Diego Police Department. A quotation from Joseph Conrad looms over each death scene; ambiguous evidence, suggesting foul play of more than somewhat elusive significance. A character in one account becomes a street name in another. Details from one account recur in others. Names connect; facts connect. Conspiracy is confounded, however, as the solid facts of one account become evanescent or peripheral in another, absent from a third, transformed entirely in the fourth.

The importance given to facts within each segment seems paramount, and yet the narrator's presence is unavoidable—in every smart-ass turn of phrase, in each manipulative revelation of detail to suggest mystery and significance, in the insistent disinterestedness, the aggressive objectivity. Each corpse ensconced in a bed of quasi-facts, conveyed to us with an air of urgent realism, these for us are the 'real' Harlow, Ruth, Einstein, and Mix. Bowering brilliantly exploits the fallacy of realistic fiction: words displace sense, syntax is the only logic essential to narrative conviction. Even knowing the absurdity of these accounts, we struggle towards conspiracy, towards a conclusion that will resolve the contradictions on some coherent plane or another. The quartet is a puzzle—it must be. Therefore it can be unlocked, if only we find the key; solved, if we can discover the proper equation. That's what narrative is all about. Why tell a story otherwise? On some level, the metaphysical, the psychological, the ontological, the facts, the design, the voice will cohere. We expect that of fiction, of narrative art (though, interestingly, not of visual art, not anymore). Why read a story otherwise?

Then, in the closing frame, the reader says yes, she got it. That's what makes her his reader; not reading, but getting it. But what does she get? We don't know. Despite our best efforts to retrieve the story from absurdity, to make it cohere on a rational plane, it refuses. And yet, when she gets it, we get it too. She says: "the only thing that puzzled me was why you decided to use my initials." Since there is no possible answer to this, either within the text or outside it, puzzle, for us, gives way to mystery. Puzzles can be resolved. Mysteries cannot. Puzzles, in the story, have been associated with death, mysteries with life. This is a mystery, this story. It amuses, it entertains, it arouses, disturbs, stimulates, intrigues, but it does not answer. It is. Reading, we get it! Not what it is about, but the story itself. Our experience is the story. We enter the text and are contained by it, we enter the fiction and contain it. Our presence completes it, yet it remains incomplete. This is a wonderful story about us the readers, wrapped in mystery, containing the puzzle, becoming ourselves.

"Four California Deaths" is a mystery story in the true sense. It cannot be resolved; it remains a mystery. And it is not an upbeat version of interactive fiction, like those whodunits of the 1930s that involved the reader in choosing among a cluster of options in order to shape the final story (the precursor to the game of Clue, or the controlled-option story making a comeback on home video, or the options for closure in *The French Lieutenant's Woman*). Like a Borgesian garden of forking paths, such stories will ultimately coalesce on a rational plane. But in this story Bowering deploys conventional devices of realism to create a dynamic narrative that goes nowhere, to involve us in a puzzle that cannot be resolved. In the end, the mystery remains, surrounding us from within.

Bowering displays a tremendous sense of fun in demolishing the barriers between his own life and the art he makes out of it. By being there among words in his text he opens up the narrative for us to be there too. In *A Short Sad Book*, he writes of writing, of the novel being written, of himself being written as he writes. At the narrative centre is the revelation of process, whereby the reader is inveigled into sharing in the novel's creation, to see it through or see it falter. The latter is unlikely. We are conditioned, perhaps only by the force of syntax on procedures of thought, to perceive meaningful order even where there is none. We make narrative, as we read, out of grammatical construction. If a text audaciously defies expectations of coherence, we impose coherence nonetheless. If Bowering says, let's see where this will go, we go with him. The narrative writes us, and him, into being within the text.

Amid quips and gibes and jokes and various asides, the textual Bowering tells the reader what this novel would be about, if it were a novel at all—which it isn't, not until we join him there and complete the narrative design. From our own experience and personalities we provide continuity, shape, and significance to the narrative his text implies. Amid a riotous display of images and allusions we make a novel together, Bowering and I. Surrounded by references to staking peonies, to pursuit of the

Pretty Good Canadian Novel, to rootless cosmopolites, baseball, the West Coast Experience, *Evangeline*, postmodernism, and the "*Tercentenary History of Canada*, Volume III, From Laurier to King," Bowering expresses himself—he squeezes, pours himself onto the page. I, as reader, we, surrounded by the same detritus of a manic mind, we, to find order, impose our separate selves upon the page. To make narrative out of this, we must see ourselves there, watch ourselves at play within the text, making sense. Even, perhaps especially, where there is none.

A Short Sad Book is the most successful anti-novel of my acquaintance. One of my favourite books. One of the few books in which I am a featured participant, while not being its author (the only one, actually). This novel/anti-novel opens to me as I read. We coexist by mutual consent. Mutual affirmation. Bowering too. He's there as well. Here and there.

When I run with Bowering, striding across the gulf between actuality and text, I also run smack into W.B. Yeats. Sailing to Byzantium will lead to a foundering in the postmodern sea. Writing such as Bowering's does not refute Yeats, for what project could be mounted against an argument that places art above life? You do not reason against fascism, even when expressed by the most beautiful of poets. You provide an alternative. Life and art, you insist, can be interpenetrating and inseparable. I have seen Ben Bulben from the churchyard near Sligo and thought poetry. But if the choice were mine I would rather have had William Yeats share the experience with me in person, than lie buried there beneath a modest stone, under a legacy of the finest of words.

The point is not to achieve immortality through self-exposure, nor to make the text a vehicle for self-expression and personal transcendence. Rather, it is a refusal to be transparent, to do a Yeats, yield being to art.

Postmodernism thrives on paradox and anomaly. When we are brought to an awareness, simultaneously, of opposing realities, when we accommodate within consciousness the contraries of a particular text, then our experience of life and of art becomes equally the experience of ourselves. Yeats left behind a marvellous legacy, but nothing of Yeats. And we marvel as we read his work that he can mean so much through us, while excluding us, in effect, from what is there.

In the novel *Burning Water*, there is a character called George Bowering. There is a character called George Vancouver. If you know enough of the world to find your way into the text, you know that both Georges are based on, or somehow related to, actual people in historical time. You also know that, at the time of writing, George Vancouver had achieved historical completion —that is, he was dead. And George Bowering was not. But the textual Vancouver is very much alive, while the Bowering persona moves through the narrative towards inevitable annihilation. The fictional Vancouver becomes inseparable from his fictional author, however, and as Vancouver dies into textual immortality, the fictional Bowering disappears into the words of his character's death. The reader is not left, though, with absence, a vacuum. Another George Bowering, the personality surviving the text who has been at play with you throughout the narrative, is still very much a presence. While the fictional Bowering has kept you at a distance from the text he claims to be his own, the fiction he says is his, the living George, at play within the fiction, has subverted the distancing effect with weird and dazzling word games, games of paradox and contrariety, that demand awareness on your part of both yourself and the author together creating a narrative of marvellous design.

Reading *Burning Waters* you repeatedly bump into yourself, reading. The narrative does not thereby collapse, the illusion somehow shattered. Rather, you exhilarate in finding yourself alive among words. How does he, the real George Bowering, do it? Primarily, I think, by playing thought and feeling off against each other, rational response against emotional. We are moved, when reason says there is nothing here to move us, only nonsense and the bizarre; we are made to think, when feelings render thought absurd. George Vancouver is a ridiculous character, utterly improbable, yet we care for him. His penchant for Blue Mountain–brand coffee, his comfort in the arms of Captain Quadra, his inept anachronistic utterances, his bombast and spleen, all make him historically unlikely, rather unlikable, yet textually real, beyond disbelief.

Between intellectual and emotional response, we find ourselves reading. Such fields the postmodern writer cultivates assiduously in pursuit of art as an act of, not work of, imagination. An avant-garde modernist such as Graeme Gibson in his rigorously experimental novel, *Five Legs*, commits to print his finished work. We, the readers, immerse ourselves amid the brilliant flashes of fractured syntax, thought shifts, voice-mood distortion, and other such devices by which Gibson attempts to transform conditions of consciousness into art. Gibson—as Faulkner does in the opening phase of *The Sound and the Fury*, where the reader is caught up in Benjy's crippled mind, or as Joyce does in the closing of *Ulysses*, where the reader is surrounded by the injured mind of Molly Bloom—deploys elements of style quite radically to fix in print the procedures of a particular imagined consciousness. These modernist models, paradigms, or artifacts do not evoke conditions of mind within the reader, but rather arouse our response to them. We are not meant to be dissociated, distracted, or mad, but rather to contemplate the replication of such conditions in print.

By comparison, a Bowering fiction is often radically incomplete. In a story like "Arbre de decision" it is only grammar that urges the reader towards the conclusion (although certainly not to either completion nor closure). Narrative design is displaced by syntactical coherence—not displaced in the sense of being pushed aside, but rather as in 'taking the place of.' Only grammar in certain Bowering fictions offers sense. The text then becomes an open field or con-text in which the dynamics of the reader's response quite literally bring the narrative into being. Sentence by sentence, scene by scene, events occur in the reader's mind. They do not logically follow one from another, and are, in the sequence offered, often contradictory, often mutually exclusive. Yet as read, they exist with equal probability. They have happened. Narrative use of the past tense is affirmation of this—although the act of reading, of entering these events into consciousness, would suffice as evidence of their having already occurred.

In the normal course of things, our minds, conditioned by several thousand years in service to the doctrine of logical causality, would sift through the conflicting possibilities in a story like "Arbre de decision" and select the most likely combination as the dominant reality. Everything else would then be accounted aberrations due to a character's imagination, altered states of consciousness, or authorial ineptitude. But what of a story that refuses coherence, that makes sense, paragraph by paragraph, but will not submit to rational inquiry; a story that proceeds with casual eloquence but yields upon analysis no structure, only pattern, no architectural form at all, but only a fine and intricate design? The convolutions of "Arbre de decision" reverberate through the apprehending mind. From the possible or possibly imagined ringing of a telephone, a number of bizarre narratives emerge. None would be especially bizarre on its own, but each precludes the possibility of the others. They are related, usually paragraphed to keep them apart, with equal verisimilitude and in much the same jaunty third-person voice. There is a certain sequential, chronological development as attention shifts from one account to another, but this is periodically violated. Arthur Cuff inhabits all of the narratives although, as I said, each precludes the others. Passages of fear, bewilderment, erotica, and pedantry follow one after, but not from, another. Darlene in bed, Judy on the phone or in the bathroom, Valerie in the office, Elena in the taxi. Or not. Oral, anal, inverted, sado-masochistic, and ordinary acts of sex. Or not. Propositions, threats, queries, conjecture, and discussion. Murder, torture, grammatical dysfunction. White slacks, blue slacks, bathrobes, towels, covering, revealing, disguising nakedness/fear/loathing/lust. There is so much to this story, and. Or not.

It is not given to us, the readers, to resolve the narrative complexity of "Arbre de decision." Bowering has not created a puzzle in which, if we are smart enough, we will perceive the narrative intent, what he was up to, what the 'real' story is. That, ultimately, is a trivial activity. We may be driven or drawn through the story by an innate desire for coherence. That's what motivates us to fill spare corners of our lives doing crosswords and playing Scrabble. In both, intersecting clusters of meaning bear no relevance to one another, yet exist at each other's pleasure. As the reader-players, our purpose is not to make connections on a rational plane, to sort out the story line. It is, rather, to discover within ourselves the knowledge and the tolerance that will lead to completion of the game.

Perhaps less tolerance is needed to accept the syntactical discontinuities of Scrabble than the narrative anarchy of "Arbre de decision," but the rewards are correspondingly less satisfying. Neither, ultimately, admits analysis. We accept all word-realities as possible. In exploiting our capacity for doing this, both text and game demand a reassuring intensity of consciousness, although perhaps we gather more of ourselves and give more when reading. We are amused and changed by Bowering, distracted by Scrabble—perhaps edified by the discovery of a word or two in Scrabble or the crossword that was previously hidden from us; but not changed. Knowledge itself does not change us.

"Arbre de decision" is puzzling, but it is not a puzzle. The various erotic, psychotic, confused, and distracting events surrounding Arthur Cuff are not offered as options from which either he, or we, must choose in order to make sense of his life/story. As readers, everything we read is equally valid. We can hold many narratives simultaneously in mind. We are used to doing so in conventional fictions, where plots and subplots are woven together in complex structural patterns. We can hold opposing responses simultaneously in mind: it is on this basis that irony has evolved as the voice of modernism. But here, Bowering confounds sense—the narrative fragments will not cohere. They are for the most part mutually exclusive, yet they are equally possible. The responses they demand are not ironically modulated but often utterly in opposition, and irreconcilable on a logical plane. It is not Arthur who conjures the diverse lives each fragment of the narrative implies. We are used to imaginary alternatives. But here, each possibility for Arthur is as real as every other, and as real or as plausible for the reader as well.

It is the author *as* text, the text as a manifestation of an authorial persona, that allows the reader to participate in the multiple realities adhering to the narrative presence of Arthur Cuff. With reason and emotional response thrown thoroughly askew, we hold all that the textual personality conveys to be possible, and we respond without reference to logic and the outside world. We are contained within the text, although not the narrative, and of necessity become a part of what happens there—for otherwise there would be only an agglomeration of contraries. Our own presence is integral to the narrative design. And in seeing ourselves caught up among the contraries, we are brought to a deeper understanding not of grammar, sex, and mayhem, or alternative realities, but of ourselves within and, as readers in the living world, outside the text.

The principal thrust of Bowering's postmodern fiction is the revelation of being. I'm not talking here about epiphany, where variations of Stephen Dedalus expose themselves in a glare of intersecting narrative beacons. Nor about propriocentrism: that's a matter of subject matter, a lyric concept, what poetry can be about. No, not revelations about, but of, being. (It is tempting to bring in a discussion of *dasein*, but Heidegger would lead away from responsibilities of the text, not deeper into them.) What I mean to say is that, in these words, this text, in Bowering's fictions, consciousness is intensified and the self revealed—the individual personalities of writer and reader both.

In "Four California Deaths" and "Arbre de decision" the impress of authorial personality is flamboyant, and yet in the lovely melancholy tale "The Clam-Digger," the Bowering presence is exquisitely subtle and the reader achieves the revelation of self only by implication. There are many ways to the same end. The purpose of all such fictions is to be life-affirming. The content of each of these stories wears the tattered shroud of death, and yet each celebrates life, proclaims the author's presence and evokes the reader's consciousness of being. I know of few new-written tales to match "The Clam-Digger" for its poignancy and beauty. It calls to mind Antoine de Saint-Exupéry, or even Hans Christian Andersen. And yet (and this is the third use of a qualifying conjunction in this short paragraph), it is West Coast contemporary; upbeat, laid-back, and lots of fun.

Woodruff, the poor and lonely clam-digger, is recognizable from the pages of fairy-tale romance, or perhaps from a passing encounter, perhaps on Wreck Beach the last time you were in Vancouver, or as someone you once saw on the streets of Winnipeg, or in a pub in Halifax. Then Woodruff rides the back of a giant turtle into the depths of the ocean where he lives in languid splendour as Prince Woodruff, marries, has children, and is adored by all in his realm. But he longs to visit one more time the world he left behind. Once back, he is suddenly aged beyond recognition; he is stranded in the world of barbershops and city streets, and another young man prepares to take his place. As you read of Woodruff, you find yourself tumbling forward through the lovely prose, wonderfully anxious to know the outcome. And even on your third or seventh reading, as with all good fairy tales, you still yearn towards the end, towards completion, so that what will happen can happen, and will happen again.

Each telling of it, each reading, plays on the delicious certainty that it will be the same. And yet, it never is. In the course of telling Woodruff's story in such a way that it seems to tell itself, Bowering occasionally and whimsically intrudes, riding a twist of phrase, an unruly word, or a lovely inappropriate image such as the one about ocean layers as the shifting colours on an old-fashioned jukebox. Look, he says, this enchanted world, it comes from somewhere, comes from me, I'm here. And for the reader, his presence adds poignancy; the enchanted world is accessible, and yet it isn't ours. As it contains the writer, but only while writing, so too does it contain us, but only as we read. There is a timeless quality about any fairy tale that with bittersweet allusiveness affirms our presence outside it, in time.

If one wanted to, one could offer up a reading of "The Clam-Digger" in which exactly what I've said above about time and timelessness, the illusions of parallel realities, the relativity of stasis and change, is shaped as fiction. But why, when, as with so much of Bowering's work, "The Clam-Digger" is an exemplar of its own inherent argument?

Nowhere is this same truth more evident than in the novel *Burning Water* . . .

or in such rough and brilliant fictions as "Looking for Ebbe," "Carter Fell," and "A Short Story."

Only by watching the birds fly do we know there is sky between the trees.

No notes.

Critical Readings: Urquhart, Butala, Gibson, Wiebe, Marlatt and Michaels

(When reviewing is done well, it is transparent and immediate; and there is a sense of loss in the doing, an awareness of ephemerality, of transience, because reviews are usually for newspapers and periodicals. When criticism is done well it is a creative work, with a life of its own. Sometimes as a critic you want to rescue reviews you have done from the oblivion of periodical indices, not for the genius of their creation but for the modest light they might reflect on the objects of their attention. Sometimes a review written not in critical contemplation but as a spontaneous record of the experience of a text, abandoned to your files, seems later, for the value of its subject, worth sharing. My reviews of Jane Urquhart's The Whirlpool *and Daphne Marlatt's* Taken *were not written with publication in mind; the review of Sharon Butala's* The Fourth Archangel *was published in the* Globe and Mail, *March 9, 1992; the review of Graeme Gibson's* Gentleman Death *was written for my own files, possibly to be included in a future* Reader's Guide; *the review of Rudy Wiebe's* A Discovery of Strangers *came out in* Canadian Forum *in October of 1994. The review of Anne Michaels'* Fugitive Pieces *was written to be included here.)*

I

Jane Urquhart's *The Whirlpool* (1986) is not a perfect novel, but it is so powerful, well crafted, and of such narrative sophistication that the reader is almost relieved to find here and there touches of writerly self-consciousness. These small scars perhaps save it from being too slick, too carefully formed; reminders that this is art, and art of the highest order.

Set in the summer of 1889 on the Canadian side of the Niagara River, *The Whirlpool* is historical fiction only in the sense that the events of the novel take place in a time other than our own. They are conveyed to us with contemporary immediacy. We are not transported back into the past, but rather the past is catapulted with astonishing force into the reader's presence. The action occurs as it is being written, and, in good postmodern fashion, it appears to be written as we are reading it into narrative reality.

Yet, ironically, history and historicity are of great concern within the novel. One of the main characters, Major David McDougal, is obsessed with the War of 1812, the Battle of Lundy's Lane, Laura Secord, and the death of General Isaac Brock, a British military leader who, in death, becomes quintessentially Canadian. For McDougal, our skirmishes with the Americans define our origins and tell us who we are, if we would only pay attention. He collects battle artifacts as souvenirs of warfare made bloodless by the passage of time. In marked contrast, Maud Grady collects corpses and the detritus gathered in their pockets as they whirl, drowned, in the Niagara River and are retrieved for burial at public expense. She runs a funeral establishment and meticulously catalogues the river's yield each season, sadly aware of the stories of the unclaimed bodies that will never be told.

The story of Urquhart's novel is that there are many stories. Each is modestly eccentric and mildly dramatic, yet the pattern into which they are woven suggests epic obsessions intersecting in a pattern of luminous, mythic intensity. The different characters, like facets of a prism, are startlingly separable yet parts of an indivisible whole. Maud's young son seems autistic, with an obsessive compulsion for verbal mimicry. Her former husband, who leaves her a widow in the opening pages, was obsessed with spiders. McDougal's wife, Fleda, whose eccentricities he strangely indulges, abjures society to live in a tent on the site of their planned house overlooking the Niagara whirlpool, reading obsessively from the pages of Robert Browning. And young Patrick, the poet, convalescing at his uncle's nearby farm from a clerical job in Ottawa and an uninspiring marriage, is obsessed with the whirlpool, the landscape surrounding it, and Fleda, whom for the longest time he cannot tell from the landscape.

Chapter by chapter, Urquhart takes us deep into her characters' secret lives, to the very edges of the unconscious mind so that we know as much as they do about what they are thinking and feeling—little about *why*, perhaps, but even more than they, themselves, about *what*, since the whole surrounding world of each is conveyed to us in imagery appropriate to their mental and emotional condition. This is one of her great achievements and what sets her writing off from most so-called historical novels of early Canada: the imagery we experience, whether streetcars running along the escarpment, American factories in the background across the river, trees in the rain, the pages of a book dappled by shadows of the wind, all comes to us through the minds of her characters. She does not create their setting in pictures; she allows us the experience of their intersecting perceptions.

The Whirlpool is splendidly chauvinistic. At a lecture given by McDougal, Patrick "did his best to appear as if he were thinking Canadian." And later, McDougal explains to Patrick that his wife, Fleda, has "never had one single authentically Canadian dream." Urquhart plays with notions of national self-consciousness, as she does with the aesthetic sensibility that seems to be an affliction for both Patrick and Fleda, in a fine balance of cynicism and sensitivity. There is no question that this novel is about collective or communal identity, yet like Robert Kroetsch, Urquhart seems to be arguing that it is our lot to draw who we are, not from heroic and inflated events but from the mythic idiosyncrasies of our myriad past. To connect us with the immediate world, not separate us from it, as Browning does in the minds of her characters here, that is the true function of art and the creative imagination.

Robert Browning is perhaps the most fully realized character in the novel. The entire narrative occurs in the season of his death as an old man in Venice. The Prologue and Epilogue describe the final December in Browning's life with exquisite pathos. The old poet dies in the shadows of Shelley, a poet who dared to seize life, to enter the whirlpool of mystery and wonder that at some time or another offers itself to us all. Browning dominates the summer in Niagara preceding his death, dominates the lives of Fleda and Patrick, each obsessed with the other, who never become lovers, nor even, quite, friends. Fleda's husband is a Browning of sorts, bloodlessly reliving battles; and Maud is Browning, in arranging artifacts of the anonymous dead to give them meaning, however arbitrary; even her child echoes Browning, as he apes the world around him in words reduced only to meaning. By the novel's close, only the Major, like Browning, seems still to be leading the lives of others. Maud discovers the power of the present, within which her son lives in a sort of inspired innocence. Both Patrick and Fleda throw off Browning's studied passion and, like Shelley, enter whirlpools of their own. Their ends are both sad and fitting.

Urquhart won a prestigious French award for *The Whirlpool*, the *prix du meilleur livre étranger*. Her prose has a sensuous, sensual quality, offering a visceral connection between the sometimes strange and distracted tenor of her characters' inner lives and our own capacity to be delighted by language used with dazzling originality. She weaves a complex web of motif and allusion that is quite astonishing to experience—this is not transparent writing but writing that brilliantly calls attention to itself being written. She is capable of relating the imperfect meeting of two obsessed minds with a palpable sense of wonder as if she, the wickedly omniscient narrator, cannot quite believe the audacity of her own imagination. She writes from inside the minds of women and men, of a damaged child, of an alcoholic derelict, of people obsessed with themselves and with death, with authority and quirky charm. She has created, in *The Whirlpool*, a novel that will change the way we write about the past in Canada and, perhaps more important, the ways in which the past writes us.

II

It would be as easy to miss this novel as a Prairie town from the highway bypass. Sharon Butala's *The Fourth Archangel* (1992) envisions at the imminent turn of the millennium, in a southwestern Saskatchewan town called Ordeal, just over from Crisis and Upwards and down from Horizon, an unpretentious Armageddon. Unless you pay close attention, or stop for directions and linger awhile over gossip at Mrs. Henwick's café, you might just not notice it happening.

This novel captures the collision of worlds in a few crumbling grains of sand. It celebrates community and the Prairie landscape, the precarious grasslands in particular. It sings the praises of place and laments the afflictions worked upon it in the service of progress. Sharon Butala does not write nostalgia, as Sinclair Ross does in *Sawbones Memorial*, a comparable novel about the life and dying of a Prairie town. Her novel is not a eulogy but a celebration, and at the same time it is an indictment. From its perspective in the year 2000, it is the calling to accounts of a beloved enemy.

Sharon Butala has written a casual narrative; the style is offhand, at times closer to spoken than written language, and the structure somehow colloquial. Occasionally, her prose takes on a lyric elegance as she, or one of her characters, describes untrammelled landscape, but for the most part the words and syntax are comfortably appropriate to a Prairie parlour. Precision is generally associated with names like Hoechst, Avadex, and New Holland found on the men's caps, or the brand names of farm machinery. Otherwise, there is an evanescence to her imagery and language that simultaneously suggests the familiar and the extraordinary.

Butala is a shy but not a modest visionary. Her future includes an extensive past; her small corner of Saskatchewan implies our entire civilization in microcosm. Around a handful of key players in the town of Ordeal, she creates a community of distressed witnesses to the town's demise, whose plight echoes the mythic dehumanization of the Western world.

All that sounds very expansive and somewhat daunting. But

The Fourth Archangel is also about Amy Sparrow, a political activist and widowed potter who makes trinkets to pay the bills, and about her lover, Neil Locke, an errant scientist in retreat from a suffocating marriage and enthralled with the grasslands or at least with reminders from books and the edges of fields of what they had been; about Val and Jessie Sheridan, the viability of their farm threatened by careless ambition, who lose their heritage but not their hope; about Alma Sheridan, a slow-aging virgin obsessed with abortion and her violent dreams; about the revolutionary *esprit* of the town's many widows; about Melody Masuria, her conversion, subsequent stigmata, and eventual apotheosis through TV evangelism; and about her mentor, Uriel Raven, the small-town prophet.

The narrative develops in fits and starts, moving among the lives of these and a scattering of their relatives, friends, and lifelong acquaintances. What seems at first sketchy slowly coalesces as small insights into private lives and public behaviour accumulate against a gradually revealed background of history, memory and dream. Nowhere has the small town in Canada been brought better into narrative focus—even, paradoxically, as it fades from existence.

The curious twist to Butala's Ordeal is that her town in its dying offers hope for the future. In part this comes from her notions of community as a reservoir of dreams; in part from its intricate design which holds even when separate threads fray or snap; and in part because she provides it a context of landscape that is at once fragile and transcendent.

It is the land that most excites Butala's sometimes haphazard prose into life. Again and again her narrative falls back on descriptions of its beauty, evocations of its geophysical, aboriginal, and historic past. It is the land that gives dimension to the lives of her characters. She writes with deep regret about the transformation through settlement of grasslands teeming with life into poisoned fields subject to machines and the bank. And she also writes with deep affection for the people who live there—and it is this splendid naïveté that separates her writing about the country and community from that of others.

Without the promises of sunshine and Empire to be found

in the Prairie towns of McCourt or McClung, the stolid virtues of farms by Stead or the silly virtues of farms by Stringer, the sullen panegyrics of Grove, or the dire constraints infecting the towns of Ross, Laurence, and Blondal, her Prairie haunts the reader with what might be called spiritual authenticity. More like Matt Cohen's Salem, in *Flowers of Darkness*, or Robert Kroetsch's Notikeewin, in *Gone Indian*, Ordeal is such a blend of the ordinary and the tolerably fantastic as to be reassuringly gothic in its Canadianness. Let us rage with decorum, perish gently, and do as little damage as possible in our passing.

The Fourth Archangel is realistic, but it is not realism. It obscures boundaries of literary convention with insouciant aplomb. If you could imagine Kroetsch's *What the Crow Said* crossed with a novel of ideas like Douglas Durkin's *The Magpie*, a novel of fractured zealotry like Bertram Brooker's *Think of the Earth*, laced with the intimacies of a Gabrielle Roy or a Patricia Blondal, the sardonic wit of Aritha van Herk, the expansive conscience of Rudy Wiebe, and the vision of St. John of the Cross on Demerol, you would have some sense of the generic indiscretions in Butala's novel. Yet so assured is her narrative, and so elusive the vision, so restrained the fantasy, that it all seems quite plausible.

In fact nothing extraordinary in the novel happens in public, apart from a political rally or two, a possible visitation of the divine, a few intrusive dreams, and the falling away of people from the land. And: a phantom herd of cattle, a dispossessed family from the thirties still on the road to Peace River country after seventy years, a pack of coyotes in search of a homeland, a coyote dreamed as trickster, then seen, stalking from the pages of *The Double Hook*, and a few other oddities. Dreams are important in this novel; some are souvenirs of the past, some prophetic; at least one is possibly demonic and another shamanistic—perhaps, in its natural innocence, even holy.

The land withholds, in retaliation for the farmers' abuse; and the banks foreclose. Businesses shut down; in a clamour of gossip, charlatans prosper; and too many leave or die. A huge cross is built on the hillside overlooking town—shades of Lily Dougall's *What Necessity Knows*, an undeservedly obscure nineteenth-century novel that echoes here with renewed vitality. The cross comes tumbling down in a storm—shades of *What the Crow Said*, *The Resurrection of Joseph Bourne*, and how many others. Part of the wonder of this book is that while its discursiveness is contained by the fiction, it leads to so many other texts and other fictions.

The rich allusiveness of *The Fourth Archangel*, its insistent validation of dreams and denigration of progress, its refusal to despair, its quiet affirmation of women's experience and assured insight into men's, its determinedly Canadian, Prairie and essentially populist narrative sensibility, its excoriating vision of the past and gentle vision of the Apocalypse and beyond, its stylishly postmodern denial of style and its bountiful explication of ideas and the Prairie landscape, make it a book worth reading and as memorable as a Prairie town, if you took the time to stop and explore.

III

Discontinuity in the hands of an accomplished postmodernist can be stunning, in the hands of a modernist sometimes merely the textual evidence of authorial ineptitude. Graeme Gibson's fourth novel, while not quite postmodern, is not modern either. The discontinuities in *Gentleman Death* (1993) convey to the reader the stunning ineptitude of an authorial character. Whether by intention or chance Gibson has devised a hodgepodge of conventions entirely appropriate to the confused consciousness of his middle-aged death-centred creatively-challenged protagonist.

Gentleman Death is concerned with what could be called the 'Solieri effect,' after Thomas Solieri, the protégé and rival of Mozart, who was doomed to relentless awareness that as an artist and therefore as a man he would never quite measure up to the achievement and standards of others. Robert Fraser is a Toronto-based writer, fifty-six years old, burdened with a distracted attitude towards himself that hovers somewhere between boredom and bemusement, indifference and fear, a benignly self-absorbed attitude that is curiously engaging. Only the prospects of death seem able to draw his life into focus. His father dies, his brother dies, an old friend dies, with whom, on her deathbed, he discusses inappropriately haunting images of death from Bergman's *The Seventh Seal.* His domestic life is unremarkable; his fantasy life mundane; his takes on the contemporary world for the most part passionately banal. Only in his writing is there the possibility of meaning and order, justification for being the man he is. Only in his confrontations with Gentleman Death is there the possibility of finding himself at home in his own life.

One of Fraser's problems is that he is not a very good writer, not nearly so good as his author. Yet his author, of course, writes the long passages for Fraser's several works in progress, allowing facts from one life to slip over into the others, from one narrative into the others. Fraser, Dunbar in Berlin, Simpson in the Shetlands, and possibly Gibson himself share indeterminately common experiences. The urgency impelling Gibson seems to be literary immortality, but Fraser creates Dunbar and Simpson more fecklessly, to sell books. Their stories are vaguely to do with spies and foreign intrigue and are not nearly so interesting as Fraser's self-absorbed ruminations in downtown Toronto or Gibson's, as author, juggling ironies to avoid bathos, fictions to position himself as a witness to truth.

Gibson can be a very good writer. There is an extended anecdote about the death of a squirrel that stands out brilliantly, as well written as anything the reader could want; and there are descriptions of Robert Fraser's relationship with his father and of his father's death that have an emotional precision that is intensely moving. But descriptions of his relationships with his movie-making wife and with his daughter and his virtually absent son are bloodless and trite. Even granting that the sub-genres into which Fraser is trying to write his own fictional characters are intentionally superficial, there seems little excuse for: "Of course there were Good Germans, he suddenly thought. But which ones?" There is no reason why fiction cannot include the ordinary and the banal, but surely the trick of good writing is to make them extraordinary or, at the least, interesting.

Robert Fraser addresses the reader in the first person, sometimes conversationally, sometimes intimately, even confessionally, and sometimes ruminating so that we seem like eavesdroppers on another's mind. Every once in a while the dominant narrative voice breaks into a diatribe on contemporary events affecting the life of a middle-class Canadian male, splenetic at Brian Mulroney for being a sleazy sellout with a branch-plant mentality, frustrated by the cultural devolution of a disintegrating nation. The effect is, curiously enough, to trivialize great events as Fraser's mind darts from Tory politics to the inconsequentiality of death among the Masai, to factoids about global population, or, out of nowhere, to quotations from Bruce Chatwin, James Reaney, or references to Graham Greene or Ingmar Bergman, et al. The effect is a very old-fashioned modernist replication of a jumbled and self-absorbed mind. Everything connects on a logical basis—only, some of the parts have been removed to create the illusion of consciousness at play.

What redeems this novel from inconsistencies in structure and style and the pedestrian ruminations of its protagonist is the voice of its author, tremulous between self-mockery and sincerity, that presides over all. It is the personality of Graeme Gibson that elevates *Gentleman Death* to the level of literature. This is a postmodern notion; the flaws in the novel, the distracted sensibility of the main character, the inconsequence of novel fragments that could never quite make it on their own, the inappropriate turns of phrase, displays of anecdote, cohere as the expression of an authorial presence behind the fiction with an urgency we can all share, an urgency against time, meaninglessness, and death. Even when the language gets patently silly, benignly sexist, Waspishly decentred, we remain always confronted with a man struggling, sometimes with wit and sometimes sadly, with consciousness of closure and his own mortality.

Gibson's first novel, *Five Legs*, stands as a very important work in experimental modernism. Along with a few others, like Dave Godfrey's *The New Ancestors* and the early novels of Audrey Thomas, it rings the changes from one era in Canadian fiction to another. While modernist novels continue to be written, writers like Margaret Atwood and Matt Cohen, Timothy Findley, Jane

Urquhart and Robert Kroetsch reach into the resources of postmodernism to create fictions that genuinely reflect the chaos of human experience. Gibson's *Communion* and, especially, *Perpetual Motion* seem to get lost between eras. *Gentleman Death*, however, is an urgent attempt to bridge them, to be contemporary even when it doesn't make sense—Gibson, the postmodern writer in a modernist world, or, perhaps, the modern writer thoroughly engaged in a postmodern world.

IV

What you have to realize when you read Rudy Wiebe's *A Discovery of Strangers* (1994) is that this is the author's dream-vision. It is not an authentic rendering of Indian reality or of nineteenth-century exploration or even of the Barrenlands as an austere and prophetic context for the confrontation between irreconcilable worlds. Authenticity and historical insight are quite beside the point, despite some silly things that have been written and said by reviewers. While the novel may seem to explore John Franklin's disastrous first overland expedition to the polar sea in the early 1820s and to illuminate the gathering awareness among Yellowknife Indians that these whites would forever change their lives, while it seems to document conflicting social values, the sub-Arctic landscape, and the affair between a young English officer and an even younger Indian woman, while it apparently uses these materials in a sort of revisionist postmodern implementation of narrative strategies designed to expose anomalies in our present perspectives on the past, a responsible reading suggests it is a very personal expression of Rudy Wiebe's interior vision. *A Discovery of Strangers* is a confessional exposition, a confabulation of private dreams.

The Indians in this novel, despite obvious research, inhabit no world that ever is or was. They are remarkable creations, as are Franklin and his men, but they exist entirely as projections of the author's own sensibility onto a story gleaned from a wide and sympathetic reading of historical records and anthropological texts. Rather than being re-creations, the novel's characters are the metonymic populace of an imaginary landscape, terrain born out of Wiebe's obvious familiarity with the taiga and waters of the sub-Arctic Barrens.

Wiebe tries to create a sentient world of nature in his highly stylized prose, with its emotionally charged imagery, evasive syntax, and juxtaposition of voices and improbable perspectives. His Indians are human consciousness within this world, although their minds are by no means the measure of its limits. They often dream beyond their own experience and merge with animals or with landscape they have never seen. Neither in the context of their own envisioned world nor in their encounters with the Franklin party do they truly represent alternate perceptions of reality or variant ontologies, although on the surface it may seem otherwise. The success of Wiebe's Indians as figures in a fiction is that they inhabit a thoughtful white late-twentieth-century middle-aged male's imagining of what their world might have been if he had been its creator—as, indeed, he is.

Wiebe circumvents charges of appropriation not by profound insight into 'the Indian mind,' nor into the most secret corners of women's lives, but through a kind of solemn playfulness which alerts the reader to his narrative presence as metaphysician within his own text. He enhances character roles as vivid ciphers in his dreamvision through gyrations of imagination at once splendid and alarming. The novel displays no hesitation at all in merging Wiebe's versions of researched native stories, drawn, for example, from *The Book of Dene*, with animistic or fabulous accounts of his own devising. His notion of The People's knowing-through-dream, whereby they hunt, and their necessary enthrallment with story, whereby they share values from person to person, generation to generation, he collapses into dream as a prophetic narrative device so precise, for example, that a suffering old woman foretells the exact location of the travellers' tragedy a full season in advance.

It cannot be an accident that Wiebe's Yellowknife Indians pun in English, a language they do not speak: Dr. Richardson becomes Richard Sun; Snow Man, a phrase used to describe whites, rhymes in an Indian woman's chant with "woe man"; the names of both Hood and Back evoke wordplay, and Franklin is known as Thick English, a nickname grounded in no language at all. When the reader considers how casually Wiebe enters into Indian consciousness, male and female, young and old, at a most cataclysmic and confusing time in their social history, it must be taken that he creates their reality according to his own design(s), quite separable from origins and actuality. His characters do not seem intended to be real, either within their narrative context nor within the reader's mind.

In Wiebe's visionary polemic, the British officers are made, ironically, to represent the reader's perspective on the native and the natural world. Especially Midshipman Robert Hood, with a sweet and open disposition and a baffled affection for his hosts, provides us as outsiders (if only because we are necessarily outside the text) with an entry point into alien experience that has somehow, perhaps because less 'human,' been spared The Fall. While Midshipman Back has sex with anyone available and Lieutenant Franklin holds himself entirely abstemious, and the good Dr. Richardson provides cerebrated links from his journal entries, and the Canadian and mixed-blood voyageurs are differentiated to the extent of their threat to British stability and the one British servant, an Orkneyman known to the Indians as Hep-Burn (the cross-cultural pun, again; the Indians associate him with a burning flag) hovers on the margin, all of them endure the travails and indulgences of Wiebe's carefully constructed envisioning of a dialectically alternative reality. They provide a context within which Wiebe's visionary world is revealed.

Consistent with the dreamvision as a mode of metaphysical inquiry, *A Discovery of Strangers* is not always forthcoming in the articulation of its philosophical argument. Certainly it is clear the author is on the side of nature as opposed to civilization, and of dream, which he holds in contradistinction to rational thought. He has a fine sense of snow, wind, and the elements of weather, season, and terrain in which fragmented and elliptical narrative episodes transpire; and against which the sensibilities of his outsiders seem mawkish, mean, and willfully brutish. He has in this envisioned world, above all, with absolute authority celebrated the ephemerality of the moral, the ambiguity of the mortal, human condition. Whether or not the originality of his materials, drawn from dream and document, sustain his vision is open to the individual reader's discretion.

Wiebe showed a moving capacity for moral outrage in *The Scorched-Wood People*, his 1977 novel excoriating Canada's malfeasance in response to the Métis of the last century and their political aspirations. In 1973, *The Temptations of Big Bear*, for which he won a Governor General's Award, offered what were at the time wondrous insights for the non-native reader into the soul of the land northwest of all the power centres threatening it, and into the heart of its original Peoples. It seemed inevitable that he would eventually round out his survey of the impact of the nineteenth-century trader/settler invasion by writing a novel from the white perspective, whether in pursuit of his own personal roots, fulfilling his Mennonite canon, or through an illumination of the remarkable hardship endured by early immigrants from Ontario and beyond. The muscular lyricism of his 1989 meditation on the Arctic, *Playing Dead*, seemed a haunting prelude for a novel, the third in a triptych, yet to be written. *A Discovery of Strangers*, which also won a Governor General's Award, is the novel anticipated. In many ways it is the completion of interlocking projects. However, as a sort of spiritual and moral autobiography it turns familiar and arcane materials to a profoundly personal end, and stands on its own as the enduring dreamvision of a writer addressing himself to the world.

V

Well into Daphne Marlatt's *Taken* (1996), the narrator shares with her reader the central problem of the text, which is also, perhaps paradoxically, the source of its disingenuous magic: this is a story of listening to the past, but how is it possible to distinguish memory from fiction, how is it possible to arrange the bits so that they will fall behind as the reader moves through them, leaving an illusion of continuity to offset the pain of irremedial loss? This is not an account of the past retrieved or of the past redeemed. It is the exquisitely poignant arrangement of its remnants, vivid with colour and mood, in the fleeting, sometimes ephemeral, present. It is a grieving and an affirmation, all at once; a celebration of loss due to time and the vagaries of human affection, out of which we invent our own stories and refuse closure.

It is impossible to distinguish between the narrator Suzanne and Marlatt herself, or between the facts of her story and Marlatt's own life. This novel is so intimate and intense that its author is absolutely inseparable from the telling. There is no one else writing in Canada or, to my knowledge, elsewhere who so wholly translates her being in the world into an aesthetic creation. Reading Marlatt, and especially this novel, the reader is exposed to emotional realities so authentic their fictional representation, their poetic manifestation, seem merely the media through which to connect with the memory fragments and imagination of the personality informing the text. To read Marlatt's writing is to read Daphne Marlatt; not as confessional artifact but as art, her life most courageously turned out as a passionate and lyrical poem, a sad proud witness to our shared condition in a fallen world.

Taken is a novel of brief evocative gestures, not episodes or even vignettes but emotive image clusters, lyric asides that seem to drift on the passage of time. It is a novel about mothers and lovers, about war and men, about wives and fathers; it is a novel about being white in Malaya before the Japanese conquest, about the Pacific War, especially from the perspective of Katoomba in the Blue Mountains of Australia, from the perspective of Esme, the young bride whose husband, Charles, writes dutiful letters home to a besieged England while living close by Esme's mother and father who have no country except in their minds, as British functionaries abroad in Southeast Asia with nothing to look forward to after the war except the ruins of Empire. It is a novel about Esme's pregnancy and the births of her three daughters, the eldest being Suzanne. It is about Suzanne, telling the story, telling things she could not possibly know, creating imagined brief encounters with the lives of her parents and grandparents, scattering shards of the past into the air where, as they fall, they invoke a past that is both absolute and unreal. It is about Lori leaving Suzanne and their island home in British Columbia to visit her own mother in the United States, currently embroiled in the Gulf War, and about the slow longing of Suzanne's realization that Lori will never return.

The British Empire falls, the Japanese empire rises and falls, the American empire unleashes its fury in Desert Storm; generations live, pass away; lovers endure terrible separations, dislocations; people die, love evaporates like a mist in morning. All this comes to us in brief stanzas of imagery, evoking smells, sounds, accents and, most of all, moods. Marlatt trusts details—she trusts her reader to fill in the grand and intimate narratives from knowledge and imagination. She writes with such confidence, is so deft with the details, her novel resonates with what has not been said. So much happens, and so little. It is a remarkable achievement.

In some respects, *Taken* is a reconstruction of the myriad past in the mind of a narrator in the ongoing present. Yet the present is not somehow valorized over the past; nor is the past cast like a flamboyant pall over an insipid or disingenuous present. The past is rendered as fiction from an omniscient perspective. However, in the present tense, the narrative is in the first person, the 'I' reduced to 'i' in assertive self-effacement. The effect is not to distance the past from the present but rather to make it immediate and visceral, memory as much of the body as of the mind. It is this from which Suzanne's lover retreats and this which leaves us, the readers, as enriched and bereft as she—taken, occupied, resistant, yielding only to change, to the beauty and sadness of the story itself.

Daphne Marlatt is a poet, a very fine and difficult poet whose sculptural shaping of words on the page sometimes fiercely resists comprehension, yet if the reader surrenders to the nuances of language, of sense and of sound, while maintaining a separateness of mind and emotion (giving in without giving up), her poems are infinitely yielding. Her prose is poetic, but far more accessible. It invades the sensibility every bit as much as her poetry, but after you have left the text behind it haunts you, not like the poetry does, with words in artful disarray—rather, as emanations of memory or dream indistinguishable from your own, seeming to have been born from the elusive darkness within, not from words at all but from the depths of personal time.

VI

I did not want to finish reading *Fugitive Pieces* (1996) by Anne Michaels, but not for the reasons you might imagine. Narrative closure meant critical response and seldom have I felt less inclined to comment on a work of contemporary fiction. This is not exactly a judgement in itself, but implies an attitude best characterized by the notion of enthusiastic ambivalence. I am genuinely disconcerted by my response to this novel. There is writing here so poetic I was left gasping for breath; there is narrative dexterity as plots elliptically collide that is astonishingly sophisticated; there are brief glimpses into human misery, the tortured human soul, that chill to the bone. Yet the self-conscious aphorisms and contrived profundity, mawkish exploitation of horroric events, vapid characterization and self-conscious cosmopolitanism left me cold. The desire to celebrate what is right about this novel is in conflict with the need to say what is wrong with it. The extent of its critical reputation precludes the tantalizing alternative of silence.

Fugitive Pieces is a first novel by an established poet. It received modest acclaim when it appeared, but it was not until a clamorous foreign reception that it really had an impact on Canadian sensibilities. Perhaps this is an echo of the old dictum that to be appreciated in Canada a work of art must first be celebrated abroad, but I do not think so. It seems to me that Michaels' novel is determinedly neo-colonial, insisting that elsewhere is more real than here; that Europe is authentic, however grotesque its recent history, and Canada is a kind of characterless limbo for the spiritually destitute, the psychologically brutalized, the socially dispossessed. An ephemeral urban shadow world of intellectual expatriates in Toronto evolves in the narrative out of the lyrical and grisly realities of a child's experience of wartime Europe which is imposed like a nervous palimpsest over fragmented documentary reports of Holocaust atrocities. As the substantiating European perspective accommodates to Canadian reality, Canada becomes real. We must be; we can write about Europe so terribly well.

And Michaels does write well. Her account of a young boy, Jakob Beer, who escapes a roundup of Polish Jews after hiding at play behind a wall when Nazis take away his parents and sister Bella, is told in stark and elusive minimalist images that evoke a deep terror and profound empathy. As the narrative follows Jakob's rescue by a Greek scientist, Athos Roussos, who takes the boy back with him from an archaeological dig to his island home of Idhra for the duration of the war, then to Canada where Athos secures academic employment commensurate with his apparent qualifications, Jakob's haunting becomes more and more internalized but no less obsessive, as he relates nearly everything in his life to his dead sister, Bella. Athos dies; Jakob achieves stature as a poet; at sixty, he is hit by a car in Athens and dies, and his young second wife, pregnant with his only child, dies a few days later. We know of his death through a brief prefatory note before the narrative opens.

The second part of the narrative offers a curiously oblique account of Jakob as an established poet from the peripheral vantage of a somewhat feckless academic expert on the conjunction of weather and biography, whose parents are Holocaust survivors, and who follows Jakob, posthumously, to the Greek island home he had shared with Athos, and has an affair that, we are to understand, saves his marriage. In this second part, Jakob is reduced to a suffering-poet figure, somewhat between icon and caricature, whose own life has been consumed not so much by war as by his inability to come to terms with living through it, and by his memories of the dead, more present to him than anything of his experience, alive, and by his devotion to Athos which verges on incapacitating idolatry. We see little of him as a poet. Oddly enough, we see little inside him as a person, beyond surface mannerisms and images of obsession.

Paradoxically, Michaels is at her best in the same areas where she is also at her worst. Peppered through the narrative like fragments of brilliance in an otherwise profoundly sober design are graphic vignettes of horror drawn from records of Nazi atrocities.

This is what apparently upset European critics; not for their untruth but rather as gratuitously vivid reminders of horror and shame. In telling one story, from the perspective of a small boy who grows to manhood under the burden of a terrible conflagration, it is sometimes necessary for the author to remind the reader of such terrors as it is within our power as humans to commit. Yet sometimes it does seem arbitrary, her introduction of yet another documentary fragment of depravity; an expression of outrage, not design, or of design only, and not of intrinsic value to her narrative.

Another paradoxical aspect to *Fugitive Pieces* is the author's devotion to local detail as the narrative moves about Europe. Michaels effectively co-opts the vocabularies of place, especially Greece, to create atmosphere; but at some point a kind of pride takes over and she uses foreign words for food and drink, weather and terrain as a sort of poetic mantra, as if to say, this is my specialized knowledge, I have learned these words, and they are unlikely to be familiar, so applaud their use. The result is alienating.

It is disconcerting with a novel that speaks so much out of historical experience to find yourself as a reader alienated, whether by language, attitude, characterization, or event. I felt locked out of Jakob's inner world; in this I think Michaels fails the challenge to make a severely injured consciousness accessible. Principal characters are introduced amid a catalogue of characteristics, not as people in a field, complex figures in a convincing environment. I often admired her fiction but I did not often believe it, so much was I kept on the surface of minds, so much was I given words turned nearly to perfection in place of raw feelings, inchoate thoughts, the inarticulable but nonetheless necessary details of individual response to the dangerous, threatening, depleted, or beautiful surrounding world.

Who has ever written so beautifully of the Jewish dead: "If sound waves carry on to infinity, where are their screams now? I imagine them somewhere in the galaxy, moving forever towards the psalms"? This is a novel to embrace, to celebrate for its verbal passion, for its controlled outrage, for its vision of spiritual disaffection and small consolations in random acts of love. It deserves better than to be celebrated for its improprieties, and less than to be mistaken for a work of stunning moral insight or extraordinary aesthetic achievement.

Works Cited

Butala, Sharon. *The Fourth Archangel.* Toronto: Harper Collins, 1992.

Gibson, Graeme. *Gentleman Death.* Toronto: McClelland and Stewart, 1993.

Marlatt, Daphne. *Taken.* Toronto: House of Anansi, 1996.

Michaels, Anne. *Fugitive Pieces.* Toronto: McClelland and Stewart, 1996.

Urquhart, Jane. *The Whirlpool.* Toronto: McClelland and Stewart, 1986.

Wiebe, Rudy. *A Discovery of Strangers.* Toronto: Knopf, 1994.

THE SEXES AND NARRATIVE FORM

Mrs Bentley's Gender

(This essay is part of an ongoing consideration of the relationship between gender and narrative form. Men have told their stories in certain ways for millennia and insisted that if women's stories must be told, they must be told in ways appropriate to male convention. Such an assumption has been radically challenged in recent decades. What is related here is an acknowledgement of change. Through orchestration of rhetorical discontinuities as well as in argument and observation, this essay is a celebration of the freedom change brings. It echoes sentiments I had expressed earlier, in other contexts, and anticipates the 1996 essay "Gender/Wilderness" as a companion piece. An alternative version was delivered as "Transitions and Transformations: The Feminization of Narrative Form" at the Convegno Internazionale di Studi Canadesi, in Torre Canne, Italy, in 1990, and published under the same title in Canada Ieri e Oggi *3, edited by Giovanni Bonanno, in 1992.)*

Bronwen Wallace, who died of cancer at forty-four, in the summer of 1989, entitled her last book of poetry *The Stubborn Particulars of Grace.* The poems of this book and of all her life are one poem. There is no rhetorical structure to their gathering. Yet in their denial of form, there is tremendous power. Some of her poems are dramatic, some exquisitely lyrical, some touching, and funny, and sad, and all are so filled with the miracle of ordinary living that they take the breath away. The structure of each poem and the movement among them is discursive. They are poems that insist on the reality of women's experience, that insist on reality; poems that insist we are surrounded in the world by unyielding details that in arrangements with other details become important. It is in the accumulation of particulars, seized in her poetry and articulated with intensity and compassion, that Wallace shares the beauty of her vision and the courage to endure. Her title is a poem itself, a brief narrative about female reality: *The Stubborn Particulars of Grace.*

IN 1954, ETHEL WILSON published *Swamp Angel.* It is a very engaging novel to read and, at the same time, unsettling. It is not a great novel. But it is very good, good in the sense of being well written, and good, also, as an affirmation of the good life, a fragmented life made whole and lived well. Maggie Vardoe deserts her husband (there is no word in English for leaving marriage that does not imply negative responsibility); she leaves Vancouver and travels by taxi and bus into the Interior of British Columbia. At the village of Hope she intentionally veers away from her route to fish along the Similkameen River. After three days, she returns to Hope and continues her flight or quest, towards Kamloops and Three Loon Lake, where she settles in for the rest of the novel. A lot happens in the first third of her story, then it seems that not much happens, and then her story is over.

Swamp Angel is the modest manifesto of a woman's will to prevail over the divisive forces against her. On her journey, Maggie Vardoe reverts to the name of her first husband and becomes Maggie Lloyd, preferring that to Maggie Macdonald, the name of her father, and then she becomes Maggie, alone. In the last two-thirds of her narrative, she learns, in the rich imagery of the novel, to reconcile the seal and the angel, swimming and soaring, substance and essence, the present with the past and future. She becomes complete in herself, a whole woman—although a woman whose self-possession depends on the nurturing of others.

Swamp Angel relates two stories, or, perhaps more accurately, it conveys Maggie's story in two ways. One is on the level of meaning, in which themes, motifs, symbols, and images relay to the reader a progression in Maggie's life towards wholeness. The other, through a discontinuous narrative structure, arrives at the same end on the level of being, and allows Maggie finally to be herself. Within time and space determined by the vision of the novel as a whole, the first or temporal narrative coheres in a sequential and rational continuum. This is radically subsumed by the other, spacial, narrative, which is analogic, synthetic, holistic, and for Maggie, as well as the reader, immensely satisfying. Structural ambivalence leads in the end to narrative closure.

THIS PAPER IS BEING composed on a computer; I can see what language does, observe the process of composition. Language becomes spacial on a computer screen. You can leap around among your ideas; make alliances, juggle and juxtapose, and ultimately share your thinking and not just the artifacts of thought. It is more like speech than writing, except it is visual and there is perfect recall. It is the inversion of orderly eloquence; it is rhetoric meant to deny the hegemony of rhetorical structure. If the conventional argument is a linear progression through time, towards meaning, then this is a discursion through space, towards awareness and the complexities of being.

THE SHORT STORIES of Bronwen Wallace were published as a collection shortly after her death. Their title itself holds them together, frames them as a single narrative. The collection is called *People You'd Trust Your Life To*. The reader shares in those words a grave responsibility with her characters, although one easily sustained.

Wallace's stories have something of the same easy familiarity and impact as her best poetry, which seems due as much to their exuberant form as to specific content. Her stories explode gently and settle as memory in the reader's mind. She literally writes the female body into fiction, writes an entirely female perspective on the world, but what gives her narrative such authority are the insistent discontinuities in her presentation of women's experience, of female reality. Each story develops in layers, and by indirection, implication, and apparently free association, until even the most intimate acts of joy and madness seem inevitable.

THERE ARE TWO EXTREMES in narrative structure. The model for one is the labyrinth. The model for the other is the jigsaw puzzle. Think of a labyrinth. At the heart or centre of the labyrinth is meaning; to arrive at the centre of a labyrinth is the only means of escape. A well-constructed labyrinth is a maze; that is, the walls of every corridor are walls of adjoining corridors as well. There is no wasted space. To arrive at the heart, you must experience every wall and corridor in your journey. You could lay a string behind you, or bread crumbs, or film where you have been, but you don't know where to go until you get there. And when you're at the centre, paradoxically, you are on the outside looking in. But now the labyrinth is contained inside you, and what you see there is a projection of your own desire.

This is a paradigm of reading, as well as of narrative structure. But it is only one approach to reading, one kind of structure. There is also the jigsaw puzzle. It, too, is a paradigm of reading; the model for another, perhaps subversive, form of narrative. Consider the puzzle. Like the labyrinth, it is arbitrary, an intrusion on the silence of time and space, an ordering in the chaos of experience. It, too, has its edges. But the edges of a jigsaw puzzle are determined by the integrity of each separate piece. Each piece is its own centre.

You can place the pieces on a plane according to intuition, to your general knowledge of the world. A light blue piece goes high; it is the sky. A deep blue piece goes low; it is water. And light comes from one direction, and shadows fall away from it. But after a while, you realize that a particular piece of sky is reflection and lies within the water, while the shadow of a rock is in fact a tree, and what you took to be a tree is part of a cart. You begin outside the puzzle, but as the puzzle-pieces fit together you enter the picture more and more, until your perspective is in the end among its many parts. You are contained by the puzzle, and its reality is inseparable from your own.

Unlike being in a labyrinth, your location in a jigsaw puzzle is in a constant state of flux. As you set the pieces down, each new piece alters the alignment of those already there. Bread crumbs and picture puzzles are incompatible. You can't go back the way you came. Balls of string unravel uselessly around the margins. The fixity of film is irrelevant. Where you have been changes with every present instance of where you are. You could take stills, slides, and layer them one atop the other. When the puzzle is complete, you could look through the stack of slides, but by then, of course, your vision is opaque; your perception, a part of the puzzle.

READ *BLOWN FIGURES* by Audrey Thomas, or read it again. You cannot move forward through it with any certainty. You keep sliding off the page. The picture keeps changing; you move through its changes. In the end you read with rapt attention a series of blank pages. She is *that* successful at engaging you in sorting out the narrative chaos, in finding form and the hell with meaning, in holding everything together long enough to see it whole, that the printless pages of her puzzle are a narrative delight.

THE LABYRINTH IS TWO-DIMENSIONAL, although it gives the impression of being three. The pattern of the maze itself is on a single plane. You move through it sequentially and no matter how disorderly your progress may seem, it still follows one thing from another. It is experienced as a temporal construct. The picture puzzle, by contrast, insists on its two-dimensionality; but it is, in fact, a three-dimensional experience, a spacial construct, for its resolution depends on cumulative shifts in perspective as you enter with each new piece into the picture and withdraw to review the whole before entering again. You provide the third dimension.

In his 1975 novel, *Badlands*, Robert Kroetsch develops two separate narratives: an existential male quest for meaning and a discontinuous female account that contains and, ultimately, discards it. Margaret Atwood's novel *The Handmaid's Tale*, published in 1985, chronicles a woman's displacement within what has been officially legislated as a man's world, only to have the female story rendered ephemeral in an extended postscript by male academics in pursuit of historical significance. Both novels isolate particular modes of narrative according to gender; both place the male and female modes in opposition, articulate them as mutually exclusive, and allow one to override the other. Yet the overall narrative strategy of each novel depends on the interaction of these modes: reality in Kroetsch's vision lies in ultimate complementarity between the sexes, and in Atwood's, in perpetual conflict between them.

In *Badlands*, William Dawe's journey down the Red Deer River in pursuit of dinosaur bones that will bring him fame and immortalize his name is an archetypal quest for meaning through experience. Anna Yellowbird watches from the riverbank; occasionally and in a random pattern she connects with the different males on Dawe's expedition, and then withdraws to watch again. Some fifty-six years later, with Dawe's daughter, who is also called Anna, she travels to the river's source while the Dawe account is re-enacted as their common dream. The female narrative, both structurally and thematically, is spacial, not temporal, embodying not progression but transformation. The two Annas provide the necessary witness to bring Dawe's field notes to life. But in the end, with a bear suspended from a helicopter passing overhead, its testicles dangling stupidly through the net, they are moved by male absurdity and copious quantities of gin to tear up the notes, the photographs, the artifacts of Dawe's adventure. Both women are set free from Dawe's story, from the impositions of male reality, to be, at last, themselves.

Offred's story in *The Handmaid's Tale* is related through a series of discontinuous revelations about her life in the future-world of Gilead, without the author detailing that world beyond Offred's limited experience. In the dystopian vision of the novel, Offred is a handmaid, a woman whose sole function is to bear children as a surrogate womb. The primary activity of Offred's narrative, however, is in the reader's mind. The reader extrapolates a coherent if terrible world from Offred's pathetically narrowed vision, projects beyond the severe emotional constraints of her conditioning, and literally shares with Offred, and with Atwood who is a guiding presence in the text, the dilemma of how to construct a woman's narrative within a misogynist nightmare.

The Handmaid's Tale closes with a section entitled "Historical Notes" that is a transcript of a symposium on Gileadean studies held at the University of Denay, Nunavit, in the year 2195. This is two centuries after Offred's narrative. Her identity, even her existence, are called into question. The academic inquisitors, in pursuit of history, in deference to data, in their quest for meaning, historical relevance and objective truth, virtually deny this woman reality. After we share in Offred's struggle to write herself, or be written, into being, we are appalled as her account is reduced by a male set of mind to documentary artifact, as her existence is reduced to merely an historical possibility.

THINK ABOUT THE SHORT stories of Alice Munro. Each is a jigsaw puzzle. As you read, you encounter piece after piece which you hold in mind until the story is complete. Each piece seems arbitrary in design, each is an episode, or a thought, a feeling, an image, a discrete and separable entity from all the others. As you read, patterns take shape, perimeters fall into place; the patterns shift, perimeters change. Munro leaves out just enough pieces that, in the end, when you tilt her narrative to the light to admire your readerly craft, it collapses. The elusive genius of a Munro story lies in its refusal to be still, to convey meaning. It is not a delivery system. In the end, it is only itself. For most readers, that is more than enough.

Think about the design of a jigsaw piece. It has narrative significance, enough to be recognized as a part of something else. But its shape is arbitrary. Its shape is jigged by a saw to fit adjoining pieces without reference to content. It is forced by its shape to be its own centre of interest. Yet, when it is aligned to fit another, both the content and the cut of its edges hold it in place, and another centre of interest comes into being. And so it goes, until the end, when all the centres become one. Read an Alice Munro story, and think about the pieces in a puzzle. When the puzzle disappears, the story is complete.

In *Lives of Girls and Women* and in *Who Do You Think You Are?* Munro links her stories into sequences determined more by chronology than anything else. The main characters in each, Del and Rose, get older. Their lives change, they learn more about themselves, and they become tentatively reconciled to who they are. The structure of each book is based on the model of the labyrinth, even though the separate stories so beautifully exemplify the narrative as puzzle. Even Munro is confused about form; and with good reason. In reaching for continuity, she writes in response to the dominant mode in our culture, which has come down to us as an existential quest for meaning. Yet the separate stories in these two books, the stories in all her other collections, are intricately shaped in narrative patterns that reflect the subversion of meaning, the importance of being.

THERE IS PATHOS in reading Gwendolyn MacEwen, who died of suicide, when she writes in "The Tao of Physics" of her own reckless vulnerability. This is a woman's story of defiance and defeat, for even as she hurls her poems against death and change, she accepts their primacy, submits to the terrible beauty of her lord. Male over female, time over space, might over matter; in such reality the grace of her poems gives tragic assent to her own demise.

> In the vast spaces of the subatomic world where
> Matter has a tendency to exist
> The lord of Life is breathing in and out,
> Creating and destroying the universe
> With each wave of his breath.
>
> And my lord Siva dances in the city streets,
> His body a fierce illusion of flesh, of energy.
> The particles of light cast off from his hair
> Invade the mighty night, the relative night, this dream.

Here where events have a tendency to occur
My chair and all its myriad inner worlds
Whirl around in the carousel of space; I hurl
Breathless poems against my lord Death, send these
Words, these words
Careening into the beautiful darkness.

THE FICTIONAL WORLD of Sinclair Ross's 1941 novel, *As for Me and My House*, is revealed to the reader as an intricate conversation between the intersecting functions of Mrs Bentley as both a character and the novel's recording consciousness, and the two sides of her mind as emissary for the radical subversions of her author's ambivalence in regard to conventions of gender and narrative authority. The double split, one involving Mrs Bentley's mind as text, and the other, Sinclair Ross's absence from the text, gives rise to a narrative design of remarkable indeterminacy.

Mrs Bentley's mind is bicameral. One side is dominated by words and meaning, by linearity, logic, and progression. This, she as a character associates with the masculine. The other side is dominated by form and pattern, by intuition and discontinuous transformation. This, conforming to the undeclared tenets of structuralism, she associates with the feminine. Narrative reality, however, refuses reduction to a simple arrangement of antitheses based on gender stereotype. Opposing ontologies are free of a fixed association with one character or another, one sex or another.

Mrs Bentley wants to see her husband as the existential hero of her account, and herself as his nurturing feminine complement. But Ross's text insists that Philip animates a structuralist reality, with Mrs Bentley a far more convincing existential protagonist than her husband. In contradistinction to gender stereotype, Mrs Bentley yearns towards meaning and Philip towards inarticulable form. She tries desperately to submerge herself in his personal mythology, while trying, as desperately, to lift him out of it. She manipulates to gain control of his life, with the intent to yield control of her own. In trying to make Philip more 'manly,' by her account of things, she makes him less; in trying to make herself more 'feminine,' she becomes less a woman. Her journal is from an existential perspective an act of self-creation. What she writes, however, is beyond her will, an account of her failure. In the text, structuralist and existential conceptions of reality converge. The genius of the novel is to accommodate both, while submitting to neither.

DI BRANDT SAYS in a poem:

> the meaning i say through clenched teeth is related to
> the structure
> of the sentence for godsake anybody can see that you
> can't just take
> some old crackpot idea & say you found it in these
> words even the
> Bible has to make some sense the Bible my father says

IN HER POEM "Bartók and the Geranium," Dorothy Livesay arranges a peculiar pair of opposites in parallel. The music of Bartók "explodes in space," and then is ended, while the geranium, "heaven's held breath," endures in self-absorbed serenity. The magnificent image, "heaven's held breath," is a typo. The text actually reads "heaven-held breath." The error is serendipity. What of this earth could be more powerful than heaven's held breath?

IT IS A TELLING IRONY that in a much-to-be-admired novel such as Daphne Marlatt's *Ana Historic*, so urgently concerned with the marginalization of women's reality through language, the story is narrated in an intricately devised linear mode which accedes to the male dominance it is attempting to overthrow. Marlatt urges the creative reunion of language and the female body. Words that pre-empt female reality are of narrative concern throughout the text, yet the novel's narrative structure reinforces notions of historical progression and rhetorical coherence through which male language sustains authority. It is chilling to realize that the word 'vagina,' with its regal sound in Canadian parlance, rhyming as it does with the city of 'Regina,' which itself echoes colonialism of another sort, in French is masculine: "*le vagin.* there must be some mistake, I thought, not knowing its history, a word for sheath, the cover of a sword." Yes. But for the reader to discover this in an essentially conventional story pattern isolates the linguistic denial of women's reality as an aberration, when it is in fact embedded deep in the structures of literature as well as language.

MOLLY BLOOM'S STORY of herself in *Ulysses* goes nowhere. In a single sentence, which is the syntactical denial of progression or change, Joyce creates a puzzle of magificent complexity, and Molly Bloom lies at its centre. Her husband Leopold and Stephen Dedalus are moved about in the first parts of the novel with great deliberation, as Joyce scours the streets of Dublin for meaning. Maundering male sexual desire becomes a constituent part of female desire, as Molly's yearning towards sensual completion subsumes their pedestrian quest. The tyrannies of religious and racial, aesthetic and masculine meaning are put in their place.

IN HER BOOK *Drawing on the Right Side of the Brain* (1989), Betty Edwards applies current knowledge about the asymmetrical functioning of the human cerebral hemispheres to the enhancement of artistic skills and appreciation. Her book bears the same relationship to an instructional manual as *Zen and the Art of Motorcycle Maintenance* does to a Honda owner's guide, or *A Hitchhiker's Guide to the Galaxy* to a backpacker's Baedeker. Edwards' intent is to liberate the intuitive, synthesizing, analogical, spacial, nonrational, holistic functioning of the right side of the brain from the suffocating dominance of the logical, analyzing, abstract, temporal, rational, linear functioning of the left side. Only then, when imagination and the unconscious are freed from intellectual constraints, when consciousness finds access to unfettered perception, will the mind rise in the act of creation to its fullest potential.

The vocabulary and syntax of language in service to the left hemisphere impose linear coherence on such linguistic emanations from the right as analogues and tropes. The left, which is associated with right-handedness, corresponds to what through human social evolution we have taken to be the masculine side of things. The right, and left-handedness, have been deemed the feminine side. The left or male hemisphere long ago seized control—reason over discord, order over anarchy. But discord and anarchy from the right are freedoms, the freedom to be different and the freedom to create. These, our human cultures for the most part have deemed to be subversive and female, to be discredited or ignored.

Literary precedent brings imagination, the tropes and analogues, symbols and images, rhythms and patterns, into line. Literally, into line. The female, in this model, provides the materials of art, but the male arranges them in sequence. Guided by intellectual awareness of tradition and the conventions of genre, as well as society, the male arranges them to yield meaning. She may be the muse, but he is the artist. He is Bartók, and she the geranium.

Betty Edwards argues that you can learn access to the suppressed right hemisphere and restore its proper functioning through discipline. Whatever led us in the distant past to yield authority to reason, we can usurp such power by an act of will. Whatever led to acceptance of meaning over being, of memory and dream over present desire, of the existential quest over existence itself, we can deny its continuance through creative anarchy. That we can do so is evident in works of great and original art that combine the so-called male and female principles. *Ulysses*, for instance. It is also evident in the birth of every human child.

THERE IS SADNESS in reading the opening stanza of Gwendolyn MacEwen's poem "Breakfast at Midnight," as the speaker opens herself with such urgency to the tyrannies of language and of time, to male authority and power:

> There are times I look at you with such shock and surprise
> I cannot breathe. Who are you? Why do I hear
> Speech of your seed, languages, voices of your
> Million unborn children?

THE NARRATOR IN Margaret Atwood's *Surfacing* begins her story in a quest for her absent father that would seem the very expression of Lacanian doctrine. Fortunately, Atwood seems guided more by the psychoanalytics of R.D. Laing than Jacques Lacan. Granted, there are many replications of Lacan's 'primal mirror' crisis in the motival patterns of *Surfacing*, but the narrator's search for her father is not motivated by Oedipal considerations or a need to recover the 'law,' enforced by his absence, that sustains the split in her experience of herself. Atwood rejects the dissociation of self as an absolute, and founds its reintegration on the grave and the gifts of her mother.

After seeing random souvenirs left by her mother and piecing together the remnants of her father's scholarly research in an effort to resolve the mystery of his disappearance, Atwood's unnamed narrator dives into the depths of a lake, where she comes face to face with death. In a rush of horrific images, she surfaces. She has seen human monsters, her drowned brother, dead frogs, an aborted foetus, and herself. When she hears that her father's drowned body has been recovered at that exact place, where it was weighed down by the camera he was using to record Indian pictographs, a victim of rational technology in confrontation with the bestial side of natural man, she breeds with her lover and then retreats into the utter solitude of primeval, prenatal, preternatural consciousness. She is transformed into the beast she has been forced to recognize within herself. She is an animal waiting for the fur to grow on her skin. She is beyond reason, beyond language, but she is aware. When she comes across the picture she drew as a girl, which her mother saved, suddenly the ordeal is over. The picture shows an unborn infant looking out from its mother's womb. The narrator sleeps, sure now that she is pregnant, wakes up and prepares herself for the surface world of language, men, and apparent surrender to the realities into which her child will be born.

While much of *Surfacing* follows a linear pattern through the labyrinth of a deeply troubled mind, envisioning reality from the narrator's increasingly dissociated perspective, it resolves in a brilliant splash of images that, once given, swirl through the text towards wholeness and completion. It is a little as if the walls of a maze in which we found ourselves reading were suddenly transfigured into a picture puzzle that only depicts a maze. The temporal pattern has become a spacial design. This transformation reflects a radical change in the narrator's understanding of herself. Her long and rapid descent into the genetic past, from acquiescence to male power, willing victim in the intellectual games that separate her from the animal within, to the asexual condition of animate awareness, collapses suddenly with her recognition of maternal continuity. Her surrender is categorically provisional.

IN A REVIEW of a book by Steve McCaffery, Thomas Willard writes: "Indeed, the book is 'dynamite' and, for better or worse, it detonates between two final quotes from Wittgenstein: 'The book exploded in his hand. / Slowly, at first.'"

BP NICHOL PUBLISHED the novel *Still* with Pulp Press in 1983. It is very obscure. In both senses of the word. It is largely unknown and as a text it is difficult, teasing the reader at the edge of incomprehension. Red Deer College Press published *The Prowler* by Kristjana Gunnars in 1989. Despite a structure that could best be described as chaotic, it is a narrative of exquisite clarity and coherence. Few people have read either novel. Perhaps few ever will. *The Prowler* offers splendid rewards to those who seek it out. Among the discord and the anarchy of its discontinuities, the quiet voice of a solitary woman achieves the echoed resonance of multitudes. *Still* is more of an enigma, as haunting and elusive as a memory of somewhere between nightmare and dream. Both novels must be reread rather than read, recollected, inseparable from other private memories of the reader's life.

Still is the narrative as labyrinth. Think of a movie camera scanning across the planes of a still photograph, recording the architectural patterns of its journey as it passes. And at the same time, think of a conversation of the most terse dialogue possible, laid over the accumulating images like a soundtrack. There are two people talking. They are unseen. One is a woman. One is a man. We know this by the way they talk. By syntactical nuance. By subtle assumptions and prerogatives in their discourse. Tensions and momentum build around him more than around her. In the beginning they discuss their end. In the end they agree to go on exactly as they have been. Somehow this seems, for him, a triumph. For her, it is an acceptable compromise.

That is the story. They talk. And interspersed between the discontinuous moments of their conversation are beautifully detailed descriptions of a house, inside and out. Overlapping visions of the grounds and environs gradually give way to a room-by-room tour of the interior. Words are a camera: Nichol moves with meticulous care through his scene, sometimes zooming in for a close-up, sometimes panning across a wall, sometimes angling a shot for intentional distortion, sometimes withdrawing to a neutral distance and at other times forcing an intimacy on the reader by such proximity to artifact that you feel implicated in a violation of some sort. This is a lived-in place, yet never do we directly encounter, there, a living soul. All motion is in our shifting perceptions; all duration, in the time we take to read. Occasionally the scene suggests whole seasons, and at other times we see a table set, a toilet-paper roll half gone; and we are haunted in this place by the apparent absence of its inhabitants. They are voices only. Only the text as context, the text as an extension of the reader's mind, brings characters and setting onto common ground.

In Alain Robbe-Grillet's *La Jalousie*, the image of a woman endlessly brushing her hair lays down a structural thread, a sequence of crumbs from the same loaf, to get you through a disorienting text. In *Still*, Nichol is doing something the same but more radical. While coaxing the reader through the text with vague intimations of continuity, in the snippets of dialogue, he simultaneously denies the reader's progress with convolutions of fragmented imagery. You get to the end of Nichol's labyrinth but you don't get out.

Male cultural hegemony and the metaphysical imperatives of conventional narrative are in direct response to the discontinuities inherent in the empirical experience of men. Even now, in the post-Hegalian displacement of metaphysics, the immediate is ironically given less importance, not more, as might be expected; presence remains an echo of something more authentic than itself, whether semiotic or phenomenal. The immediate, in effect, is not a sign but only a signifier; what it implies, imitates, or anticipates is the signified. From Plato to the present there has been a relenting, in that the signified has shifted in recent times from absolute to enigma, while the sign remains a process, a site of transcendence. Through symbol and metaphor, the play between similarities and differences in a linear sequence of revelation, plotted referents acquire meaning and significance. Even when the tropes are muted with such determination as in Nichol's *Still*, and story is intentionally obscured, everything in the narrative connects. The beginning anticipates the end; the end affirms the intention of the text, which has been to illuminate its quotidian origins—the still-life brought to life by what Roland Barthes, with his affinity for Robbe-Grillet, would surely have described as a most readerly text.

In the experience of women, continuity has been an outlaw activity unless under the sanction of male authority. Presence has meaning only for what it promises. The wilderness of earth is merely a prelude to the kingdom of heaven; the garden, a haunting memory of the paradise ahead. The challenge, then, has been how to resist the imposition of narrative connection, how to usurp the authority of transcendence, of meaning beyond text, how to establish authenticity in the immediate, without lapsing into incoherence. And the response has been metonymy—set forth the discontinuities, think of narrative as thrown, thrown apparently at random, apprehended by the ways each piece implies another and another, as the picture puzzle changes and changes, and the reader prowls among the pieces, towards completion, not closure.)

Kristjana Gunnars, in *The Prowler*, refuses the linear authority of time. She prowls among the random jigsaw pieces of her narrator's life; her narrator is a prowler in her own story, and you, as reader, prowl the text among discrete passages which seem to slide elliptically across the narrative plane. There is something delightfully sinister about your progress. You share in the conspiracy of re-creation, as you piece the narrator's life together without reference to continuity or duration. Almost by stealth, you encounter, capture, and sustain the fragments of her story. Even the text is a prowler, slipping with furtive deliberation among the fragments held within the reader's mind.

Initially, the novel seems to be arguing that stories can no longer be told, that 'the novel' is dead. Quickly, though, before you are off the first page, you realize, far from slipping into silence, that this is a reinvention of narrative form. Arbitrary, self-effacing, and enigmatic, a story is, nonetheless, conveyed, the story of fragmentation in an Icelandic girl's experience growing up and in the arbitrary events of her young life, determined by a patriarchal family, a misogynist society, geographic discontinuity, and a war. Form in this novel is the perfect expression of content.

Gunnars' novel claims modesty, proclaims its own limitations. Never trust the obvious. When the writing narrator says, "It is a relief not to be writing a story"; when she echoes Joyce by saying, "Perhaps it is not a good book . . . *but it is the only book I am able to write*"; when she says, "I do not want to be clever," and "It is a book marked by its ordinariness. That knows there can be nothing extraordinary in a life, in a language"; she is giving you fair warning of her radical intent. Each denial is an invitation to participate in the novel's narrative complexity. A story is, after all, being written. It seems as if it is being written while you read. It violates the linear conventions of storytelling which dictate that the story knows where it's going, even if the reader doesn't. It is many stories, each with its own centre, some only a few words, none more than a few pages. The novel's succession of 167 numbered sections, arranged on unnumbered pages, is its only and ironic concession to continuity. All are written as surely out of the writing narrator's own life as Joyce wrote from his, but in her refusal to be clever, to be portentous, Gunnars accedes to the function of art as an expression not of the intellect but of intuition, not of the body politic or the body aesthetic, religious, or otherwise transcendent, but of the body itself, her own presence in the world.

Do we ever know the narrator's name? We are told that as a girl growing up in Iceland she is "owned" by her father, Gunnar Bodvarsson. This gives her the right to speak on certain rare occasions. Kinship with her mother gives her no such right. She is somehow less related to her mother. We learn this, and about her anorexic sister. About Iceland, about children's work. Children's silence. Growing up as a white Inuit. School in Denmark. School in California. Libraries and words. Versions of the same story. We come to know the narrator as intimately as she knows herself—even if we can't remember whether or not we know her name. Naming is an expression of ownership, and while we may become familiar with the narrator's life, she is in no way our possession or under our control. "The project was to clarify the picture. To make the patterns emerge out of a random set." And they emerge with striking clarity, but they will not resolve, hold still; it is as if we have before us only one piece of the puzzle at a time and from memory have to hold them all together, affirming, as we do, life over artifice, being over meaning, grace over transcendence.

VIRGINIA WOOLF—did you begin to think she would never enter the scene? She has been here from the beginning.

DI BRANDT writes in a poem of women:

> i have subscribed to endless circulars
> proclaiming us blood kin in these rooms
> i have rolled and unrolled with the rest
> wordless sheets announcing the damp odour
> of our common text . . .

MEN AND WOMEN have learned to tell their stories differently. Woman's story has largely been expunged from the myriad records of our progress towards eternity. But subversively her story has been inscribed upon the landscape of our consciousness, to be shared among the overlapping generations which converge with each collapsing moment, and it renders the notion of eternity irrelevant. Woman's story turns her confinement in immediate experience to advantage. She explodes time in fragments across the narrative plane. There is a correspondence between the evolution of feminist ideology and the opening of art in all its forms to structural anarchy and creative discord, to discursion from meaning, to transformation and reconciliation as alternatives to transcendence and consolation, and to the worth of life itself. Is it possible to separate this from the creative chaos of postmodernism? Without the rise of feminism to foster violations in the patrilinearity of narrative syntax, to crumble the authority of patriarchal structures, perhaps Gilead would still be Atwood's private nightmare, Kroetsch might not have merged Huck Finn and Mr. Kurtz in the image of an emasculated bear, dangling high above a riverbank, and Bronwen Wallace might never have recorded, for us, the stubborn particulars of grace.

WORKS CITED

Atwood, Margaret. *Surfacing.* Toronto: McClelland and Stewart, 1972.

——. *The Handmaid's Tale.* Toronto: McClelland and Stewart, 1985.

Brandt, Di. *Questions I Asked My Mother.* Winnipeg: Turnstone Press, 1987.

Edwards, Betty. *Drawing on the Right Side of the Brain.* Revised. Los Angeles: Tarcher, 1989.

Geddes, Gary, ed. *15 Canadian Poets X 2.* Toronto: Oxford University Press, 1988.

Gunnars, Kristjana. *The Prowler.* Red Deer: Red Deer College Press, 1989.

Joyce, James. *Ulysses.* Paris: Odyssey, 1932.

Kroetsch, Robert. *Badlands.* Toronto: New Press, 1975.

MacEwen, Gwendolyn. *Afterworlds.* Toronto: McClelland and Stewart, 1987.

Marlatt, Daphne. *Ana Historic.* Toronto: Coach House Press, 1988.

Moss, John. *A Reader's Guide to the Canadian Novel.* 2nd ed. Toronto: McClelland and Stewart, 1987.

Munro, Alice. *Lives of Girls and Women.* Toronto: McGraw-Hill Ryerson, 1971.

——. *Who Do You Think You Are?* Toronto: Macmillan, 1978.

Nichol, bp. *Still.* Vancouver: Pulp Press, 1983.

Ross, Sinclair. *As For Me and My House.* Toronto: McClelland and Stewart, 1969.

Thomas, Audrey. *Blown Figures.* Vancouver: Talonbooks, 1974.

Wallace, Bronwen. *The Stubborn Particulars of Grace.* Toronto: McClelland and Stewart, 1987.

——. *People You'd Trust Your Life To.* Toronto: McClelland and Stewart, 1990.

Willard, Thomas. "Steve McCaffery." *Journal of Canadian Poetry* 4 (1989).

Wilson, Ethel. *Swamp Angel.* Toronto: Macmillan, 1954.

Gender/Wilderness

(Over the Labour Day weekend of 1996 I participated in an interdisciplinary symposium in honour of Bruce Hodgins, hosted by the Frost Centre for Canadian Heritage and Development Studies, Trent University, at the Wanapitei Wilderness Centre in Temagami. Bruce is an old friend, one of the great canoeists of Canada, an historian pre-eminent in aboriginal studies, and the director for a generation of Camp Wanapitei, renowned for their canoe trips throughout the Northwest Territories. I took the occasion of Bruce being launched into improbable retirement to weave interests in narrative, gender, and wilderness into a brief essay that I hoped would reflect contemplative concerns and yet be provocative. There are vital issues here, and I wanted a tapestry that would throw them into realignment, for reconsideration. This essay was published as "Gender Notes: Wilderness Unfinished" in a special edition of the Journal of Canadian Studies *called* Refiguring Wilderness, *Vol. 33, No. 2, edited by Jonathan Bordo, Peter Kulchyski, John Malloy, and John Wadland. Parts of this essay appeared in the March 1996 issue of* Canadian Forum.*)*

REFIGURING GENDER, REFIGURING WILDERNESS—I thought of calling this a completed work in progress, as an attempt to set ideas of creation against the notion of closure. The structure of story usually associated with narrative authority has a focused beginning, which implies a decisive conclusion. By offering only beginnings, I had hoped to subvert the truism that endings are either possible or desirable; and perhaps to argue that story can be as much about process as progress, as much about evasions of meaning as ultimate ends.

In *The Canadian Settler's Guide* and *The Backwoods of Canada*, Catherine Parr Traill instructs her reader on the etiquette as well as the techniques of survival in the wilderness. She does not write about conquests but about accommodation. Following a crazy-quilt pattern, she leads the reader among the discontinuous procedures of establishing a new-world presence. Her sister, Susanna Moodie, wrote *Roughing It in the Bush* and *Life in the Clearings*. Anna Jameson wrote *Winter Studies and Summer Rambles*. These books were all published before Confederation. Each is related from a first-person perspective in the authorial voice. All are narratives about their authors coming to terms with unfamiliar terrain. Traill stays relatively close to the dooryard blooms; Jameson is an aristocratic tourist; and Moodie, as a failed settler and proud immigrant, is somewhere between. There is little narrative progression in any of these books, yet each woman in her own way has written herself into the Canadian landscape.

The pre-Confederation travel journals of Samuel Hearne, Alexander Mackenzie, and John Franklin describe harrowing tales of exploration and adventure along a labyrinthine maze of lakes and rivers. Each man is the hero in his own story; each inscribes his name on the North American map, writes his name into history. Hearne is an exciting writer, albeit with help from his literary friends. Mackenzie and Franklin are more plodding, both of them struggling to balance the documentary function with a desire to please. Each is responsible for stringing lines of direction, distance, and authority across what to them was an alien landscape. Unlike their female counterparts, they do not write about reconciliation with a strange new world; rather, their journals attest to the struggle of putting that world in its place.

The male accounts are about the conquest of geography over landscape; historiographic gridlock as an expression of both corporate and personal power. The women write to share their experience of the wilderness; the men, to be admired for surviving theirs. The men write to achieve meaning; the women as witness. Men, passing; women, presence.

Begin with *Genesis* or with Aristotle. Begin with the *I Ching* or with Jacques Lacan. Begin within the pages of Margaret Atwood's *Surfacing* or Robert Kroetsch's *Badlands*, or within numerous other contemporary works of Canadian fiction. Begin with documentary accounts of wilderness experience by men and by women that are true for the writer writing even if, on analysis, they are not as close to the truth as their non-fiction designation implies. What we have, in each beginning, is clarion assent to the almost universal notion of separate male and female realities. Man is one thing and woman is another. Discourse between them is an illusion. Man's story and woman's story may intersect, but they do not merge. Man writes his name into history, and woman's out of it. His story is at her expense; she, in turn, suppressed, has learned to tell her story in a different way, arranging its components to a different end. If the form of the male story is essentially linear and leads through time, ultimately, to transcendence, the female story is spacial and leads to grace. If man yearns towards meaning, woman's desire, expressed in narrative through what sometimes appears to be structural anarchy, is to be free. In a world that places imminence over presence, becoming over being, anticipation over actuality, memory and dream over immediate experience, she writes to be real. Rather than to connect with meaning, she writes to become meaning.

Imagine wilderness: what is it you are imagining? Absence, adversary, a field on which we impose ourselves like figures in an existential tourney, where quest becomes conquest and to survive is to prevail? Or a place where you find things, the context in which human consciousness connects with natural world? Reconnects—there must have been a time, perhaps paleolithic, when mind and environment were no more separable than head from body, or vision from the eyes that see. Some of us periodically enter what we call wilderness in an effort to achieve such unity of being. Like lovers, we yearn towards the condition in which it is impossible to tell where we end and the other begins. Like tandem paddlers set to run a riot of whitewater rapids, we yearn to move as one, and to become what we behold.

This may be what we desire, in what we call wilderness, not transcendence where we escape from ourselves into a more meaningful and authentic reality, but subtle transformation, metamorphosis, where the reality of the natural world is inseparable from our experience of ourselves. This may be what we reach for on our canoe trips and backpacking treks and other excursions beyond the civil limits. While we often find pleasure in these adventures, usually in direct proportion to how remote we are from human society, there is also for some of us the inevitable sense of falling short of our goals, either at the time or in the telling. Inevitable: because in the Western world the concept of wilderness has traditionally been negative. Our language and culture bring to us notions of wilderness as demonic, or, at best, a void; a place for forty days to test one's godhood, or one's manhood; adversary or absence; dehumanizing, dehumanized. It is difficult to reconcile personal pleasures in the wilderness with cultural conditioning. There is a kind of small-*c* secular calvinism at work: our unaggressive pleasure, the proof of ineptitude; the lack of correlation between effort expended and elements subdued, a cause for unease.

Our historic response to wilderness has been limned in the annals of conquest and defeat. At one extreme, the ultimate experience in wilderness is death: we celebrate the victims of wilderness catastrophe as heroic and applaud epic hardships in the wilderness, no matter how foolish the plight. At the other extreme in our experience of wilderness is the death of others, annihilation of those native to what from the venturing perspective is necessarily perceived as empty. We may admire to the point of veneration the native capacity to endure but cannot forgive their intrusion into our narratives of exploration and achievement. Between such parentheses, we envision the wilderness a privileging context for the discovery of self, for relating to other. The paradox is endemic, as much the burden of our wilderness experience as backpacks and bannock. To resolve the paradox would be to discriminate between the ways in which wilderness is culturally embedded and our own desire as wilderness travellers: we will have to deconstruct narrative strategies by which the natural world has been subordinated in our collective story to the interests of the white male protagonist who has traditionally entered it on our behalf.

This past summer I spent some time walking the Barrenlands. I travelled on my own from Kugluktuk, known until recently as Coppermine, south past the Dismal Lakes to the headwaters of the Dease River flowing into Great Bear Lake, and back north along the Coppermine Valley to the Arctic Ocean, a fifty-six-year-old Canadian hiker, fellow protagonist in my own field notes with Samuel Hearne, John Franklin, and Jack Hornby, of whom I was in a sort of metonymic pursuit and wrote about as often as I did about myself. My forty days in the wilderness took twenty-eight. I covered a total of 450 kilometres. After a month of harrowing solitude and the rushing silences of wind and water, I suspected I was closing in on Hearne and Franklin and, especially, on Hornby, the loner, the emotional outlaw; the haunting intransigence of the tundra drawing the four of us into a form of communion, the changeless landscape transcending time and the deaths between us.

Consider what I just told you: the Barrenlands are in fact teeming with life; the Dismals are among the most beautiful lakes I have ever seen; forty days of wilderness is proffered as Biblical allusion, declaring my emulation of our culture's premier hero, connecting all men as heroes who would challenge the devil without, the demons within—arguing the Barrens as a moral testing ground when actually it is a place of great solace and, sometimes, serenity. Notice the disingenuous understatement opening the passage, "I spent some time walking the Barrenlands." It was in fact tumultuous terrain, but, given what I can assume is known about the Barrens and implicit in the name, understatement implies conquest. Notice too that I was not walking *in* the Barrenlands—the omission of the preposition subverts the landscape to my own presence upon it, striding over it as a passive context. Notice the anthropocentric overstatement of "harrowing solitude" and "rushing silences," as if the sounds of the natural world were for my benefit alone, as if my isolation were nature's concern. Consider the copious numbers and geographical references, lending an aura of authenticity, the days numbered, distance measured, giving credence to expressions of personality. Notice the suggestions of preternatural connections with historical figures, giving my quest meaning beyond mere adventure—this is a favourite ploy for validation used by virtually every writer of wilderness travel from earliest to the present. Notice the closing, the invocation of death, the apotheosis implicit, the mystery implied, in its apparent defeat. And so it goes.

So it goes: a seemingly casual paragraph, an offhand documentary of personal adventure, in which the archetypal masculine quest for transcendent meaning is accomplished as a consequence of narrative closure; a travel brief in which language writes the landscape, and not landscape the language; in which wilderness is subverted to serve human ends and story celebrates the protagonist and his place in the historical continuum; in which the self is quietly inserted into the narrative, inscribed on the landscape, as a figure whose model is Jesus himself. So it goes.

Immanuel Kant inadvertently sanctions the strategies of my account: "Without man," he writes, "the whole of creation would be a mere wilderness, a thing in vain, and have no final purpose." Consider that: 1. It is man who provides meaning to creation—a statement in striking resonance with John Donne's declaration on our behalf: "Man is not a piece of the world but the world itself; and next to the glory of God, the reason why there is a world." 2. Wilderness is by definition an absence, "a thing in vain," the antithesis of what creation is all about: all about us. 3. Man is a metonym for humanity; our human being is legislated by divine and secular laws, and the natural laws implicit in our culture, to be under masculine dispensation. Humankind is taken in essence to be male. 4. The point of creation is to anticipate a "final purpose." It has no value in itself. The solipsism is embracing; the solecism comforting. The way man tells his story as man in the world is what gives the world meaning and man tells his story to preserve his privileged status.

In such a world, men and women tell their different stories differently. The notion that narrative modes are intrinsically bound to gender acknowledges polarities that have been sustained in our culture through millennia. The male and female of our species have arrived through social evolution at a curious symbiosis, based not on intrinsic difference or biological function but on the politics of power. Aristotle codified an evolving concept wherein men are the source of human energy and achievement, while women provide the base materials, body substance, which is stimulated into life by the male through copulation. In *Genesis*, God charges the first man to name the world and thereby gain ascendancy above all earthly things. With language comes control, but also consciousness of the self as other. The post-Freudian subversions of Jacques Lacan do not appreciably differ from this paradigm. God's elevation of man led to the necessity of creating woman as a vital link for Adam to his earthly origin. In *Feminine Sexuality*, Lacan likewise struggles to provide a viable reality for woman that his pre-emptive speculations have casually denied. So much for the divinity of our beginnings.

It is set in holy writ and learned text that humankind is in essence male, and in substance female. Mankind is man, and woman his female emanation. Through scientific method and visionary speculation, the complementarity between man and woman is taken to preclude equality, for the male is spirit, vision, vital force, while females are the very stuff of mortal flesh. This is a notion not peculiar to the Western world. The first two trigrams of the *I Ching*, which are called Ch'ien and K'un, are yang and yin, male and female, heaven and earth; ostensibly reflections of one another, one is active and one is passive, one creative and the other receptive, and so on. To spawn and nurture flesh is woman's lot, while man is given to create on the higher levels of art and science, religion and the law.

Woman is stranded within each generation, isolated from one generation to another by her function as the material source of life, the embodiment of earth. She is her function—and nothing more. By law, man isolates her from her daughters and her mothers. With science, man founds authority for his privileged state in the activity of molecules and stars. Through religion, man sanctions his ascendancy, sanctifies his own apotheosis. And through art, he explores and celebrates his continuity with all mankind.

In such reality—which, until recently and with few exceptions, we have taken to be categorical—life has no meaning in itself. Sustained in the Western mind, no less than in the East, is a profound discrepancy between the lived-in world and what it signifies. Everything must be named and explained in terms of something else. All our institutions, our religious, civil, and aesthetic laws, our science, our philosophies, function on this basis.

The writer of wilderness narrative, no less than any other, exists in such a world in order to invest it with meaning: with significance, relevance and continuity. To connect—that is the artist's great desire; to create analogues, correlatives, fields in text, to devise allusions, archetypes, hermeneutic encounters, to arouse, to illuminate, to affirm the presence and validity of a higher hidden self. To connect, give life meaning and meaning life. To make of life, in short, a metaphor.

To act otherwise, it would seem, to collapse metaphor, to found reality in the immediate, is feminist subversion. To say that life is not a metaphor would be the usurpation of male dominance. To evade meaning, to refuse the quest for connectedness and significance is to valorize the real, to deny art, and to deconstruct all masculine imperatives of control. To create narrative in dissociative patterns that must resolve in memory and by intuition is to insist that art is not a medium but inseparable from reality itself. To affirm that human experience is not a signifier but the signified is a declaration of female power.

Who determined men and women opposites, as black and white, day and night, hot and cold, north and south, substance/essence, energy and stasis, instead of complementary, like east and west, differences determined by direction faced, by point of view; not colours on a wheel, each implying its antithesis, but colours of the spectrum radiant from a common source?

Now imagine wilderness. Where are you, yourself, in what you are imagining? Can Kant be left behind, can you do without Donne, shake free of narrative patterns embedded so deep in our culture they seem innate, can you set aside male imperatives, the humanist assumptions, that insist on a hierarchy of being, with nature a base, the wilderness a void, and man ascendant, reaching for his place beside God? Imagine wilderness, instead, as a good place to be, where being and the world are one. More and more, as women write themselves into the wilderness, wilderness is refigured in our imaginations from object to subject, with us as outsiders, decentred, our position no longer privileged, the context of our adventure no longer a means but the end in itself. Many women refuse the headlong linearity of traditional male narrative, the metaphoric impulse to force meaning from their wilderness adventures. Without the same apparent need to inscribe their presence on the natural world and bring it to submission, women write of wilderness as metonym, of being there, not passing through.

There are several instances available for analytic contemplation in twentieth-century wilderness literature, of male and female accounts of the same or parallel events. Victoria Jason in *Kabloona in the Yellow Kayak: One Woman's Journey Through the Northwest Passage*, and Don Starkell in the extravagantly subtitled *Paddle to the Arctic: The Incredible Story of a Kayak Quest Across the Roof of the World*, both books published in 1995, offer remarkably conflicted narratives of the authors' two summers paddling together across the top of continental Canada. In 1903, Leonidas Hubbard died in what was evidently profound wilderness, in the eastern sub-Arctic. His companion, Dillon Wallace, published an epic male adventure quest, detailing their fatal journey, in a 1905 book entitled *The Lure of the Labrador Wild*. Hubbard's widow, Mina, retraced their route in 1905, accompanied by her husband's guide, survived with quiet flare, and published her contrary account in 1908 as *A Woman's Way through Unknown Labrador*. In both pairs of books, what is essentially a male conception of narrative and of wilderness is challenged by the female version, by women's narrative strategies, imagery, sentiments. In the process, conventional notions of wilderness deconstruct.

Consider the most recent pairing . . .

For those who love the journey, Victoria Jason's *Kabloona in the Yellow Kayak* is irresistible. For those who find satisfaction reading about the feats of others, *Paddle to the Arctic* by Don Starkell will be more appealing. Either way, each book is a gloss, a complement to the other. Starkell invites you to watch and witness; Jason, to come along for the ride. For several legs of their kayak journeys across the top of North America they travelled together. It was, at best, an awkward alliance. Starkell's achievement is that he managed to survive his ordeal as he conquered the Northwest Passage; Jason's, that she enjoyed so much her improbable adventure, for the best part alone, as she did exactly the same.

Starkell is not a contemplative man. His account is rough, self-serving, and arrogant. He writes as one driven to achieve goals of his own design and he makes no apologies, no concessions, to reader or fellow traveller for attitudes essential to his purpose. He is not out to win a popularity contest; he can be abrasive in the extreme. But he is wholly focused, obsessively self-reliant, and that makes him, as the protagonist in his own account, mesmerizing.

Jason is not contemplative either. No more than Starkell does she attempt to plumb those depths of personality that urge her on, through four summers, to cover an astonishing 7500-kilometre journey through the Canadian Arctic and sub-Arctic between Churchill, Manitoba, on the western shore of Hudson Bay, and Fort Providence, where the Mackenzie River flows out of Great Slave Lake. Despite Starkell's histrionic style (as writer, as protagonist), she is the more complex character, both elusive and enthralling, as she glides through the pages of her narrative.

Starkell is compelling to watch, like observing a kayak swirling on the edge of a sluice-hole vortex, waiting to see if it will spring free or collapse. Jason is charming, despite vile weather conditions, enervating illness, danger on every horizon —a woman insisting, always, that she is the same as the rest of us. Jason's attempt to connect, to merge her experience with the reader's own, contrasts vividly with Starkell, who is obsessed with establishing difference, that he is one of a kind. He is not. We are used to the existential odysseys of angst-driven males in a realm where failure is perhaps the greatest success. We are not so prepared by tradition or convention for the protagonist in an adventure narrative who pines for her grandchildren and carries among her survival gear mascara and an eyelash curler, along with a shotgun for bears, forty-eight Nutri-Bars, and a dictionary as her only book.

Victoria Jason is forty-six years old and a grandmother when she joins Don Starkell in 1991 on his second attempt to kayak out of Churchill, north and west through the Arctic archipelago sprawling tumultuously across our northern reaches, with Tuktoyaktuk at the edge of the Mackenzie Delta as their goal. That summer they make it as far as Repulse Bay, losing a third member of the party along the way (through choice, not disaster). Much of Jason's account is taken up with details of weather and landscape; yet her stormy relationship with Starkell dominates. It is almost unbelievable, then, when the two make amends during the winter and set out from Repulse Bay in early June 1992, hauling their kayaks across the land and frozen sea.

Suffering from severe edema due to muscle breakdown from overexertion, Jason is forced to drop out at Goa Haven. She mentions in passing that Starkell, who continues alone, is eventually rescued a day's distance from Tuktoyaktuk, following which all his fingers and some of his toes are amputated. Even after they go their separate ways, she is unrelenting in her descriptions of Starkell as overbearing, bombastic, and obsessive. Starkell, in remarkable contrast, writes of Victoria Jason with warmth and admiration; he is ingenuously contrite about his grating behaviour, never apologetic about his ambition.

During the next two summers, Jason paddles on her own from west to east, from Great Slave Lake to Paulutuk, Paulutuk to Goa Haven. Despite Starkell's claim to accomplishing "the longest self-propelled kayak journey in Canadian Arctic history," she covers one-third more distance. But conquest is not her goal, whether of territory or personal demons. That is where her book is revolutionary. Jason documents her experience with casual eloquence and a thoroughness that makes her reader feel a part of the adventure. She describes wind blowing the hair on the back of her neck, the feeling of cold wet clothes, tired muscles, a warm sleeping bag, wariness of bears, the ecstasies of wind on water, and a shoreline of infinite variety. She introduces everyone she encounters by name, from a man we suspect becomes her lover to companions of an hour's duration over steaming pots of tea with bannock.

Jason's account is a narrative of transformation, an implicitly feminist refusal to participate in the male quest to inscribe one's singularity on history. Starkell's account is a celebration of the obdurate self. He is Homer to himself as Odysseus. His narrative declares that nothing will touch him, change him, keep him from his course, nothing but death—which he flirts with like an aging satyr. Jason, in contrast, grows, matures, opens to herself. Hers is a voyage of discovery; his, an existential evasion.

Starkell has a gripping story to tell, and often, in spite of his breathless declamations that once again (and again) he stares death in the face, the fact is, he does. Many of his problems arise out of his own doing, his own character. That does not make any of them less of a problem. He is a fool to travel with no extra paddle, without all-weather gear, with no winter mitts or gloves. But he genuinely suffers for his foolishness, is maimed for life, and shares the confusion of his agonies with remarkable candour —as he writes himself into the mega/mono/macho/narrative of wilderness adventure, inserting the names of numerous Arctic explorers into his text, to be known by the company he keeps.

Victoria Jason seems as oblivious to historical precedent as Starkell claims she is to the dangers of Arctic adventure. She shares with her readers a present perspective; and the beauty of presence. Starkell is bent on closure, on getting it all over with, one way or another, and having the story told. Experience is merely a link between past and future. Jason shows with eloquence her genuine affection for the people she meets, the solitude, the landscape, the experience. She is concerned with the telling. In spite of her lack of grace about Starkell—she did after all travel with him for two summers on an expedition he organized and for which he was the driving force—her book is important for rewriting the rules of wilderness narrative. Starkell's book is a good example of why they need to be rewritten.

Men and women have learned to tell the stories of their reality in different ways. In accounts of wilderness experience, the structural anarchy and creative discontinuity of women's narratives deny absence, refuse adversarial conflict, find instead the wilderness a place where people find things, sometimes themselves. In reading women who have learned to revel in freedom from meaning, from numinous tyrannies, women who, in denial of male authority and privilege, write to dismantle the constructed world, the male world where this life is merely a prelude, a rehearsal, a trial in preparation for the next, for some other, women who subversively explode notions of conquest and reduction of the natural to metaphor, in reading such writers we can break from the narrative conventions that determine perception and shape our experience, we can rediscover wilderness as a good place to be, *dasein* with a difference, and ourselves at home in the lovely amplitude of time.

Works Cited

Atwood, Margaret. *Surfacing*. Toronto: McClelland and Stewart, 1972.

Hubbard, Mina. *A Woman's Way through Unknown Labrador: An Account of the Exploration of the Nascapee and George Rivers.* Toronto: W. Briggs, 1908.

Jameson, Anna. *Winter Studies and Summer Rambles in Canada.* London: Saunders and Oatley, 1838.

Jason, Victoria. *Kabloona in the Yellow Kayak: One Woman's Journey Through the Northwest Passage*. Winnipeg: Turnstone Press, 1995.

Kroetsch, Robert. *Badlands: A Novel.* Toronto: New Press, 1975.

Mitchell, Juliet, and Jacqueline Rose, eds. *Feminine Sexuality: Jacques Lacan and the école freudienne.* New York: W.W. Norton, Pantheon Books, 1982.

Moodie, Susanna. *Roughing It in the Bush, or Life in Canada.* London: R. Bentley, 1852.

——. *Life in the Clearings Versus the Bush.* London: R. Bentley, 1853.

Starkell, Don. *Paddle to the Arctic: The Incredible Story of a Kayak Quest Across the Roof of the World.* Toronto: McClelland and Stewart, 1995.

Traill, Catherine Parr. *The Backwoods of Canada: Being Letters from the Wife of an Emigrant Officer.* London: Charles Knight, 1836.

——. *The Canadian Settler's Guide.* Toronto: W. Briggs, 1857.

Wallace, Dillon. *The Lure of the Labrador Wild: The Story of the Exploring Expedition Conducted by Leonidas Hubbard Jr.* New York: Revell, 1905.

THE REACHING SEA

UNDER LAKE AGASSIZ: MANITOBA REDUX

(This essay was intended to articulate the ineffable. A much appreciated invitation to Japan in December of 1996 was contingent on giving at least one lecture on Manitoba literature and culture. I gave a series of three talks in the Tokyo area. One was on images of the North in Canadian literature, meant to be accessible for students with only a basic working knowledge of English; another, delivered at Kyoritsu Women's University under the title "The End of Exile," offered a more challenging critical perspective on Canadian writing at the close of the twentieth century. The third, a version of this essay, was on Manitoba. It was given at Chiba University where our host, Professor Yuichi Midzunoe, teaches Canadian literature. Playing through convolutions of language and extended conceits is my attempt at a sincere tribute to a province I know mostly as a reader, and deeply admire. The essay was published in Tokyo in a book edited by Professor Ikuko Mizunoe entitled Aspects of Multiculturalism in Canada and Elsewhere, *Kyoritsu Women's University Press, 1998.)*

I

Manitoba is not what you think it is. Having come to Japan from Australia where the separate states and territories pride themselves on belonging to the federal community (with the possible exception of Tasmania, an island in space and time that sees itself quite separate from the Australian nation-continent), I am particularly aware of our tendency in Canada to define ourselves in terms of provinces or regions within the larger Dominion. This seems especially true of Manitoba, at least from my perspective as a Canadian from Ontario. (Not that Manitoba is insular or unaccommodating to outsiders.) I have lived in other parts of Canada for extended periods—on the West Coast and in the Maritimes, in Saskatchewan and several times in Quebec—and I have travelled on a dozen expeditions through the Canadian Arctic. I have never lived in Manitoba. However, I feel at home there. I am at home in Manitoba not because it is my constitutional right as a Canadian. I am at home because Manitoba yields access to itself as an illimitable place of the imagination, a place you can apprehend as part of your real life, even if you have never been there.

Manitobans are a seafaring people. That may seem a surprise, given its Prairie location. Most of Manitoba was once submerged under a freshwater sea called Lake Agassiz. The Canadian Coast Guard has a contingent at Gimli, on the western shore of Lake Winnipeg, which is the principal remnant of this primordial flood. The Canadian Navy built a prototype aircraft carrier out of ice-blocks in Jasper National Park during World War II. If the iceship had been built near Gimli, the Coast Guard could have offered it an official escort on one of the great lakes of the world, at least until the melting season, which comes annually in Manitoba (as it does in Alberta, where Jasper is strategically located).

Manitoba was once a mouldering bottom that has risen to good health and prominence. Perhaps the variegated landscape of Manitoba emerged from under Lake Agassiz at the end of the last ice age, to the astonishment of early émigrés from Asia. Or possibly Lake Agassiz retreated underground back when the dinosaurs, wallowing at its attenuated edges, began turning into oil. Whichever is true is a matter of time, of concern only to pedants who care little about the mythologies of place. Truth is elusive from our perspective outside Manitoba. What is true is that Manitobans are a seafaring people—although seafaring may be misleading since I think of Lake Agassiz as a freshwater lake, but then 'freshwater lake' is redundant for if a lake is salty it is not a lake but a sea, and if it is a mixture of fresh water and salt water, its salinity determined by the ebb and flow of saltwater tides, it is mareotic, a word not used in common parlance, as rare as the lake it describes.

Icelanders coming to Manitoba in flight from the tumultuous upheaval of the earth and the hardness of weather in their homeland, to which they had first ventured a thousand years before in open boats across ocean-roads both treacherous and beguiling, were cast adrift on Lake Manitoba and made their way to shore only long enough to settle, build boats, provision themselves, before taking once again to the water, discovering in this ocean-lake such bounty that, ashore, they prospered, and some of them, salt in their veins, spread out across the landscape, inscribed their heritage in Manitoba history, shaped the lives of all who live there.

One might perhaps with less irony call Manitobans a sea-crossed people, since everyone, some a thousand generations ago, arrived over bodies of water, came not as wanderers but as people with a purpose, a vocation to find food or to build from the crumbling rubble of their old homes a new home; some came as migrants over a hypothetical land bridge, drifting from one location to another within the perimeters of adjoining lands, from Africa, Asia, Europe—this was when all the world was America, as John Locke once said—until at last they crossed over onto this continent which then, despite Locke, was no longer America; some emigrated more recently, in the last few centuries, and in the process experienced a sea change.

Imagine that you travelled water to what, in the tyranny of language over time, we call Canada. Manitoba. As the ice age retreated, you envisioned yourself indigenous, the time of your presence no longer measured by ancestral memory. You have always been in this place. Your dreams are of nowhere else. You do not call yourselves Indian, but in your several languages you call yourselves The People. To be human is to be who you are. For the rest, more recent newcomers, dreams of elsewhere fade, become myth, metaphor, displaced fragments of history caught up in a surname, residual in the shaping of flesh to bone. For a generation or two you might think you are an Icelander in Manitoba, a Japanese Manitoban, a Manitoban from Jamaica, from the Ukraine, from England, from France. But the truth is, when you cross the sea you become one of us. Even if you pause in the United States for a while, a decade, a century, when you set foot on Canadian soil your feet sink into earth and you walk submerged, the immense space of this place enclosing you like a lover; the land not an unwritten text pressing you down but a context, making you free. You belong to the land and are also its heir. You have exchanged the gnawing awareness of your absence from history in the old world for an incontrovertible presence in the new. Although you now belong to a sea-shaped people, your reality is inseparable from the land itself.

If you look at a detailed map of Manitoba and squint a bit, it will seem as if much of the province is still underwater. This is largely an illusion: the northern reaches are a blur of blue lakes and blue rivers. If you look at a larger map or a world atlas you will see that Manitoba is at the geographic centre of the continental land mass, both latitudinally and longitudinally. You can drive thousands of kilometres east from Manitoba to Atlantic Canada, or you can drive thousands of kilometres west to the Pacific coast. You used to be able to cover the same vast landscape by train, before the railways were allowed to atrophy under the ignorant auspices of unimaginative bureaucrats. You can begin at the American border and travel north by car, canoe, on foot, until you reach the provincial boundary, and you are only halfway to the Arctic Ocean.

Strangely, considering its continental location, Manitoba has its own seaport. This is at Churchill, on Hudson Bay; not a freshwater port like Chicago or Montreal but a real saltwater seaport. You can travel south from seeing polar bears at Churchill and without too much trouble find yourself in the headwaters of the Mississippi, which flows into the alligator-infested bayous off the Gulf of Mexico, or on rivers draining into the Great Lakes, or on great Prairie rivers flowing from the Rocky Mountains to the sea. The landscape of Manitoba cannot be defined by its geographical features.

Manitoba is not the result of history arising out of geography. It is an example, easily recognizable in a postcolonial world, of history being arbitrarily imposed on the land and its resident people; geography by political or imperial fiat. Manitoba is a political entity. It is a province of Canada. It is a community of common political interests, a state. In defiance of nature its borders are straight, ruler-edged, with a bite taken out by the sea. It is not a folk society; it has not the cultural coherence of a nation; it is not an ethnic collective. While a Manitoban may easily feel that provincial boundaries form palpable dimensions to his or her experience of the world, what an outsider sees is a remarkable diversity of culture and landscape which could not possibly be contained by lines on a map or parliamentary acts of entitlement.

Manitoba refuses to submit to definition. It is not like other provinces; it is not like other places. The orderly mind will find it contradictory and inconsistent, an enigma, an anomaly, a labyrinth of improbabilities and the unexpected. The inquiring mind will find it a rich and varied world, as simple and complex as a constellation. Elusive as it is, and allusive as well, the best access to understanding Manitoba is through the imagination, in the works of its writers.

David Arnason writes beautifully crafted stories about fish that talk and improbable coincidence and fairy-tale figures in realistic settings, settings that are sometimes Manitoba and sometimes places of the imagination, say Europe, most recognizable for not being Manitoba. His stories directly or indirectly are about how to make the story. A wise postmodernist, he knows at least for himself the pleasure of text is not in the resolution of contrived complexity but in showing us the secrets of magic while still making the magic work. Sandra Birdsell writes beautifully crafted stories about things that happen to people who live in Manitoba because she imagines them there. They live in the town of Agassiz, named for the primordial lake. These people could be your own family or members of hers, they are brought to life with such quiet extravagance. Only distractions from outside the text as you read startle with reminders that these are created characters and their real world is a world of words.

Reading Arnason is to watch the juggler dancing one-legged on a tightrope with no net below. Reading Birdsell is to witness the aerialist on her wire, poised, breath held, standing absolutely still. The visions of both are wondrously innocent. We attend their literary show amazed at their diverse sensibilities on display, but in Manitoba, if these two writers are an indication, to our delight it is the circus performers themselves who are most astonished.

You might find 'innocent' a curious word to describe contemporary writers, both of them in their middle years and worldly. David Arnason and Sandra Birdsell might be thought to know better—and they do. They are not naïve. Arnason, who has published a sensitively cynical novel called *The Pagan Wall*, a brilliant and sadly uncelebrated fiction about conspiracy surrounding a superannuated Martin Heidegger, the German philosopher best remembered by the public for his personal attachment to Nazi doctrine—Arnason wears innocence as armour, knowing full well the fallen world and arguing the necessity of imagination to counter its foibles and depravities. Birdsell is perhaps a more natural innocent, less cerebral but by no means foolish. In the face of the flood, she avoids carrying rocks in her pockets. She celebrates those who float to the surface.

The powerful anomaly of innocence as antidote to Armageddon offers a good entry into a broader discussion of Manitoba fiction. This is not because Manitoba writers share in perversities of virtue but because their work shows the extreme range possible within a recognizably common context. In Arnason's writing, it is more the quirky old-fashioned postmodern sensibility on display in his work, characteristic of his being an intellectual entrepreneur in Winnipeg, at the centre of a world where there are no margins, rather than the setting of his fiction, that articulates its Manitoba origins. This is true even when he is writing directly out of his own particular memory-bank heritage of Gimli, the Icelandic community on the shores of Lake Winnipeg where he grew up. His fiction shows him equally at home in contemporary philosophy and postmodern critical theory and among the sagas of his Nordic forebears, Hebrew chronicles of the Old Testament, classical mythologies, Indian legends, lore of the Red River Valley, Canadian history. Arnason writes not as an innocent through lack of experience or in spite of it, but rather because of it. To be Manitoban in a world-weary and worldly world is a matter of choice, of survival.

In Birdsell's writing, the unwavering specificity of Manitoba life, place described in absolute terms, makes the lives of her characters real. Setting not only shapes their actions but also reflects their psychological, spiritual, and moral condition. The sense of authentic particularity her fiction conveys transcends the limits of modernism to bring the reader alive in the text. In allowing us access to her characters' reality, she offers us access into the hidden reaches of our own. In a world where everything is particular, the particular is universal. We are all Manitobans.

Two writers who are outsiders to Manitoba, although not as much so as myself, and have shown remarkable facility for drawing Manitoba as a regional context into their fictions are Rudy Wiebe and Carol Shields. The writer who is perhaps Manitoba's most renowned outsider, Robert Kroetsch, falls outside this discussion: Kroetsch is an Albertan and only someone as untutored in national diversity as Jean Chrétien would presume therefore to describe him, generically, as a representative Westerner. Having worked at the University of Manitoba for the latter part of his career, Kroetsch has gained from Winnipeg a lovely perspective on the world, but the world itself is another place.

Carol Shields has lived most of her writing life in Canada, and some of it in Winnipeg, but in consequence of her having maintained American citizenship her novel *The Stone Diaries* qualified a couple of years ago for the prestigious Pulitzer Prize, attainable only by citizens of the United States. We are a more open society in Canada, and honoured the same novel with our highest literary distinction, the Governor General's Award. Rudy Wiebe is an Albertan—here, despite Chrétien referring to everyone west of Ontario as the constituent of a singular political community, the West, 'Westerner' might be an appropriate appellation, for Wiebe was born in Saskatchewan, has lived and worked most of his life in Alberta, is an avowed Prairie writer, and expresses a sensibility informed by imperatives that historically precede the arbitrary laying down of territorial boundaries.

In Wiebe's moving requiem for the ways of life that sustained the Plains Cree through hundreds of generations, *The Temptations of Big Bear*, political borders are irrelevant to his vision of the Canadian West as the dying fields of a tragic race. However, in the foreshortened history of the sequel, *The Scorched-Wood People*, his account of the visionary renegade Louis Riel, who was the founder of both Manitoba and Saskatchewan and was executed for his revolutionary efforts, provincial boundaries are inseparable from the action itself. To be morally indifferent to alien notions of territoriality does not mean to be ignorant of their implications.

Both Wiebe and Shields write Manitoba into myth, although it would be difficult to conceive two novels more dissimilar than *The Scorched-Wood People* and *The Stone Diaries*. Shields, like Arnason, invokes reader self-consciousness to make the problems of narrative the subject of fiction. Is it possible to construct a dynamic and engaging account of an ordinary and uneventful life within the conventions of fiction in the autobiographical mode? Yes, according to Shields, if an exploded view of the conventional mode begins with a haunting tale of mythic origins, contains random elements of the improbable and the absurd, and ends after the narrator's death in a touching residue of postmodern triviality. The fictional rendering of Daisy's account of herself is inherently more interesting than she is. Her birth, for example, is conveyed in rhythms that transform Manitoba into a mythic oasis. Myth happens in a real place in a parallel dimension of time. Manitoba provides the place, and fiction the time. Daisy is real, a valid life, because her story is founded at the intersection of sonorous language and a narrative setting as substantial as rock, as stone. The rest of her life, in the United States, in Ottawa, never ceases to elicit from the reader an aura of sustained astonishment that from these origins she is nevertheless so ordinarily expendable.

Louis Riel, the main character in Wiebe's novel, is an historical fact. The challenge for Wiebe is to make the truth of Riel's life accessible through fiction, to make the truth seem true. Wiebe takes the reader on a spiritual journey through the mind of a man for whom Manitoba, as the projection of a messianic dream, became and remains a mythic creation, the only province of Canada to have been conceived in an act of revolution, quite possibly the only place in the world where revolution has been conducted in so discreet and decent a manner, albeit its leader, duly elected to Parliament, was eventually hanged. Writing in what might be described as the historically prophetic mode, Wiebe places Manitoba at the mythic centre of a visionary quest that somehow through time has come to seem appallingly ordinary, redeemed here only by his own visionary zeal and the power of his voice.

Wiebe's Manitoba is the focus of a sad triumphal, celebrated in a lament for what history denied. For Shields, Manitoba recedes smaller and smaller as her fiction progresses, a myth of origins swallowed up by the mundane details of an ordinary life. Possibly because both writers are outsiders, they are able to exploit the splendid possibilities of Manitoba as a regional context, to provide both literal and metaphoric shape to their characters and the aesthetic strategies by which we are allowed entry into their fictional realities. Arnason and Birdsell, who are at home with Manitoba as a literary environment, write more out of the specificity of their own real or imagined experience. They are not regional writers. They are writers for whom the particularities of Manitoba, rather than its peculiarities, provide access to the universal.

Manitoba does not lend itself to fictional regionalism in the same way as the Prairies do, or the Arctic, or the Maritimes. Not that Manitoba is not in part a prairie landscape, as it is also an Arctic and even a maritime landscape. But that is the point: Manitoba is prairies, is bushland, is Winnipeg—one of the great small cities of the world whose streets extend into every corner of the province—is wheat fields and marshland, small towns and village crossroads, taiga and tundra, is American borderland and the shoreline of Hudson Bay, is east of The West, west of The East, south of Nunavut and the Northwest Territories. Manitoba makes no big fuss over geographical or cultural characteristics peculiar to itself but shares in the attributes of many places and peoples. Manitoba, proud as it is, is a somewhat arbitrary designation. It is a convergence of regions, a myriad of regions. To twist a Biblical aphorism, it is a house of many mansions. Or perhaps an ark. Yes, what could be more arbitrarily the vessel of our survival; an ark.

II

The following is a Manitoba reading list, fiction, perhaps idiosyncratic, slightly annotated.

Two of the best and most celebrated Manitoba writers:

Margaret Laurence (her writing is not regional in the strictest sense, where locale both shapes and reflects character, but it is thoroughly grounded in Manitoba, wherever it is set); especially *A Bird in the House* (1970).

Gabrielle Roy (published first in French, her fiction of 'innocence' is set in Manitoba and her fiction of 'experience' is set in Quebec); especially *Where Nests the Water Hen* (1950).

Others:

Agnes Laut, *Lords of the North* (1900). Historical documentary and conventional romantic fiction; a rousing and rare good read.

Nellie McClung, *Sowing Seeds in Danny* (1908). Heart-wrenching sentimentality by a renowned early feminist.

Frederick Philip Grove, *Over Prairie Trails* (1922). Seven journeys through the landscape; contemplative.

——. *Settlers of the Marsh* (1925). The best of Grove's Prairie novels; psychological realism contorted by a deterministic outlook.

Douglas Durkin, *The Magpie* (1923). A passionate novel of ideas built around the Winnipeg General Strike of 1919, by Martha Ostenso's life partner.

Laura Goodman Salverson, *The Viking Heart* (1923). An epic saga of Icelandic immigrants to Manitoba.

Martha Ostenso, *Wild Geese* (1925). Gothic, penetrating; psychological romance verging on realism.

Robert J.C. Stead, *Grain* (1926). A sleeper; early Prairie fiction at its best.

Bertram Brooker, *Think of the Earth* (1936). Proof that a Governor General's Award bears no relation to merit; visionary bathos; evocative details.

John Marlyn, *Under the Ribs of Death* (1956). A theme novel; anatomy of the immigrant experience; Winnipeg.

Adele Wiseman, *The Sacrifice* (1956). A stunning great novel; Jewish immigrants in unnamed Winnipeg; reworking Abraham's story, a testing of its implications in the New World.

Patricia Blondal, *A Candle to Light the Sun* (1960). Another sleeper, a triumph; small town as central character; falters slightly in the closing pages, written as Blondal approached untimely death.

Arnason; Birdsell; W.D. Valgardson. There are many more, still writing.

Waves Break Stone

(The title of this previously unpublished work is taken from one of David Arnason's most beautiful poems. The piece as a whole is probably best served by an absence of commentary. It began as a celebration, in response to an open invitation from Prairie Fire *magazine for contributions to a special Arnason issue. It became what it is, a critical fiction. This transformation and modest apotheosis is, I hope, a tribute to David—it is as much his doing as my own.)*

I FIRST BECAME AWARE of a Manitoba conspiracy late in October of 1970, while living in Fredericton, New Brunswick. There, under the commodious shadow of David Arnason, both of us new to the justly famous graduate program in Canadian literature, myself feeling a little in everyone's way and David as genially loquacious as a Prairie sunrise, I learned that Gimli is the axis of the world, if not earth, and Winnipeg is the cultural capital of Canada. The progress of my awareness may have begun decades earlier, for as a toddler I passed through Winnipeg by train with my mother and brother, on the way from Waterloo County to Rivers, Manitoba, where my dad was stationed with the RCAF; and as a student I stopped over in Winnipeg on my way to Jasper Park Lodge, where I was to drive a tour bus for the summer, long enough to stand at Portage and Main and remark to myself that I was standing at the most famous intersection in the Dominion. In retrospect, I may have had premonitions of the sinister importance Manitoba was eventually to assume in my life, but it was not until one evening at a party in 1970, sitting in the Arnason living room in Nashwaaksis and listening to David share with a makeshift symposium of conspiring academics the pleasures of his home province, that I realized, what I am absorbing is beyond my control to resist. Here in greater Fredericton, the most beautiful small city anywhere, I am falling dangerously in love with Manitoba.

My dissociative affection for a part of Canada I hardly know came to mind recently, owing to the strange convergence in my life of a discarded newspaper and a nasty bit of bad weather. A North Atlantic storm combined with mechanical difficulties in the aircraft forced an unscheduled landing in Iceland, which loomed as our flight descended like an apparition, an isolated refuge or asylum edged by grey weather streaming at the limits of vision, submerging the unseen landscape in a morbid pallor. Stranded at Keflavik International Airport, preoccupied by the inconvenience and desiring distraction, I picked up a newspaper that had apparently been thrown at random upon the bench I now occupied. I do not read Icelandic, but, since it shares a common alphabet with those languages I know, I began working my way through the unintelligible sequence of letters laid out with seductive precision, looking for recognizable combinations. My flight was delayed indefinitely; transportation into Reykjavik was impossible. The terminal was a world on its own, and being there as I was, I had no other purpose than to endure the passage of time.

Reading Icelandic struck me as an act of redemption for time otherwise squandered. Before my attention had begun to flag, midway through column four on the first page, the whole of which was arranged to accommodate a shadowy photograph of two men and two women, suddenly I encountered the words

"Martin Heidegger." Here was a configuration of letters I knew. Almost immediately, my eye scrolled down and then over to alight on "David Arnason," in the fifth column. Four words in a page of indecipherability around which a narrative could be constructed that might take in my whole life, or so it seemed at the moment, in this place so completely severed from anything familiar. Four words to fill the time, the undifferentiated hours until takeoff, and to endow with mystery this gaunt structure, the sole purpose of which is to process people, pass them through from one place to another, like the portals of heaven or hell.

I could not immediately discern the relationship between Arnason and Heidegger. I knew that David knew the philosopher, although not as Martin, or so at this point I assumed. The resistance of text to the yielding of meaning meant their true relationship was tantalizingly inaccessible. Yet, since my determination that they must be in the same story established a connection between them, I could not help being drawn into the unfathomable plot of their coincident representation. Driven by the prospect of intrigue and looking for something I could comprehend, I turned from the encoded Icelandic text to consider the photograph that divided the columns in which the four known words now shone from their enigmatic field of alphabetic obscurity like beacons of absolute light.

What you have to realize about David, who as you know is a writer, is his genius for writing his reader into the text. If he loves Manitoba, then you love Manitoba. If Manitoba provides the cultural apparel that David wears like a mantle of justified privilege, then you are bereft for having Manitoba as an absence in your own past, you are naked without his memories of place, haunted by the presence of emptiness. In his living room across the broad surge of the St. John River from Fredericton, in 1970, a strange province far away was invoked deep in the crenellated passages of my brain, as if it had always been there, awaiting discovery, and I was homesick for someone else's world. As in conversation, so too, that is the way with his writing. You cannot separate David's words in your mind from what they describe.

I often remember a dog called Skrag, for example, especially when I am trapped like I was at Keflavik, in a secure place—like Skrag, I cannot always be sure of the difference between safety and bondage. I have never actually known a dog called Skrag, but David Arnason has; he wrote the Skrag poems. The poems do not argue his affection for Skrag, do not articulate passion. You read about Skrag and love him yourself, the way you love anything that speaks to you from within, even though you may fear it or loathe it, which you do not, in Skrag's case. Skrag transcends language, is alive in your mind. When he lopes away from the imponderable awkwardness of conflicting emotions and over the farm bridge, it is because he has things to do in the south pasture, he has things to do. Between words and what they describe there falls no shadow, there is no mediation. I would rather have written David Arnason's few stanzas about an old dog than all the love poetry of Elizabeth Barrett Browning or of Shakespeare himself, for those writers are driven to metaphor, and I can admire their tropes, even borrow them on occasion, but Skrag, who is only a dog, inhabits my life, is affirmation of my being in the world. Metaphor reduces everything to meaning, and Skrag and I, we simply are.

David as a writer, that might have explained his name encoded in the newspaper among words of his ancient lineage—Icelandic, to him, being both a mystery and familiar as blood, if suddenly his blood were encountered in a pool at his feet or in a spreading stain just out of reach of an outstretched hand. Strange it is to have something as intrinsic to your genetic design as the language in which your forebears dwelled inaccessible except in translation. As I contemplated the extent to which this profound dissociation conditions the experience of most Canadians, myself included, immigrants in a settler society, I observed with a slow awakening of surprise that the photograph was not a picture of David. Yet if it was meant to illuminate the article, one must assume it related to his prodigious canon as a poet, storyteller, playwright, and critic. If so, whatever it might reveal of his accomplishment was obscured by a swarming of letters that refused to coalesce. Just as he appears in his own writing, David among Icelandic words in the newspaper was an astonishing revelation, and utterly elusive. Elusive, but intriguing. Inviting complicity. But complicity in what? If I were to commit sufficiently to his story, as I felt compelled to do, I recognized there was a risk of being caught up in something beyond my control, the very contemplation of which summoned tremors of anxiety from deep within.

The uncaptioned photograph, the gloom of the emergency lighting in the terminal lounge, the scratched lenses of my reading glasses, combined with my uneasiness at being stranded in a place without sufficient comfort for a traveller plucked out of the air, as it were, from a determined trajectory, a place with no substance to the senses, without diversion for fibrillating nerves, all this conspired . . . but why would a picture be deliberately blurred? It could be archival, I thought. Yet the people in the photograph wore contemporary dress. It could be an aesthetic phenomenon, the prioritizing of medium over message. But it was singularly uninspired in design. It could be a mistake. Icelandic editors, however, are no more prone to technical error than others, I thought, in this age of desktop publication, when even the most esoteric ephemera appear correct and substantial. Finally, the blurring could have been intentional, done for me alone—solipsism was sanctuary in a setting that seemed eerily otherworldly. What might appear paranoid in fact allowed solace. The blurred photograph: for a soul disembodied by the ephemerality of its present surroundings, palpable affirmation in the possibility that the picture was printed just so, for my sole benefit; left, just so, for my discovery.

If this fourth and final explanation was true, then my strange solitude was part of some larger plot. I was not stranded as I had supposed, but positioned. A piece in a game, perhaps virtual chess. Not knowing my own value, whether pawn or bishop or king, or even for sure if the game was chess, I could not anticipate my next move nor deduct from preceding events what moves led to my presence here, now. Should I look to the last few hours or days for the pattern that would allow me to anticipate what lay ahead? Since I could divine neither the game-master nor the scale of the game, perhaps I should look for a larger design—but given that time from a human perspective is two-dimensional, could I as a piece on a game board comprehend the relative movements of myself and the pieces around me: can a pawn know only the movement of pawns, and a king of kings?

With mounting anxiety, I contemplated the paradoxical notion that almost any conclusion the mind can seize upon is retroactively prophetic; ends anticipate the process by which they are achieved, although the beginning and the end of things from my perspective within an arrested continuum were presently incomprehensible. In need of definition, compelled to align myself with the familiar, I returned my attention to the blurry photograph, looking for Arnason. I held the newspaper at arm's length. I squinted to throw everything out of focus except that portion of the picture under assessment. I examined each face in turn, the two men and two women. I did this repeatedly until my arm was tired and my eyes watered from the effort. On the final survey, the last of my looking, I suddenly realized in looking for Arnason I had missed the indistinct but undeniable image of Martin Heidegger on the extreme right. It was knowledge preceding experience that allowed for what amounted to revelation. In looking for Arnason I had nearly missed the point of the photograph.

There was Heidegger, standing in front of the Manitoba legislature. The building itself was in focus, as if the photographer had purposely hidden the figures not behind but in front of an architectural form that would be generically familiar to any viewer of the Western world, and thus a distraction from the foregrounded subject. An impulse to narrative took hold, generated by a clamour of questions. Who were the other three people; why were they apparently indifferent to the man on their left, who was of course on the right from the viewer's perspective, unless the photograph was reversed? From the way shadows fell in a thin bar across the snow to the right of the figures I surmised it was evening; the sun in the west, on their left, meant the picture was printed correctly: I could tell this because I happen to know the legislature faces northwest. It is a key element in the Manitoba geography I carry within me, which I long for with the irrational nostalgia of a lover for his imaginary beloved. I can see it all. Winnipeg straddles the fiftieth parallel and thus in winter the sun rises from the southeast. If it were a morning shot, the sun would throw shadows in front of the figures, casting their silhouettes forward across the snow, and the legislature would itself be shrouded in residual night, as would the figures being photographed.

Who were these people, posed with such deliberation, like permanent tourists? Why was their photograph taken, what event does it record; or obscure? Why was it printed on the front page of an Icelandic newspaper? Was it printed on every copy of the edition, perhaps indifferent to the bewilderment of Icelandic readers, or only on this one copy, left here for me to find by someone who anticipated the bad weather and my condition as a castaway surrounded in a pool of dim light by the sounds of terminal emptiness? Where was David in all of this?

But even as I asked the question, I knew—Arnason was the photographer. Once realized, it was obvious. This was a photograph of David Arnason, he was there, within the shadows and textures and contours and depths, as surely as if someone at that moment had taken a candid shot up close of the photographer photographing. It was a portrait, not unlike those *trompe l'oeil* compositions which at a distance seem to be of James Dean but up close reveal scenes of motorcycles and Porsches and fifties paraphernalia. Looking around me to confirm my relative solitude, I then said aloud, this photograph is not what it seems! My voice echoed with such resonance I peered into the dismal reaches of the terminal to see if there was someone mimicking my words, mirroring my presence. Finding no one, I subsided into contemplative trepidation and, nurturing my fears, dozed for a few moments while sitting absolutely upright as I always do in public places.

I may have dreamed Icelandic sagas. I remembered nothing on awakening. Yet I felt an affinity with the location of my estrangement that only a subconscious rehearsal of the stories first told to me by David over beer in Fredericton could account for. Possibly I had dreamed the *Islendingasšgur* or perhaps in that infinite moment of suspended time between waking and sleep I had actually lived the entire narrative as if it were my own story—and then in the jarring journey back into consciousness and time, it had escaped. In any case, while I fell asleep a Canadian, I awoke robust with imagination. Perhaps I was Icelandic at last, my ancestral affinity for Manitoba no longer neurotic divination.

Being a diagnosed narcoleptic I have a vested interest in dreams. I cannot always distinguish between wakefulness and sleep, nor do I always have the urge to try. The two states of mind are not mutually exclusive: asleep, I sometimes dream I am awake, and awake I often suspect myself to be sleeping. Normally, the elision of boundaries between one mode of consciousness and the other is not problematic. Many of my university colleagues seem to share the same condition. But sometimes it can be disconcerting, not knowing whether the Cartesian notion of *cogito ergo sum* affirms the solidity of my foothold in the waking world or is proof that in dreams the reality of thought is as absolute as it is ephemeral.

If I was now Icelandic, I reasoned, it was because I was either still asleep and dreaming wakefulness or I was awake but someone other than the person I had thought myself to be. To test this new sense of myself I picked up the newspaper again and began to read. The words tumbled by, nearly making sense, their unintelligibility no longer an affront. If I was not Icelandic, then why, while I sub-articulated the Icelandic text, was the letter *r* rolling against the back of my mouth, as I had so often heard it in David Arnason's own peculiar accented vernacular?

Newly centred by my unremembered dream, I shrunk away from the surrounding gloom that seemed to reach like strange dismembered limbs towards me, out of the architectural twilight. Finding myself Icelandic after a lifetime of being Canadian, you might have thought there would be great comfort in being marooned at Keflavik. You might think I had inadvertently discovered relief from the lack of definition by which I have been haunted all my life. Instead, I felt afraid. If an interlocutor had asked at that moment, what is the farthest place in the world from here, I would instantly have replied, Manitoba! That is where in imagination I am most secure, and where the world is most sure. But I was centred, now, in mounting terror. Despite myself, my pride in being emotionally self-reliant and a rational anarchist, impervious to the conflicting implications of intellectual apperceptions, I was transfixed within the singularity of my present experience in Keflavik Airport. This, I reasoned, must be what it is like to know you are dying.

What you have to realize about David Arnason is that in October of 1970 he was the most imposing man in Canada. His scowling grin, voluptuous beard, fearsome girth, the shambling authority of his movements, the precision of his articulation that seemed to envelop him in a luminous carapace of words, the tremors of earnest enthusiasm in his voice, the thundering resonance of his convictions and his sweetness of disposition, all this, once met, became the measure of what a fully authentic person could be. He carried Iceland in his blood, although at that time he had never been to Iceland. He could play any musical instrument, after watching it shape sound for only moments. One simply expected he would do well, and he always did. Whatever my own mark in a graduate-school essay or project, Dave always got one mark better. It was the way professors like Fred Cogswell and Tony Boxhill acceded to and sustained the natural order of things.

David was an accomplished storyteller, even then. He spun out sagas where the truths of his own life were indistinct from wry and wondrous fictions. You knew his dog Skrag would become a book one day. And as with all good story-tellers, the better he got, the more inseparable he was from the telling. When, some two decades later, he came to publish a novel, *The Pagan Wall*, it was inevitable that I would look for him there, in its cadence and vocabulary, and in the lives of his characters. And of course he is there. It is and is not his own story. But do you know who else is there? By name. Martin. Heidegger. David disguises his own presence in exquisitely controlled misdirection, turning confessional into narrative strategy, but the old Nazi philosopher he draws into public display, neat as a pin. There he is, Heidegger, among words.

That, in itself, should not be surprising. There is a connection between Heidegger and residual colonialism coursing the veins of most Canadians, invisible and deadly as a low white cell count. For Heidegger death is the key to being; we must each accommodate the knowledge of our inevitable end, live knowing we are incomplete and that on completion we no longer exist. So it is with Canadians of a certain age, alive with the burden of being on the edge of being British; and for younger Canadians, being not-American. Much as we may fidget on the outside looking in, that is our perpetual condition. If Canadians were at the centre, we would experience perfect annihilation—to be British, or American, would mean we cease being Canadian. We live in a state of becoming, our ongoing anxiety a constant reminder of who we are not. We hover, never truly ourselves.

That is the Manitoba conspiracy, in a nutshell. In a world where we are what we are not, there is an insistent reminder coming from the province at our dead centre—that phrase, I use fully aware of its implications: it is not Manitoba that is dead but the absence it signifies for the rest of us deep within our collective psyche, nurtured by the knowledge that there is at our centre a place that for most of us is accessible only in imagination, a place so special we long for it with a kind of misbegotten longing that is for some of us very much like grieving. The insistence by Manitobans that the measure of Manitoba is Manitoba itself is a profoundly Heideggerian notion in our collective Canadian cosmology. In my own private dislocation, not unlike unrequited love, which is a sort of grieving if you think about it, David Arnason is the prime mover. In his conversation, in his writing, even in *The Pagan Wall*, which is set entirely in Europe but informed with uncompromising fidelity to authentic experience by a Manitoban sensibility, I am continually reminded that such authenticity as some of us can only imagine, others can actually live.

At this point in my ruminations, I promised myself that I would reread David's novel, if ever I escaped the dreary confines of this terminus, the ominous theatre of my isolation and conjecture. In the dismal light I seemed to be making a pact, let me escape, move onwards in my journey, and I will explore once again the confluence of an Arnasonian protagonist and Martin Heidegger in a context more coherent, less disturbing, than the present situation allows. I am not sure whether the pact was with God or the Devil, and it was not important since I believe in neither, although I am frightened by both. Perhaps it was with David, who had been conjured by the letters of his name, so that he seemed to be there, standing just back from my field of vision whichever way I turned to peer into the murky gloom, or perhaps the pact was with Heidegger, an old old man in *The Pagan Wall* who was now middle-aged and standing with an air of expectation in front of the Manitoba legislature, insisting I resolve the puzzle of his appearance there as a perfect example of the living dead, for while I knew he had expired on May 26, 1976, he had clearly posed for this picture in the 1990s and, while not entirely in focus, did not seem the worse for wear.

I did not start this; David, as well, has him alive after death. Arnason's contextualized Heidegger animates a vision of moral decadence in Europe that is offset by the loves of a man and a woman from Manitoba who are caught up in its machinations, yet as innocents abroad are able to resist its power. Heidegger as the living dead seems less an intellectual vampire haunting the shadows of a post-war continent and more the sly superannuated attendant of inexplicable Being.

David can talk to fish. That is one of the strange things about him. To mermaids, yes, but given their imagined being, that is not surprising—accomplished mermaids can appear wholly human if they wish, and will listen to almost anyone. But David talks to fish. I have seen him, drink in hand, sitting eighteen inches from a tank of tropical fish, engaged in esoteric discourse, as if his reflection in the glass were responding point counterpoint to his argument, and the fish meanwhile were scurrying in phalanxes of meaning, careening as rhetorical signifiers across the front of the tank.

The terminal now appeared to be empty, save one despairing soul, myself. If my dread and insubstantiality seem intemperate, consider: I was alone in the gloom of emergency lighting, caught up in the purgatorial limbo of waiting, waiting for nothing but time, for time to resolve, as if time were suspended and I had no choice but to endure until it resumed its normal function as a context of consciousness, into which I might rediscover myself thrown, like clay on a wheel, spinning beneath the hands of an unknown potter, shaped by an imagination beyond my control. Where the others in the terminal might have gone, who had been swarming as apparitions at the very edges of my awareness, less seen than understood to have been there—flight personnel, security people, passengers in transit caught like myself between departure and arrival—I could not tell. There was no evidence of egress, yet if others had been there they were now absent. Fighting panic I clutched at the newspaper as the only familiar object at hand. In my agitation, I ripped the front page lengthwise from top to bottom.

Offended by what seemed my incontrovertible cowardice, I flung the paper's several pieces against the dismal air. Two parts of the torn page caught an edge of atmosphere; swirling upward, they looped and fluttered to my feet. Between the written Arnason and the written Heidegger a shard of marbleized floor obtruded like caesura in a sonnet; in the torn photograph of the Manitoba legislature a neatly severed Heidegger now stood apart from the other figures as if observing them from across an insuperable abyss. The precision of this apparent accident, far from making me wonder at the meaning to be drawn from chance action, served rather to affirm my suspicion that not only had the photograph been tampered with, to make it tear just so, but my every action was being monitored and manipulated by an unseen witness.

It stood to reason, there must be a purpose to all of this. Someone must be in control. I immediately suspected it was David. Somehow I had found myself in an Arnasonian plot. I had become a character in an Arnason narrative. Even more disconcerting, perhaps it was only my awareness that was new, this epiphany representing a shift in my perception, not my condition. Perhaps I have always been a figure in the narrative design of David Arnason. That would explain my sense of Manitoba as a home-place, although I have never lived there. That would explain my present discovery of myself as Icelandic, for I had long since acquiesced to the probability that, just as the heart of the Canadian nation lies in Manitoba, Manitoba itself is transcendently informed by its heritage of Icelanders, including the Arnasons, who fled from the conflagrations of fire and ice in the nineteenth century to settle on the shores of Lake Winnipeg.

Here is the problem. At what point did Arnason and Heidegger come together in my mind? In terms of philosophical verities, they converge only at the vanishing point, where each might be abandoned to the other from the inquisitor's perspective, although this is an illusion fostered by post-Cartesian valorization of the viewer's eye, the witness reconfiguring the witnessed, seeing perception as reality. Here is the problem. David is and is not Heideggerian. Of course he is, for how could a thinking being not be? But he is not, for how can the spirit resist imagination? David, in his fine morose and whimsical, diffident and erudite, generous and solipsistic renderings of himself as fiction, constructs a personality where soul and imagination are undifferentiated, imagination being the spontaneous presence of the self, and soul the accumulation of these myriad selves through time. David is a pretertextual phenomenon. Heidegger lies soulless among words, never quite lifting himself from the pages of an endless text.

Heidegger does not understand irony: to do so demands awareness within language but also beyond it. Incapable of irony, he could not comprehend the unnatural nature of Nazi atrocity. Unable to distinguish between living-with-death as a set of mind and as a social condition, Heidegger committed himself to the latter, to death as the measure of society's authenticity and hence of his own. Oh David, I murmured, my words penetrating into the dismal air of the terminal lounge. How did you ever get involved with such a man, you of the powerful bones and immeasurable capacity for being alive?

I slept again and thought I heard Umberto Eco speaking. It was October in my dream. I was in a large room with a gaunt cathedral ceiling, like a holy place abandoned to ordinariness. There was a big crowd. He spoke in English. He said that some things cannot be improved upon: he named the spoon. He named several other things but in the dream I did not agree with him on anything except the spoon. The bicycle was one of the other things; but the bicycle has been manifestly improved upon over years and may be infinitely refined. The spoon is what it does. A good spoon has perfect shape and balance. Some spoons are better than others for one purpose or another, but once found, the perfect spoon retains perfection. Eco named other things but they have slipped from my mind, all except the book. He named the book, and it too is what it does and does so with perfection. I agreed with him on books. On spoons and books.

It is October 6, 1998. Umberto Eco invites his listeners to think. A number of people get up and walk out, not angrily but not awkwardly; more as if they suddenly remember they have appointments elsewhere at precisely the moment of their departure and of necessity walk headlong through his words and into the adjoining corridors. He says dictionaries are systems; the dictionary is a limited cache of words but its contents offer infinite possibilities, possibilities of infinite meanings. He says that in a democracy hypertext can be dangerous, offering as it does a kind of intellectual anarchy, but in an authoritarian state its refusal of authority can signify freedom. Freedom signified, he says, is revolution. The alphabet, he says, is so small it takes the breath away, and it is infinite in disposition.

I listen to Umberto Eco. He offers an overhead projection of plus signs and minus signs, and using this he explains permutations of the relationship between text and hypertext, books and the Net. Unfortunately, as he does so, he moves in and out of microphone range. Much of his explication is lost, but he seems happy. Most of us share his happiness. When he stops talking there is much applause, after which I awaken.

As I looked around me in the shadows of the terminal for alterity, for assurance that I was no longer sleeping, my gaze included a long window overlooking the runway, then projected through the glare of the glass into the murky atmosphere outside, then fixed upon a fuselage at some distance across the tarmac, on which I read 'nada' which I assumed to be Canada encrypted by my line of vision into an ominous abbreviated cipher. Had I created Umberto Eco? Stunned at such power, I did not immediately recognize the corollary as equally possible. From nada, a nada, had I made him happen, written his books, spoken his words? I knew we must have a vocabulary in common or I could not have read his books, never mind written them. Had he ever been to Canada? If so, if I could prove he had been there, would that establish that I had not created him? But then of course it could open the possibility that he created me.

This latter seemed unlikely since I had already arrived at the possibility that I was a peripheral figure in a David Arnason fiction and could not very well also be an Italian persona. In any case, I felt Icelandic; I was marooned in Iceland, estranged from Manitoba, and had a personal history, or so I believed or was allowed to believe, rooted in Waterloo County, in southwestern Ontario. I was Italian only in that dim connected way the whole of Western civilization is Italian.

No sooner had Waterloo County appeared in my mind, however, superimposed over the vision of an Air Canada fuselage in the streaming fog, than I grasped a terrifying connection which brought the significance of my present situation into sharp relief. Erb Electric! The manufacturers of wire conduit used on Canadian airliners; the company is a family affair. I possess the original Erb birth certificate, Johannes Erb, born in Lancaster County, Pennsylvania, 1754. Fled the American Revolution. His son, Christian, married a Mohawk woman from the Grand River valley. One line of their progeny begat the founders of Erb Electric, another begat the line that begat me.

In consequence of having been borne here on the grounded wings of Canadian technology and at this precise moment having become aware of convergent narratives, my own and that of the manufacturers of a critical component in the aircraft's function as a vessel of safe passage from this tedious place, an involuntary shudder reverberated throughout my system as if someone had desecrated my grave. Such convergence forced me to the realization that my presence here might be part of an unresolved narrative equation, the working out of which was inseparable from my own end. That might seem to verge on the psychotic, but consider the ineluctable irony: if someone else was in charge of my story, how could he or she resist bringing me down as the absolute and arbitrary consequence of Christian's birth in a small cabin on the edge of a Mohawk village where the Speed meets the Grand, two hundred years previous. If my story was in the ironic mode, would resistance be possible?

My affection for Manitoba led me on this venture in the first place. I was on my way to give a lecture at a congress in Strasbourg on Manitoba writers. These included such Icelandic Canadians as W.D. Valgardson, Laura Salverson, and David Arnason, and here I was, suspended from the normal progressions of time in an Iceland that swirled with elemental fury beyond these walls, this impossible labyrinth of my own mind and destiny. Being a man of my age, however, I was able to look at death square on. The imminence of death was not absolute.

The trick was to anticipate it and find alternatives. The convergence of forking paths that in retrospect would provide my survivors with an overweening sense of synchronicity could be avoided. Everything that had happened had to happen just so, to bring me here, waiting to board a plane in which a faulty strand of wire would cause the plane to explode in mid-air, its residue to fall plummeting through layers of weather and crash piecemeal into Arctic seas. The past could not be changed but its implications could be denied. Of this I was relatively certain.

I looked once again at Arnason's photograph, now lying on the floor. The Manitoba legislature adorned with a golden icon—that, I realized, was the very fulcrum of my own peculiar cosmology. If there was a visceral heart to my visionary sense of myself in the world, this gilded bronze was it, in black and white. Somewhere along the way, I had come to understand Manitoba as the vital throbbing heart at the centre of the dying organism that was all I could ever hope to be—the conspiracy was to make me accept this. Such sentiments could not have been self-induced, for who would knowingly accept such morbid dislocation, even in an immigrant society such as ours?

Feeling arbitrary, utterly, I almost gave up at this point, nearly submitted to the inevitable. To dwell in meaninglessness, that is nothing; to be conceived, to conceive oneself, as arbitrary, that is more than mortality can bear. I looked to Heidegger, then across the abyss to the other three. They were not couples, but stolidly individuated, despite the pixillated blur of the newsprint. They occupied their severed rectilinearity on the torn page like gladiators in ordinary modern dress, each turned in upon his or her own private darkness, each turned out to face the dying light. Why was Heidegger here like this, just now, just so? Precisely, it occurred to me, because there was no reason, no explanation.

As I accepted the arbitrariness of Heidegger within language beyond my comprehension, in a photograph of my own dislocated psyche, the meaning of the other three leapt immediately to mind. Heidegger, separated, was spectral; presence without substance. The second man was a configuration of impotent lechery. The two women—a lesbian, and a nymphomaniac. The four of them were David's joke, borrowed perhaps from Jean-Paul Sartre. The conspiracy, to make me submit. It was through David that I now perceived them in this fashion. The story was his. In a story by someone else, or by David stranded elsewhere in time, in Fredericton, perhaps, in 1970, instead of his beloved Winnipeg to which he returned after graduate school, the same four figures could be something else again, a troupe of deadpan mimes, four strangers, swans in human form.

Caught between Heidegger and Sartre, as it were, trapped in a discontinuous world, I could embrace meaninglessness as justification for submission to text and my fate, or I could seize my own being, turn from the unholy foursome and embrace freedom, instead. Believing David was providing me the option, that this entire situation was somehow his doing, and that as a figure in his narrative I could choose to be free, I realized it was up to me to create my own future. That meant, of course, I must avoid getting on the plane which, if I were aboard, was destined to crash in an extravagant and gruesome display of ironic inevitability.

With self-preservation in mind, I rose from the bench and strode to a door at the end of a short hallway in front of me, stepping as I did so on the torn newspaper, grinding it to cryptic fragments. The door opened into a windowless room that was empty but for a single chair beneath an overhead light, a bare bulb that swayed on its corded wire in the still air. There was an exterior lock on the door. No one could find me here. The flight would proceed in due course and the threat of my presence would be eliminated. I turned the lock on the outside of the door, stepped in, pulled the door shut behind me. There was no escape, no turning back. Sooner or later someone would come, open the door, and set me free. Meanwhile, beyond a world of meaning and control, beyond even Arnason's reach, I would endure with grace and with the conviction that an entire universe was unfolding as I wished.

In locking myself in, however, I now realize I have committed an unpardonable narrative offence; what is, in effect, a mortal error. In this empty room, there is no longer the possibility of a witness to my life, no one to relate the closure by which this, as all human stories, must come to an end. Out there, someone would surely have emerged from the shadows to provide dimension, if nothing more, to my isolation; but here, whether or not I am even alive is of no consequence. I have placed myself in an untenable position. While I can negotiate how the story is to be told, the story itself is beyond me. I have anticipated the disaster of the plane, which I am not aboard, plummeting into the sea as an inexorable consequence of my own genetic destiny. I have evaded the fate that would have left me, bits of flesh dissipating on estranged currents of the mind as the chessmaster gathers himself or herself into separate consciousness, awakening, perhaps, into a separate dream.

But where to, from here? If, perhaps, my existence is unreal, if Descartes is wrong, must I remain in this room forever? If so, then time is meaningless. In a world without meaning, all meanings are possible. If that is the case, then all stories that are possible will occur as equally authentic. In at least some of them I will be Icelandic, I will be the protagonist, in some the witness, in some an omniscient narrator so inaccessible in semantics and syntax, a truly absent presence in the text, that language itself will seem to be saying whatever is said. In at least one of these stories I will know what the future holds for the man locked in a room in the terminal who anticipates closure, believing time merely a projection on the infinite moment of his tenuous life. If all stories are possible, in one of the possible stories the reality will be that only one story is possible. In one story, only the future will be known, while the present will be virtually indecipherable.

In this story, I am sitting on an uncomfortable chair under a naked light bulb, immobilized by the certainty of my impending death. There is no other reality accessible into which I might insert myself, driven by my desperation to alter the inexorable.

This, of course, is not a matter of preordination, since while the future is known the present is not—such is the knowledge that separates us from animals and angels alike. I am sitting, immobilized, in reckless contemplation. Then with a crash the silence falls. My mind goes still. The end is about to begin.

They will find these notes among the debris. This collapsed corner of the building will have given way to structural fatigue at the precise moment that I finish writing. I had not even been aware I was writing these notes. From the outset I thought I was recollecting all this from some indeterminate safe vantage at my eventual destination. The notes will be close to my outstretched hand, as if I had let them slip away carelessly. In order to extricate my body from the rubble, they will have to bring in power-jacks to hoist the imponderable weight of a steel girder from my chest. On the twisted side of the girder will be a single word, printed as the construction company's logo, repeated in a sans-serif font from one end to the other. Arnason, it will say. Arnason, Arnason, Arnason. At one point in the line of words the letters will appear stretched to indecipherability. That is where the bend will occur, the break in load-bearing equipoise that caused the collapse.

In the unalterable course of this particular story, these notes which I now realize I have been making from the beginning as a means of coping with the emptiness of time between arrival and departure, and of constructing a perspective from which to observe myself as my own witness, these notes will be forwarded to my daughter, Laura, in Winnipeg where she is a colleague, in this version, of David Arnason at the University of Manitoba. At my family's request, my remains will be rendered into ashes in Iceland and my ashes will be delivered for scattering to Waterloo County, my ancestral home in southwestern Ontario. The notes will be examined by David who will marvel at the ironies of my demise and explain to my daughter that his cousin's construction company had never before had a problem, and that it was an earth tremor, Odin's whim, an act of God, and not a faulty girder, that imposed an end to my story.

Once alone, David will light a cigar in his office sanctuary and with the same match he will set ablaze the original print of the newspaper photograph. As they burn, the four figures will briefly share their common plight, like four gates to a beleaguered city, four heads to an immolated beast: for a moment in the contorted paper Heidegger smiles; in a twist from the flame the other man's face leaps with sudden passion, before shrinking into the heat; the two women turn intimately towards each other, then fall away into the fire's embrace. The Manitoba legislature crumbles. David will see all this. It is dangerous to write as he does, where meaning is in the service of being. He will not take notes. He dreams, perhaps, of Gimli or maybe of Fredericton, and of how much he loves Manitoba. So much, in imagination there is nothing he cannot do.

AUTHOR / TITLE INDEX